Sermons on the Blessed Sacrament

JOHN M. KELLY LIBRARY

SERMONS ON THE

BLESSED SACRAMENT,

AND ESPECIALLY FOR THE

FORTY HOURS' ADORATION.

FROM THE GERMAN OF
REV. J. B. SCHEURER, D.D.

EDITED BY

REV. F. X. LASANCE,

Author of "Visits to Jesus in the Tabernacle,"
"Manual of the Holy Eucharist," etc.

NEW YORK, CINCINNATI, CHICAGO:
BENZIGER BROTHERS,
Printers to the Holy Apostolic See.
1900.

Nihil Obstat.

HENRY BRINKMEYER,
Censor Deputatus.

Imprimatur.

✝MICHAEL AUGUSTINE,
Archbishop of New York.

NEW YORK, February 10, 1900.

PREFACE.

"DAS GROSSE GEBET" is the title under which this volume of Eucharistic Sermons originally appeared in German. *Das grosse Gebet* is a term employed to designate that particular form of Perpetual Adoration of the Blessed Sacrament which has been established in several dioceses of Germany, notably that of Mainz, and corresponds very nearly to the Devotion of the Forty Hours, as it is practised in many parts of the United States. It is the great event of the ecclesiastical year to devout German Catholics and pious adorers of the Holy Eucharist In a certain rotation fixed by the Ordinary, *Das grosse Gebet* is celebrated in every parish of the diocese, one following another, in a continuous succession from the beginning to the end of the year. The celebration is opened with a grand procession, in which the Blessed Sacrament is borne with every demonstration of public honor and respect through the streets and meadows of the place.

The present volume of English sermons bears a double title The main title: *Sermons on the Blessed Sacrament*, indicates the general utility and adaptability of these discourses for all Eucharist celebrations;—the sub-title: *And Especially for the Forty Hours' Adoration*, announces their special purpose, and is most appropriate, since the devotion of the Forty Hours is the nearest equivalent in the United States to the German festival of public exposition and adoration of the Most Holy Sacrament, for which they were originally written by the Rev. Dr. Scheurer. *Das grosse*

3

Gebet, as practised in Germany, differs from the Forty Hours as celebrated in our country, mainly in this respect, that there the loud praying and singing goes on without interruption by alternate bands of adorers, whereas here the devotions, excepting at the opening exercises and at the close, are more quiet and private.

The *Instructio Clementina,* regarding the manner of celebrating the Forty Hours, is obligatory only in Rome; elsewhere, Bishops who introduce this devotion into their respective dioceses are at liberty, in some things of minor importance, to deviate from this regulation. In Rome, public prayers are not in vogue. In the United States of America, where are found so many nationalities, it would hardly be advisable for each class to follow the custom existing in its mother country; at least some uniform rules are desirable in each diocese. For the sake of uniformity, the Archbishop of Cincinnati, for instance, has laid down special regulations for holding the Forty Hours in all the churches under his jurisdiction.

In the *Synodus Diœcesana Cincinnatensis Tertia* we read under Article Seventy: " Quoad Adorationem Quadraginta Horarum, stricte mandamus, ut *conciones, publicœ preces* tempore Quadraginta Horarum omittantur. Permittimus tamen, ut pueri puellæque scholares, si in corpore SS Sacramentum visitent, simul publice orent, quod etiam concedimus tempore Vespertino ante repositionem. Fiat modo descripto in libello, cui titulus: *Manual of the Forty Hours' Adoration* edito ab *American Ecclesiastical Review.*"

While the Archbishop does not permit sermons to be preached *during* the Forty Hours' Adoration, His Grace exhorts and encourages pastors to prepare their flocks for the worthy and earnest celebration of this Eucharistic devotion, by preaching sermons on the Blessed Sacrament *before* the opening of the *Quarant' ore.* Such legislation is no doubt in accordance with the spirit of the Church. The Forty Hours' Adoration should be *preeminently* a glorification of the Blessed Sacrament,—a devotion of reparation and atonement.

The custom which has crept into many places of giving a *series* of sermons or even *lectures* during the Forty Hours on various subjects, and thereby giving to this devotion the character of a mission, is to be deprecated. Sermons on the Blessed Sacrament *only* are in order during the Forty Hours, if any sermons can then be tolerated at all; they would be rather more appropriate and more fully in conformity with the spirit of the Church if they were delivered at the *opening* of, or even on the Sunday previous to, the celebration. And it is precisely in this connection that the present volume of sermons may be found of great value to pastors.

To the saintly Bishop Neumann belongs the honor of having first introduced the devotion of the Forty Hours into the United States. It was introduced into the Diocese of Philadelphia in 1853, and into the Archdiocese of Baltimore in 1858; finally, by Papal Indults, it was formally approved for all the dioceses of the United States in 1866, in answer to the petitions of the Second Plenary Council of Baltimore. The following modifications of the *Clementine Instruction* were conceded to all the dioceses of the United States in 1868: 1. The Exposition may be interrupted during the *night;* 2. The procession may be omitted at the prudent discretion of the pastor; 3. All the Indulgences granted by the Constitution " *Graves et diuturnæ* " of Pope Clement VIII. can nevertheless be gained by the faithful.

The " Manual of the Forty Hours' Adoration," issued by the *American Ecclesiastical Review,* gives us the following sketch of the early history of this devotion:

" The Forty Hours' Adoration of the Blessed Sacrament, in memory of the forty hours during which the sacred body of Jesus was in the sepulchre, began at Milan about the year 1534. It soon spread into other cities of Italy, and, in 1551, was introduced into Rome, where it was celebrated on the first Sunday in every month by the Archconfraternity *della Trinità dei Pellegrini,* founded by St. Philip Neri in 1548, and on the third Sunday in every month by the Archconfraternity *di S. Maria dell' Orazione.*

By the Apostolic Constitution *Graves et diuturnæ,* dated November 25, 1592, Clement VIII. provided that the Blessed Sacrament should be exposed for public adoration, in continuous succession, on the altars of certain churches in Rome. He enriched the devotion with special indulgences. On the first Sunday of Advent of that year the devotion was commenced in the chapel of the Apostolical Palace.

Paul V., by the Brief *Cum felicis recordationis,* May 10, 1606, confirmed the decree of Clement VIII., and established the devotion *in perpetuum.* Succeeding Pontiffs issued various rules and directions for this devotion, which were collected by order of Clement XI. and published January 21, 1705: these are called after him the *Instructio Clementina.* The *Instructio Clementina* was confirmed and promulgated anew by order of Clement XII., September 1, 1730. The Instruction has the force *of law* in the city of Rome; outside of Rome only a *directive* force.

The Rev. Dr. Joseph Keller, in his *Anecdotes of the Blessed Sacrament,* relates the following: "Somewhat later (following the institution of the *Quarant' ore* in Milan) it happened that a troupe of actors came to Loretto at the carnival time for the purpose of performing a highly objectionable play. A pious Jesuit Father who was there did his utmost to prevent the acting of this play, but he failed ·in his object. He then determined to offer a counter-attraction to the people and to present them with a spectacle of a very different character, one, indeed, calculated to raise the heart and soul to God. Having obtained permission from the Bishop, he caused the church of his college to be most beautifully decorated, the high altar lighted up with countless tapers, and the Blessed Sacrament exposed during forty hours; meanwhile, at intervals, hymns and anthems were sung; there were *spiritual readings* and *two or three short sermons* each day. The people were, moreover, exhorted to approach the sacraments. This plan proved most successful. The sacred entertainment, if it may be so called, found more favor with the inhabitants of Loretto than the performance of the comedians. Almost the whole population repaired to the church, and the gain to souls was immense. From Loretto this devotion spread to the whole Church."

At first the Forty Hours was celebrated most commonly at Shrovetide, or the Carnival season; *later,* without any definite order, at all seasons or at any time of the year; but *now* the beautiful and commendable custom prevails in many dioceses of appointing a fixed time for each and every parish at which the Forty Hours' Adoration is to be celebrated, and from which no deviation is permitted without the knowledge and sanction of the Ordinary, so that, as nearly as possible, there is a continuous exposition of the Blessed Sacrament throughout the entire year, one church following another in the celebration of this festival, till the circuit of all the churches in the diocese is completed, and thus the Church Militant on earth imitates the Church Triumphant in heaven in the perpetual adoration of the "Lamb that was slain."

"And I beheld, and I heard the voice of many angels round about the throne, and the living creatures and the ancients, and the number of them was thousands of thousands.

" Saying with a loud voice: The Lamb that was slain is worthy to receive power, and divinity, and wisdom, and strength, and honor, and glory, and benediction.

" And every creature which is in heaven, and on the earth, and under the earth, and such as are in the sea, and all that are in them: I heard all saying· To Him that sitteth on the throne, and to the Lamb, benediction, and honor, and glory, and power forever and ever" (Apoc. v. 11–14).

It is regrettable that in so many dioceses of the United States it has not yet been found possible or feasible to establish the Forty Hours' Adoration systematically, in such a manner that all the churches in the diocese have assigned to them in rotation a certain time in the course of the year for the celebration of this grand and fruitful devotion.

The object of the Forty Hours' Adoration is:

1. To make a public profession of our *faith* in Jesus Christ, the God-man, as He is really, truly and substantially present in the Most Holy Sacrament of the Altar.

2. To pay a most righteous homage and a most solemn tribute of *praise* and *adoration* to the incarnate Son of God in the Sacrament of His love.

3. To offer in a becoming and deserving manner our *thanksgiving* to the divine Saviour for the institution of the Blessed Sacrament, and for all the graces and benefits that we have received through this sacred mystery.

4. To make *reparation* and *atonement* in a most public and appropriate manner for all the insults, irreverences and profanations that are heaped upon Our Lord in the Holy Sacrament by infidels and heretics, as well as by careless and disloyal Catholics.

5. To make *supplication* for the aversion of calamities, and to offer *prayers* for divine blessings in behalf of ourselves, the Holy Father and the Church.

These Eucharistic Sermons of the Rev. Dr. Scheurer aim to impress upon the minds of the faithful the *ends* and *purposes* of the Forty Hours' Adoration; they are calculated to give the people a clear idea of the dogma of the real presence, and a proper understanding and appreciation of its immense significance in the whole life of the Church and in the supernatural life of each individual soul. They throw light upon the teachings of the Church regarding the sacred and sublime Mystery of the Altar.

These sermons were delivered, as the author tells us, between the years 1867 and 1887, in the Cathedral of Mainz, at the opening of the Forty Hours, or rather of that annual German Eucharistic celebration, called "*Das grosse Gebet.*" Hence their design or purpose is obvious.

They are all intended to excite devotion to the Blessed Sacrament, and particularly to induce the faithful to celebrate the Forty Hours with fidelity and fervor. To attain this end, the author, in these sermons, portrays from various view-points and expatiates upon the *greatness* of the love of Jesus in the Blessed Sacrament. At the same time he seeks to impress the faithful with the fact that, precisely by the zealous celebration of the Forty Hours, they can, in a measure, give Our Lord a fitting return of love for His immeasurable love, and make atonement for this outraged love. While these sermons are primarily intended for the opening of the Forty Hours, and some of them may be found unusually long, they can very easily be curtailed, condensed and adapted to suit all occasions and feasts at which sermons on the Blessed Sacrament are in order. Solid discourses on the Blessed Sacrament are not too abundant in the vernacular, and hence this volume of Eucharistic Sermons ought to be well received by the English-speaking clergy.

In place of the four last sermons contained in the original edition of Dr. Scheurer's *Das grosse Gebet* we have sub-

stituted the XXI. and last sermon of the present volume.
This sermon on "The Life of Jesus in the Blessed Sacrament" is for the greater part from the German work of
Dr. Lierheimer, bearing the title "*Jesus mit uns.*" It
can be easily adapted for all Eucharistic festivals and devotions.

Dr. Scheurer's sermons are perhaps open to criticism,
not only for their length, but also for their redundancy
of words and complex diction; yet, while this defect has
been overcome somewhat in the English version, it was
not deemed necessary to depart, to-any material extent,
from the original text, since it may be fairly assumed that
priests are wont to make the sermons offered them in
books of this kind their own mental property by altering
or adapting the same to suit their own tastes in accordance with time and circumstances These sermons, though
rather diffusive, will be found to contain many precious
gems of thought, sunbursts of brilliant word painting,
splendid similes, apt scriptural references, and, above all,
solid doctrine

One of the sweetest tasks, one of the most important
duties of a priest, consists in making Jesus, who is hidden
beneath the sacramental veils, known and loved by men,
and particularly in leading souls gently, persuasively, per-
sistently to the foot of the altar, there to offer to our
Eucharistic God a worthy tribute of praise, adoration,
thanksgiving and prayer in return for His excessive love,
and in atonement for the profanation of the Holy Mystery.
May this book of sermons aid our zealous priests in the dis-
charge of this sacred obligation, and thus become an instrument in their hands for the propagation among the
faithful of a greater devotion to Jesus in the tabernacle

F. X. LASANCE.

January 1, 1900.

CONTENTS.

PAGE

CARDINAL WISEMAN'S PASTORAL ON THE FORTY HOURS' EX-
POSITION OF THE BLESSED SACRAMENT................. 13

EXTERIOR REVERENCE DUE TO THE EXPOSITION OF THE
BLESSED SACRAMENT................................ 25

SERMON I.—The Intention of the Church and the Disposition of
the Faithful in the Celebration of the Forty Hours' Prayer.. 29

SERMON II.—Adoration—Reparation........... 46

SERMON III.—The Adoration of Jesus in the Blessed Sacrament
our Most Sacred Duty, our Most Meritorious Service 66

SERMON IV.—The Blessed Sacrament the Poorest and Best-
loved Dwelling..................................... 74

SERMON V.—The Humble and Sorrowful Dwelling of Jesus in
the Blessed Sacrament........ 88

SERMON VI.—The Blessed Sacrament the Perpetual Dwelling of
Jesus upon Earth.................................. 107

SERMON VII.—The Most Holy Sacrament a Great and Munificent
Gift of the Love of Our Saviour 120

SERMON VIII.—The Love of Jesus in the Blessed Sacrament
Knows no Bounds and Overcomes all Obstacles........... 132

SERMON IX.—The Self-sacrificing, Patient and Enduring Love
of Jesus in the Most Holy Sacrament,.................... 143

SERMON X.—The Blessed Sacrament a Second Birth of Jesus.... 152

SERMON XI.—The Blessed Sacrament a Magnificent Manifestation of Divine Omnipotence....... 164

SERMON XII —The Excess of the Love of Jesus in the Blessed
Sacrament Expressed by the Granting of the Sacerdotal
Power.. 185

PAGE

SERMON XIII.—The Exercise of the Sacerdotal Power a New
Proof of the Superabundant Love of Jesus 201

SERMON XIV.—The Blessed Sacrament the Deepest Self-abasement and Condescension of Jesus......................... 218

SERMON XV.—The Voluntary and Involuntary Humiliations of
Jesus in the Blessed Sacrament........................... 233

SERMON XVI.—The Heroic Obedience of Jesus in the Blessed
Sacrament.. 250

SERMON XVII.—Jesus in the Blessed Sacrament a Hidden God.. 268

SERMON XVIII —Jesus in the Blessed Sacrament a Hidden God
(*continued*)... 280

SERMON XIX.—Jesus in the Blessed Sacrament filled with Reproaches 296

SERMON XX —The Glorification of the Sacred Body of Jesus in
the Blessed Sacrament and by the Blessed Sacrament....... 317

SERMON XXI.—The Life of Jesus in the Blessed Sacrament 329

THE LIFE OF THE CHURCH................................... 343

CARDINAL WISEMAN'S PASTORAL

ON THE

"FORTY HOURS' EXPOSITION OF THE BLESSED SACRAMENT."

THE following Pastoral, being the "Lenten Indult for the London District" for the year 1849, in which the Forty Hours' Devotion was officially and systematically introduced into the English metropolis, will be found an appropriate and useful introduction to this volume of sermons, which aims at encouraging the devotion of the faithful during the solemn exposition of the Most Blessed Sacrament. There is ample and most excellent material in this Pastoral for a beautiful and practical sermon on the Adoration of the Blessed Sacrament at the Forty Hours' Devotion:

To our dearly beloved in Christ, the Clergy, secular and regular, and the Laity of the London District:

HEALTH AND BENEDICTION IN THE LORD.

As the Almighty, dearly beloved in Christ, was pleased, at creation, to set in the heavens a bright luminary "to preside over the day," and to be "for signs, and seasons, and days, and years, and to shine in the firmament of

13

heaven, and give light to the earth;"[1] so when the same Spirit, who first moved upon the waters to give them life, again returned to renew it, in the blessed womb of Mary, and God created a new heaven and a new earth for man redeemed, no less did He bid His sun of righteousness to shine upon them both, declaring that He, too, should be set up "as a sign,"[2] to men   And from that time it is not to the visible sun that the believer looks for his division of seasons, of days, and of years, but to that "splendor of the Father's glory"[3] manifested to him, whose cycle of glorious actions, achieved for man, diversifies with beauty and energizes with life each succeeding season   We count our years from Christmas to Christmas; that is, from one commemoration of His blessed nativity to another; even in the distribution of our social year, we yet prefer to regularity of division the terms marked, at unequal distances, by the great festivals dear to our fathers,[4] and the freshness and beauty of spring are more naturally associated in our minds with the joyful solemnity of Easter, though yearly varying its period, than with any fixed day on which the beginning of that season may be marked in our almanacs.

If our days and years are thus regulated in their course by the "true light that enlighteneth every man that cometh into the world,"[5] what portion of His earthly career is represented to us by this solemn season of Lent, on which we are about to enter ? Surely not merely those forty days of fast which He spent in the desert; for the year would not thus suffice for the many great mysteries which have to be crowded into it; nor does the Church occupy us beyond one day with this, our blessed Redeemer's retreat But in those forty days, what did He symbolize in Himself

---

[1] Gen. 1. 14, 16.   [2] Luke ii. 34.   [3] Heb. 1. 3.
[4] As Lady Day and Michaelmas   [5] John 1. 9

but the Christian's life on earth, passed in banishment from his true country, in the midst of a wilderness, pathless, dreary, and waste; wherein he is " the brother of dragons and the fellow of ostriches;" [1] where there is famine and drought of all that can satisfy the soul; where he is tempted with the threefold assault of those whom he has forsworn; and which, O sole consolation! begins with baptism,[2] and closes with an angels' banquet.[3] Those forty days were as Israel's forty years' sojourn in the desert, typical of the rescued soul's pilgrimage all the way to the Land of Promise.

And similarly, dearly beloved in Christ Jesus, does the Church commemorate, in these forty days of Lent, the active life of our blessed Redeemer upon earth For having first, with great minuteness, brought before us the incidents of His birth, she seems to pause for some weeks, as though to commemorate His hidden life at Nazareth, and then, having sobered our thoughts by the recollection of man's creation, fall, speedy corruption, and nearly total destruction by the deluge, and having awfully reminded us of our frail and perishing nature as dust, she introduces before us Our Saviour laboring to repair past losses, from His fast in the wilderness to His entry into Jerusalem; when more awful scenes commence, and the Lenten commemoration subsides into a deep abyss of holier and tenderer contemplations during Passion-tide. Throughout this whole period the Church presents us daily, as she does at no other time, with a distinct portion of gospel history, which no, even greatest, feast can supersede; in which is placed before us some lesson of heavenly wisdom, or some splendid act of power and mercy, or some touching record of kindness and forgiveness; ever diversified, but all tending to fill up the picture of Our Saviour's character, and

---

[1] Job xxx. 29. [2] Matt. iii. 13. [3] Ibid. iv. 11.

place before us the model of His sacred humanity: the cheering and joyful is brought forward as vividly as the grave and solemn; Thabor indeed twice [1] for one proclamation of doom.[2]

And wherefore, then, should this commemoration be made in fasting and weeping and mourning ? Because, dearly beloved, we are so drawn away from thought of things heavenly by the world and the flesh, that we must put aside the one, and subdue the other, to enter profitably into the contemplation of that holy life. Because not only contemplation, but practice, is proposed to us, and the precepts enjoined us in our Gospel regard patience, and humility, and mortification, and weeping, and praying, and fasting, and watching, and almsgiving, the having our loins girt and our lamps trimmed, the walking on a narrow way, the denying of ourselves, the renouncing of all things; and surely it is not too much to be called on to practise these things, faintly at best, while we are presumed to be learning them Because not only practice, but imitation, is required of us; and the life of Jesus was a life of rigor, of poverty, of frequent retirement; of one who had not where to lay His head,[3] save all night long on the bosom of His Father in prayer; [4] who wept and mourned while all was joy, and triumph, and hosanna around Him. Because not mere imitation, but conformity, is demanded from us, so that not only our acts should be like unto His, however distantly, but our hearts and affections, too; as though we were the wax whereon become impressed His character and type, we sharing in His affections, His severities, His choices, His repugnances, His whole thought and heart; and how shall this be, if, we living with the world, every one of these shall run counter in us to what was in

[1] On the second Saturday and second Sunday.
[2] Monday after first Sunday.
[3] Luke ix. 58.   [4] Ibid. vi. 12.

Him; our love being for what He abhorred, and our choice for what He rejected?

But if the rule of the Christian fast is that prescribed by our blessed Lord, not to be, " as the hypocrites, sad," [1] the Church will not fail to provide you during this holy season of fasting, the means and motives of spiritual joy. She will associate with the hard, but consoling task of imitating our divine Redeemer, in the practice of His virtues, that devotion towards Him in His adorable humanity, which more than any other pours the unction of gladness [2] over the soul, and makes the spirit to exult in God its Saviour. [3] Yes, beloved in the Lord, on her behalf, and through the divine mercy, we have thought it our duty to provide for you, during this season of mourning, an unfailing source of consolation, of grace, of devotion, and of love. We have therefore so disposed, as that, throughout the whole of Lent, the Most Blessed Sacrament shall remain exposed in one or other of the public churches or chapels of this metropolis, so that every day it may be in each one's power, not only to assist at a solemn service of the Church, but, at whatever time he chooses, to pour out his affections at the feet of his Saviour. And we doubt not that every one will gladly seize any moment of leisure to pay his tribute of homage to Him, at that particular place where, on each day, He shall be more especially honored.

And as this devotion, called the " Forty Hours' Exposition of the Blessed Sacrament," is as yet but little known in this country, we will proceed, in a few words, to explain it: premising no more of its history than to say that it was first instituted at Milan, in 1534; that it was thence introduced into Rome, through the instrumentality of its great modern apostle, the holy St. Philip Neri, and was formally

---

[1] Matt. vi. 16.   [2] Ps. xliv. 8.   [3] Luke i. 47.

sanctioned by Pope Clement VIII., in 1592, in consequence, as he says, of the troubled state of Christendom and the sufferings of the Church.[1]

As a condition of the Incarnation of the Word an exchange was made, not unequal, between earth and heaven. We gave to it not only the spirits of the just made perfect, in the glorious choir of saints who fill the seats of fallen angels, but, in anticipation of the resurrection, one precious instalment of humanity glorified, in her the spotless, who rules, in the very body, over the hosts of angels as their queen. But even higher this our flesh has penetrated, yea, into the very sanctuary of God's light inaccessible. For in the very midst and centre of that dazzling radiance towards which blissful spirits bend, gazing and adoring, is to be seen the gentle "likeness of the Son of man," [2] in all things resembling us And in return heaven has bestowed on earth, not merely communion between us and its happy citizens, but the permanent dwelling of God amongst us, who under the name of the Emmanuel, or "God with us," lives ever in the midst of His Church, to be the direct object of our adoration and love.

And so it comes, dearly beloved, that heaven worships now the nature of man indivisibly united with the Godhead, and earth adores the Deity, joined inseparably to our humanity, in the Person of the Incarnate Word. Hence is our worship and theirs but one; one in object, one in value, one in sentiment, one, if possible, in form For so identical throughout this communion of saints is the essence of divine worship, that the very mode of its performance necessarily becomes similar, not to say one So that in reading the glorious visions of heaven's sanctuary, thrown open to St. John, it becomes difficult to determine whether

---

[1] Raccolta di Orazioni, &c.   Rome, 1841, p. 181.
[2] Apoc. i. 13.

he there beheld counterparts to what the Church had already instituted upon earth, or types which served her, under apostolic guidance, for the framing of her ritual. But rather would we say that the same divine instinct guided both; and taught angels in heaven and saints on earth to adore and to love with the same outward expression. And so the whole forms but one Church and one worship. There is one altar in both, beneath which the slain for Christ rest, and on which the same victim-Lamb reposes; one censer from which prayer rises fragrant from minister's to angel's hand, one bench of venerable elders, that sit or fall prostrate in rich array around; one choir, one song, one voice, one heart, one life.

In one respect only would these services appear to differ,—that theirs is perpetual, uninterrupted, unceasing; that the thrice-repeated " Holy " echoes ever through those golden vaults, while we only at brief and distant periods can unite in formal worship. But even here the spouse of Christ on earth would not be outdone; and wishful to rival the very deathless and sleepless watchfulness of those eyes that sparkle all over the cherubim round the throne of God,[1] she has instituted at different periods modes of imitating the unfailing worship of heaven In early ages she taught her religious in desert and in monastery to divide themselves into choirs, that day and night kept up the praises of God in uninterrupted psalmody; and in our days (O happy and heavenly thought !) she has instituted this perpetual adoration of the Blessed Eucharist of Him whom in heaven they so worship, with us present as truly as with them. This it is, dearly beloved, that we are going to introduce among you.

But it is not your Saviour, " as the hidden manna " [2] of which you partake, that you have here to reverence and

---

[1] Apoc. iv. 6.   [2] Ibid. ii 17.

love; it is your Lord, your God, triumphant over death for you, yet shrouding from you His overpowering glory, to whom you have to pay your open and solemn homage; not enshrined in His poor tabernacle, where, because unseen, He is often unhonored; but enthroned, as in heaven, above IIis own altar, lord of His own sanctuary, centre of all surrounding splendor, challenging, with love, deep adoration. Around Him shall flame the hallowed tapers by whose pure ray the Church symbolizes, however feebly, the bright spirits that shine around IIis heavenly throne. At IIis feet earth shall scatter its choicest flowers, as its graceful tribute to Him that bloomed so fair from Jesse's root.[1] On all sides shall be arrayed whatever of richness and splendor our poverty can collect to adorn the chosen abode of Him who hath said, " The silver is Mine, and the gold is Mine," [2] and does not disdain any manifestation of our reverence. Hasten then, dearly beloved, to bring whatever may be necessary to enrich the solemnity . of that happy day when your Lord, in His kingly progress, shall visit your own temple, saying, " I will fill *this* house with glory," [3] and, whether it be splendid or lowly, shall there abide in special state. Give proof to all that come there to visit Him that you prize, you cherish, you love this privilege which He bestows; and that, like Solomon and the people of Israel, you have " gladly offered all those things " [4] which are requisite to its becoming, and even splendid, enjoyment. And " presently the Lord whom you seek, and the Angel of the testament whom you desire, shall come to His temple." [5]

Oh, then, go forth with joyful hearts to meet and welcome Him; and leave Him not alone, so long as He shall condescend to dwell in the midst of you. From that lofty

---

[1] Isai. xi. 1.   [2] Aggeus ii. 9.   [3] Ibid. 8.
. [4] 1 Paral. xxix. 17.   [5] Malachias iii. 1.

mercy-seat whereon He hath been placed, from that bright
radiance in the midst of which, as a peerless and priceless
gem, He hath been set—beauty Himself, essential light,
and matchless splendor—there go forth on every side, not
scorching rays of glory, not burning shafts of might, but
a mild and constant flow of holiness and grace, which fills
the entire space from roof to pavement with the very
breath and air of heaven. Silent and soft, as wave impell-
ing wave of fragrance goes forth and diffuses itself around,
that savor of sweetness, that balm of life, that virtue
which, emanating from the sacred humanity of Jesus upon
earth, healed all diseases [1] And from the threshold of
this His palace now, no less than His temple, it will pass
abroad and spread itself on all sides till it reach your dwellings; and more powerful than that blessing which the Ark
of the Covenant (type, whereof you now possess the reality)
shed over the house of Obededom,[2] it will impart to them
peace and grace, and welfare spiritual and temporal. " I
will fill this house with glory, saith the Lord of hosts . . .
and in this place I will give peace, saith the Lord of
hosts." [3]

But now it is that you will practise that angelic worship lost and unknown out of the Catholic Church—the
worship of pure adoration. For beyond her pale men may
praise God, or address Him, or perform other religious acts,
but they cannot know nor make that special homage which
His presence, as we possess it, inspires; when, without
word spoken, or sound uttered, or act performed, the soul
sinks prostrate and annihilates itself before Him; casts all
its powers, and gifts, and brightest ornaments, as worthless
oblations before His altar, and subjects its entire being,
as a victim, to His sole adorable will. When first, then,
you approach the place where He is solemnly worshipped,

---

[1] Luke viii. 46.   [2] 2 Kings vi. 12.   [3] Aggeus ii. 10.

as you humbly bend your knees and bow your heads, let this deep and silent adoration be your first act. Speak not in words; forget all selfish thoughts; repress, even, all eager longings of your hearts, and receive the benediction of your mighty Lord in solemn stillness; while you, reputing yourselves but dust and ashes at His feet, a nothingness before Him, tender Him the homage of loyal vassals, humbled as the clay before the potter,[1] as the creature before its God. Then raise up your eyes, those keen eyes of faith, which, through the veil of sacramental elements, see, as John did, "in the midst of the seven golden candlesticks, one like to the Son of man,"[2] yea, the adorable Jesus, the King of your souls; and there feast long your sight upon that sacred humanity which love hath given Him, and with it kindred and brotherhood, and ties of tenderest affection with you. And now speak to Him, but with outpoured souls, with the unrestrained familiarity of warmest friendship, face to face; no longer with the awful Lord, like Moses or Elias, on Horeb,[3] but with them, and Peter and John, on Thabor,[4] where you see Him radiant with His own light, but mild and inviting love.

Pray to Him now for your own salvation and for that of all mankind. Pray for the exaltation of His holy Church, for the happiness and prosperity of its supreme Pastor, our dear and afflicted Pontiff. Pray for the propagation of the true faith, and the conversion of all in error, and especially of our own dear country. Pray that God will mercifully remove from us the scourges and judgments which we have deserved by our sins, and remember no longer our offences, nor those of our parents, but rather show us mercy, and give to us His good gifts, but principally His grace, holiness of life, and perseverance in His holy service.

---

[1] Isaias xxix 16.   [2] Apoc. i. 13.
[3] Exod. xxxiii. 11 , 3 Kings xix. 11.   [4] Matt. xvii. 2.

And then, oh, never think of rising from before Him without thanking Him from your hearts for this miraculous institution of His power and goodness, this sweetest pledge of His love ! Adore Him now again, as the treasure of your souls, the food of life, the living Bread that cometh down from heaven, your consoler, your strengthener, your surest hope in life and death. Speak to Him of the kindness, of the self-abasement, of the immense condescension which He here exhibits; of the untiring affection for poor man which He displays, in bearing with so much coldness, ingratitude, and even sacrilege, as this blessed memorial of His death exposes Him to; of the still more incomprehensible excess of love which makes Him communicate Himself daily to us, frail and sinful creatures, as our food, and thus brings our very hearts and souls into contact with His ! And offer Him your humble tribute of reverence and love, in reparation and atonement for those scoffs, contradictions and blasphemies to which He has long been, and is daily, subject in His Adorable Sacrament, and nowhere so much as in this unbelieving land.

But, dearly beloved in Christ, confine not your devotion to the time when the opportunity for this heavenly act of worship shall come to your very doors. Say rather, " We will go into His tabernacle, we will adore in the place where His feet have stood." [1] Make this, if possible, a daily devotion throughout the Lent,—this daily worship of your divine Saviour in His Blessed Eucharist. Fear not to penetrate where His humbler temples stand in the midst of His poor; let your faith guide you beyond the range of your ordinary occupations, and the beat of worldly recreations, holding that spot to be the most noble, the most sacred, and the most highly privileged for the time, in which He is manifested, to be publicly adored.

---

[1] Ps. cxxxi. 7.

And the further to encourage you to this devotion, we not only remind you of the many spiritual favors bestowed upon such as practise it, but we exercise the power conferred upon us by the sovereign Pontiff of communicating a plenary indulgence, which may be gained by each one twice in the course of the Lent, with the usual conditions of confession and communion, by visiting the Forty Hours.

And, beyond the places set down in the Table published by us of the Exposition of the Blessed Sacrament in London, we leave it to the discretion of the pastor of each other place in this district, should he deem it conducive to the piety of his flock to have it in his church or chapel, on such days as he shall think fit, in the form also published by our authority, and with the above conditions and privileges.

" Now, to Him who is able to preserve you without sin, and to present you spotless before the presence of His glory with exceeding joy, in the coming of Our Lord Jesus Christ; to the only God Our Saviour, through Jesus Christ Our Lord, be glory and magnificence, empire and power before all ages, and now for all ages of ages."[1]

---

[1] Jude 24, 25.

EXTERIOR REVERENCE DUE TO THE EXPOSITION OF THE BLESSED SACRAMENT.

By R. P. Eymard.

WE should honor the Blessed Sacrament when exposed by even greater reverence and respect than when enclosed in the tabernacle. (Our Lord exposed in the Blessed Sacrament is the King upon His throne.) If this respect be due from all, it should be shown in a more marked degree still by members of the Guard of Honor, who are the courtiers of this divine King. It is not only an honor that we are bound to render to Our Lord, but a true adoration, for He wills to be honored by the body as well as the mind; to Him is due the adoration of the exterior as well as the interior man. This is the reason why an exterior and sensible worship is observed, animated by the interior worship of charity.

As regards the exterior worship, greater ceremony and solemnity is required by the Church when the Blessed Sacrament is exposed than when it is reserved in the tabernacle, because it is a greater manifestation of the love of Our Lord. The Church wishes that Our Lord should shine out upon His throne in glory above all others, and that He should absorb all our thoughts. She will not allow upon the altar statues of the saints nor sacred relics, wishing that the adorer should concentrate all thoughts and devotion upon the adorable Person of Jesus Christ, and that all exterior ceremony may surround the Blessed Sacrament alone.

She ordains for these occasions more magnificent ornaments and decorations She requires the priest to wear his surplice when entering the sanctuary, because ordinary garb is not fitting at the court of the King

The genuflection is no longer a sufficient mark of respect; a more profound prostration on both knees is required when addressing the King upon His throne. We should study the liturgy of the Church, and by our exterior deportment in presence of the Blessed Sacrament express the deep respect and adoration that fill our hearts. We should preserve a recollected demeanor and keep our eyes cast down. I do not mean that it is better to close our eyes. On the contrary, in presence of the exposition, it is better to look at the altar. Why does the Church expose Our Lord upon His throne and adorn it with such beauty and splendor, if she does not wish that we should look upon this magnificence, in order that our hearts might by it be led to God ? Why should Our Lord be upon His throne if it is not that we might see Him better ? He clothes Himself with these exterior and sensible appearances that impress our senses only that we may say: "I see the good God through these filmy clouds; His face is hidden, but it is He !"

Strange to say, this exterior magnificence never becomes a source of distraction to the soul of the adorer. It is therefore that I say to you: Look at the altar, the burning tapers, the beautiful flowers, and let them suggest holy thoughts. It is so natural that we cannot help it. It would indeed be a mark of disrespect to the Blessed Sacrament if, instead of looking at the altar, we were looking around to see the people coming in and out, and to notice their dress or manners. Let your eyes lead you to Our Lord, and not away from Him.

I would say also: Be dignified and grave in your manner in the presence of Our Lord. Kneel as long as you can, and if you must be seated, avoid a negligent and careless attitude.

We would not loll on the seats at a reception. Surely, we would like to appear dignified and polite in the society of people of good breeding.

Do not speak in the church when the Blessed Sacrament is exposed, and do not pay any attention to what is going on around you. In presence of the King no one ever thinks of the servants, it would be a great want of politeness

Again in presence of the Blessed Sacrament, let us put aside the thought of our business, our friends, our cares, to think that we are there for God alone. It is said in the Canticle of Canticles: " Do not disturb My beloved until she awakes," that is to say, leave the soul that adores Thee to finish her contemplation. You should be respected and much respected, and be left in peace to pray when you are before the Blessed Sacrament: your whole occupation then is to adore Our Lord and listen to His divine word.

But you say: " Suppose some one speaks to me ? " Do not say in reply four words where one would be enough; do not answer even, " We will go outside and speak, it would not do here." But answer, if it is necessary, by a simple " yes " or " no," in a low voice. There is a way of speaking, gently in low tones, that is a lesson in itself. If it is any one over whom you have authority, impose silence at once; it is your duty.

If we had more respect and understood better the etiquette of the King's audience, we would never have the courage to interrupt any one at prayer; on the contrary, we would do everything possible to avoid distracting him What would we do in the world if a person were called to an audience with the king by his own desire? Surely no one would be so rude as to interrupt the interview, not even one of the king's ministers. The adoration which is an audience with Our Lord, the interview with our souls that His love has so ardently desired, does it not merit at least as much consideration as the private audiences with the kings of this world ? All this shows that our faith is not what it should be. We should practise perfectly this worship of exterior reverence in our looks, in our deportment and in our silence; it is enough that our adoration should suffer from our coldness and distraction of mind; the exterior, at least, it is always in our power to control. If our heart is a ruin, a desert, at least let us honor Our Lord by the exterior, that we may by that means reach the interior.

[From " The Sentinel of the Blessed Sacrament," Vol. II., 8.]

SERMONS ON THE BLESSED SACRAMENT.

SERMON I.

THE INTENTION OF THE CHURCH AND THE DISPOSITION OF
THE FAITHFUL IN THE CELEBRATION OF THE FORTY HOURS'
PRAYER.

"Come, let us adore and fall down."—Ps. xciv. 6.

IN establishing the devotion which is known as the Forty Hours' Adoration, the Church provides that once each year the homage of every Catholic congregation shall be offered in a most solemn and public manner to our dear Lord in the Holy Eucharist.

The Church, indeed, invites and urges us to make frequent visits to Jesus in the Blessed Sacrament throughout the whole year, and to pay our meed of adoration to Him before the altar in *silent* prayer and *solitary* devotion. Once a year, however, at the Forty Hours, every parish in the diocese takes its turn in offering to our Eucharistic King, our blessed Saviour in the Sacrament of His love, amid the most sacred and sublime rites and ceremonies, a *public* protestation of faith, a *grand* demonstration of honor, a *solemn* tribute of praise, a *united and prolonged, a devout and most worthy* homage of adoration, thanksgiving, reparation and prayer.[1]

---

[1] *Vide* Preface, pp. 5-8, for history and purposes of the Forty Hours.

My dear friends, if you have ever tasted the sweet and heavenly joy of this blessed occasion, you will not need a pressing invitation to come again and attend the Forty Hours' Adoration. That your devotion may be more fruitful, however, we will, before the opening of the Forty Hours, consider to-day some of the *reasons* which the Church had in establishing this devotion, and reflect on the holy *dispositions* with which the faithful should attend it. The Church has many ends in view in the celebration of the Forty Hours. At present we will consider only three points.

The Forty Hours should be—

I. A solemn thanksgiving.

II. A source of rich graces and many blessings.

III. A quickening and strengthening of the faith.

First Point.—In the Forty Hours our hearts are gladdened and excited to devotion by the chanting of sweet sacramental hymns, and the substance of these songs, to a great extent, is contained in that beautiful, indulgenced ejaculation:

> " O Sacrament most holy ! O Sacrament divine!
> All praise and all thanksgiving be every moment Thine "

Now, the first disposition which a devout soul should have in the celebration of the Forty Hours, is a sentiment of warmest and deepest *gratitude* to Jesus in the great Sacrament of His love. We must be incited to this by the reflection that (we owe Our Saviour an open acknowledgment that, among all the gifts and graces we have received from His merciful hand, the greatest, the most precious, the most holy is the Blessed Sacrament of the Altar.) Let us make this clear: To every Christian who has a lively faith it must be evident that, among all the sacraments, the Holy Eucharist holds the first place. We not only call this Sacrament the " supreme Good, " it is such in reality.) O my friends, arouse your faith and consider earnestly what a precious treasure, what a costly gift, the Blessed Sacrament is! Compare it with other holy things.

It is not merely blessed water by which we are purified from sin and made a child of God; it is not merely a mighty, absolving, life-giving word which calls and awakens the sinner from the grave of sin to the life of grace; it is not merely a consecrated chrism by which the child of God is anointed, consecrated, and strengthened to be a soldier, a warrior for the holy cause of God, his heavenly Father, and by which he is victorious and triumphant over the world and the devil and himself; the Blessed Sacrament, my brethren, is more, far more, inexpressibly more. It is the true body, it is the true blood of Our Lord and Saviour Jesus Christ; or, to speak more properly, it is Our Lord and God Himself, with flesh and blood, with soul and body, with divinity and humanity. He has made Himself a means of grace by a holy sacrament, and has given it to each of us.

Rise up, Christian soul, and realize how greatly thy God has honored thee. See the eyes of thy blessed Redeemer, which looked so tenderly and helpfully on all misery, which melted so many hard hearts, and, finally, were blinded with blood for thee: they are thine.

The ears of thy blessed Redeemer, which were ever open compassionately to all pleading, and at last for thy sake heard patiently the horrible cry: Crucify Him! Crucify Him! They are now thine own.

The lips of thy blessed Redeemer, which by their words of truth and consolation poured forth such light and infused such balm into the hearts of men, and at last were moistened for thee with vinegar and bitter gall, thou mayest call them thine own.

The hands of thy blessed Redeemer, which were ever open to bless, and ever ready to dry all tears, and at last were outstretched, pierced through and nailed fast, of them mayest thou say: I possess them.

The feet of thy blessed Redeemer, which went about sore and wounded bringing peace and happiness to all, and at last were fastened to the cross for thee, of them mayest thou say: They are mine.

And the Heart of thy blessed Redeemer, in which every one of His creatures, even the least, has a place, and which at last was broken by the pain caused by our sins, even of this mayest thou say: It is my own.

The soul of thy blessed Redeemer, which lived for nothing but the salvation of men, which was consumed by longing for the redemption of the world, which was sorrowful unto death, and at last sank under the abandonment of God, and gave itself into the hands of His heavenly Father, of that too mayest thou say: It is mine.

Yes, the divinity of thy blessed Redeemer, which loved thee so much that it emptied itself and assumed the form of a servant, and in this form of a servant was obedient unto death, even unto the death of the cross, of this thou mayest say it is now thine own. O truly of all heavenly gifts the Blessed Sacrament is the most sublime, the most precious, the holiest!

And now need I add a word to make it clear that we must unite this week in deepest gratitude to repeat solemnly and publicly to Our Lord in the Blessed Sacrament the prayer of praise: " Blessed be the Most Holy Sacrament! " to chant to Him our " Ave Jesu! " to cry:

"O Sacrament most holy! O Sacrament divine!
All praise and all thanksgiving be every moment Thine."

My brethren, let us not be put to shame by the faithful of the Old Law. Hear how King Dávid, by the inspiration of God, called upon the chosen people: " Praise the Lord, O Jerusalem: praise thy God, O Sion." And why should they do this ? Hear what the Psalmist says further: "Because He declareth His word to Jacob: His justices and His judgments to Israel." Therefore, since God had made His revelations to them, the Jewish people should not weary in praising its Lord. And the royal singer adds: "He hath not done in like manner to every nation: And His judgments He hath not made manifest to them." Then in what words would he have called upon them to praise God had that gift of grace, the Blessed Sacrament, been revealed to his people ? He had a slight presentiment of it. In the manna he had a faint foreshadowing of the Blessed Sacrament, but we note that words fail him in speaking of it. He exclaims: "I will praise Thee, O Lord, with my whole heart," but, he says to himself, not I alone; that is not enough, and he adds: "In the counsel of the just, and in the congregation." And how does he express this praise of God ? "Great," he exclaims, "are the works of the Lord: sought out according to all His wills. His work is praise and magnificence. He hath made a remembrance of His wonderful works, being a merciful and gracious Lord." Ah, how full of gratitude is a heart that thus rejoices ! And behold, my brethren, we find here also indicated the manner in which we should show our gratitude to Our Lord in the Blessed Sacrament.

Beloved, it is a part of gratitude to make known and to acknowledge the grace which we have received; to openly reveal how highly we value it; to seek opportunities to praise the Giver. And you will now understand and feel why the Church—the David, the divine messenger of the New Testament—should summon everything that is magnificent, precious, and beautiful in the domain of nature and art to glorify and honor the Blessed Sacrament.

Behold, Jesus has made Himself so little and hidden in the Blessed Sacrament for us, and the Church builds Him grand cathedrals, churches, and chapels; Jesus has made Himself poor in the Blessed Sacrament in order to enrich us, and the Church gives Him all riches and treasures; Jesus is so silent in the Blessed Sacrament, and the houses of God resound with prayer and song, whereby He is loudly and solemnly praised and glorified, adored and invoked.

The Church does this with a feeling of deepest gratitude, for she knows that she owes, now and forever, a great debt to her dear Lord, which cannot be paid, and must stand undischarged. She is indebted to Him for this Sacrament, in which are contained all the riches of the compassion of a God, in which is enthroned the fulness of the divinity, and she will at least do all that she can to prevent it from being a hidden treasure. Yes, being sensible of the love and ceaseless bounty of her Spouse, who has adorned her with this Most Holy Sacrament, she will publish her love and acknowledgment of it, rendering Him praise, glory, and thanksgiving, and, louder than words can express it, church and tower, the solemn peal of bells, the organ and the altar, the richest vestments and hundreds of burning candles, the perfume of flowers, the earnest prayers and sacred chants of men cry out: " Come and behold the great things that the Lord has done for me, and I will show thee the remembrance of the wonderful works of God, thy great, living God, in the little, lifeless, inanimate form of bread."

Surely, Christian soul, you must approve of the Church's action, but you must also unite yourself to her, for this great Sacrament belongs to you; is completely and forever yours Therefore the Church cries out to you: " Come with me, pray with me, and let us fall down before our God in the Blessed Sacrament."

Beloved, let us do this, and prove that to us the Blessed Sacrament is the highest Good; let us prove that we have a taste for what is divine and heavenly; let us prove that to us the lowly, lifeless form of bread that we see is not only no temptation to us to leave neglected and dishonored the majesty of Our Lord and God who has condescended to dwell therein, but rather the fact that Jesus in the Blessed Sacrament is a hidden God and Saviour shall make us praise and honor more and more this great, wonderful and holiest of sacraments. We will prove that we know whose fault it is that Jesus dwells among us so poor and humiliated. We, my brethren, because we are sinners, who stand in need of the sacrifice of propitiation, bear the guilt thereof. Oh, we know, beloved, that we owe Him thanks that for love of us He has voluntarily confined Himself in this prison of the form of bread, and shall we weary of repeating in deepest gratitude: " Blessed be the Most Holy Sacrament! " of devoutly singing our "Ave Jesu! " and of crying out:

"O Sacrament most holy! O Sacrament divine!
All praise and all thanksgiving be every moment Thine."

Another object that the Church has in view in establishing the Forty Hours is this: She wishes to apply to the faithful all the graces and blessings of the Sacrament.

Second Point —There are occasions upon which princes and kings bestow their gifts generously upon their subjects. If a whole people unanimously arose, and went solemnly to its lord to offer him publicly its homage, the day on which they did this would surely be such an occasion. The people would have gone to him because the king desired it, therefore they must retain something to make them conscious that they had been near to the king, and it would be a duty on the part of the sovereign to make the day one that his people could not forget. And this should not be merely by showing himself to them in his splendor and might, but rather by helping them. For a king is not only a lord, he is also the father of his people.

We know perfectly well that Jesus can help us, and make us feel His love and compassion even though we be far away from the holy place where He dwells in the Blessed Sacrament with His divinity and humanity. For what He did when He went about visibly among us under the form of a servant, He can do now that He abides with us invisibly under the form of bread, and not all who then experienced His compassionate assistance were in His bodily presence; many were far, far away. Even thus it is now; Our Lord sends help to many from the tabernacle, though they have not gone to Him in the Blessed Sacrament.

Yes, beloved, and there is something more. Even if we are before the Blessed Sacrament we must have that faith which we see in the centurion in the Gospel, who spoke to Our Lord and asked Him to heal his servant When Our Lord said to him. " I will come and heal him," this believing soul made a reply that not only showed his profound humility, but also expressed a great truth " O Lord," he protested reverently, "I am not worthy that Thou shouldst enter under my roof." And, so strongly was he convinced that this was not necessary to the doing of what he desired that he added: "Say but the word, and my servant shall be healed." Behold, my brethren, this faith must we have, even when we are before the Blessed Sacrament. This is so true and certain, beloved, that in the solemn moment when we are about to receive Our Lord to the nourishment of our soul, the Church puts these words into our mouth. When you are prepared, when with yearning desire you have prayed, and have invited your Lord with the words: " Come, O my Jesus, and visit me, and strengthen my soul with Thy grace; I am so weary and heavy laden; O quicken my soul," what does the priest do by command of the Holy Ghost enlightening the Church? He shows you your blessed Lord under the form of bread, and prays thrice the prayer in which you must join: "Lord, I am not worthy that Thou shouldst enter under my roof; say but the word and my soul shall be healed." You see that we Christians know quite well that Jesus can help us, and show us His love and compassion without our presenting ourselves in the holy place where He dwells under the form of bread, with His divinity and humanity.

But, my brethren, in connection with this truth, there is another fact to be considered. While Jesus was on earth He surely showed His compassion to those who were around Him. He poured forth His assistance without reserve, with the greatest generosity when the people drew near Him in great multitudes, and gave Him special proofs of their confidence. St Luke tells us in his gospel: "And coming down with them He stood in a plain place, and the company of His disciples, and a very great multitude of people from all Judea and Jerusalem, and the seacoast both of Tyre and Sidon who were come to hear Him and be healed of their diseases And they that were troubled with unclean spirits were cured And all the multitude sought to touch Him, for virtue went out of Him, and healed all." You see there, beloved, the people in a great multitude; you see an especial proof of veneration, of honor, and confidence shown Our Lord by this multitude. You see also that each one was helped according to his need, because all had approached Our Lord in a solemn manner. And so, too, my brethren, though we have just said that Jesus can show us His compassion and love and power through the Blessed Sacrament, even though we have not presented ourselves before His tabernacle, yet we must not forget that He opens His treasures more generously for those who take the trouble to come to Him in the Blessed Sacrament, and He will lavish them without reserve, in more abundant fulness still, when His faithful come in great multitudes to pay Him a particular homage, as at the Forty Hours.

How could it be otherwise ? For, my brethren, if it is true that Our Lord dwells among us in the Blessed Sacrament with the intention of helping us, then it is a special inducement for Him to open His treasures and share them with the faithful if they present themselves before Him, and come to plead with Him for them. Particularly will He bestow His treasures, and far, far will they flow out from Him, if the faithful come to Him, not singly, or in solitude to show their devotion to Him, but rather if they unite together to do this, and Our Lord sees them around Him, worshipping Him openly and solemnly.

Behold the end the Church has in view when she ordains that the Forty Hours shall be celebrated yearly in each parish. Not content with urging the people to come often to visit Our Lord in the Blessed Sacrament, and adore Him in silence, the Church desires them to come for many consecutive hours to their hidden Saviour, to come in great multitudes, and publicly and solemnly praise, glorify, and adore Him, and make reparation to Him in prayer and song; and she does this, among other reasons, that the graces and blessings of the Sacrament may flow upon us in greater fulness. Therefore she cries out to you: " Come now at this time; fall down with me before your God in the Blessed Sacrament, and adore Him with me: many and great are the blessings which our dear Lord will shower upon you."

You will certainly call this action of the Church right and proper, but you must also respond earnestly to this invitation; you must act in union with the Church, you must bear your full share in the Forty Hours; you must take care that all the hours of adoration, to the very end, are well attended. Let the stream of visitors never be interrupted. For the Blessed Sacrament belongs to you, belongs entirely to you, and forever.

Yes, beloved, do this; show that you desire the treasures and graces of Our Lord to be poured upon you from the Blessed Sacrament; show that you understand what the King of glory expects while He dwells in our midst, and what Christendom must do if it will have Jesus open His gentle hand and fill all with joy; vie with one another in the fervor of your devotion, till graces and blessings and all spiritual treasures without reservation, and in the fullest measure, flow upon you from the Blessed Sacrament. Therefore take heed, and do your part that our Forty Hours may be what it should be, a solemn homage that the entire Christian people brings to its Lord in the Blessed Sacrament, that thereby we may fulfil the intention of the Church, which is to rejoice His bountiful, loving, Sacred Heart, and send you home richly endowed with graces and blessings of every kind.

Come all of you to the Forty Hours, come so that each hour of adoration, even to the last, be well attended; see that there is ever a great multitude here who piously pray: " Blessed be the Most Holy Sacrament! " and sing from devout hearts: " Ave Jesu ! " and cry with fervor:

> " O Sacrament most holy! O Sacrament divine!
> All praise and all thanksgiving be every moment Thine."

And now let us consider the third end that the Church has in view in celebrating annually the Forty Hours. She will thereby enliven and strengthen our faith.

Third Point.—It is with faith as it is with love. (Love diminishes with time, becomes lukewarm, and grows cold; in many cases faith, too, grows feeble in the course of time, becomes weak, powerless, lifeless.) True, it may not be quite extinguished and burned out, but with many it has no longer the strength and power, the activity and life that enable it to do or to resist whatever faith dictates. For, dear brethren, to keep to our subject, (see what disrespect is shown before our altars, how irreverently people behave; what coldness, ingratitude, and distractions they are guilty of at divine service, when hearing Mass, and receiving holy communion.)

The reason that those who are guilty of these faults make so little of them is because their faith in the Blessed Sacrament is so feeble, so perfunctory; because it is not a faith deep-rooted in their heart. How necessary, then, that it should not fall away, and diminish still further, but should be raised up again, and made living and strong by a grand demonstration, a solemn celebration, which will make an impression that will waken and direct it. How necessary is this also to those whose faith in the Blessed Sacrament is still firm and fruitful, that it may not weaken and fall away, but rather retain its vigor, increasing and perfecting itself.

It surely cannot be disputed that the Forty Hours is a feast which best leads to this end, which is best suited to awaken and strengthen a sleeping and benumbed faith, and to bring it to new activity, to greater strength and perfection. For what is this magnificent celebration of the Forty Hours, during which the Most Holy is surrounded by the splendor of burning candles, the fragrance and beautiful tints of flowers placed before the tabernacle's majestic throne, and the faithful assembled in untiring multitudes from early morning into the shades of night, kneeling in prayer and singing hymns that come from hearts adoring and praising their Lord in the Holy Eucharist? It is nothing else than a renewed profession of faith in the Blessed Sacrament which the Church makes; an official and solemn profession, a public and united, and, therefore, a worthy profession of this faith.

Yes, dear brethren, this mutual example that we give one another, this universal conviction so solemnly manifested, this unanimity calls forth a faith so strong and sure that, I might say, all difficulties are removed in a moment, all doubts yield, and are scattered like mists before the sun. We see, and believe; not as Thomas, of whom it is written that he had to see in order to believe, nor like those of whom Our Lord said: "Blessed are those who have not seen, and yet believe"—no, not thus, for we see, and believe; that is, we see this sublime and touching feast; the open, public, solemn and united adoration of Our Lord in the Blessed Sacrament, and that which the Christian sees draws him to that which he does not see; to believe that—

> "Lo, the Good, supreme and best,
> On the altar deigns to rest,
> Is with flesh and blood our Guest,"

but to believe it much more vividly, much more strongly than before   Oh, how sincerely Christians sing from their hearts in the Forty Hours—

> "Here our God Himself we see,
> Knowest thou how this can be?
> Here the senses all must fail;
> Faith alone can pierce the veil,"

and the breezes are laden with the echo of our hymn.

Now, beloved, if the feast of the Forty Hours produces such an effect on the hearts of Christians, brings about such a change for good, you see plainly how right and holy, how wise and potent are the three reasons that the Church does not content herself with urging the faithful to go alone to visit, praise, adore, and supplicate Our Lord in the Holy Eucharist in silence and solitude, but has set apart one celebration in the year, in which her children in each parish should unite to bring the homage of their adoration, thanksgiving, reparation, and prayer to Our Lord dwelling on our altars under the form of bread. She does this in order to enliven and strengthen anew in the hearts of her children their faith in the Blessed Sacrament. And, oh, how many Christians there are who still believe in the Blessed Sacrament who would have long since lost their faith if it were not strengthened and enlivened each year anew by this sublime and touching feast of the Forty Hours; and in how many Christians who have now a strong faith in the Blessed Sacrament would this faith be only faint and feeble had not this beautiful feast given their believing hearts more light and conviction, more warmth and zeal, constantly growing and becoming more fruitful.

Verily, my brethren, you must pronounce this action of the Church wise and proper; but the more clearly you see that the intention of the Church in establishing and celebrating this feast is reasonable, holy, and productive of blessings, the more closely must you unite yourself to her, in order to carry out her intentions.

We must, therefore, take care that this beautiful feast becomes actually a restorative and source of strength to our faith in the Blessed Sacrament; you must bear your full share in the celebration of the Forty Hours; you must so order it that every hour of adoration, even to the last, be well attended. Beloved, do this; prove that you recognize and know how to esteem this priceless gift of God; prove that your faith in the Blessed Sacrament is sincere and deeply rooted in your hearts; prove that you comprehend what must be done that our faith may not decrease, become faint and feeble, but rather that it may increase, growing ever greater and stronger. And take care to do your part that our Forty Hours may be what it should be, a homage to Our Saviour so solemn and affecting that it will influence all, drawing all hither that faith in the Blessed Sacrament may be strengthened in all. Take care, therefore, to come in such numbers that it may be said our whole congregation has paid this solemn homage to Our Lord, and that the few who neglect their duty may be ashamed to have stood apart in their indifference, which arises from their lack of faith.

Once more then, beloved, hear the invitation: Come ye all to the Forty Hours! But so come that each hour of prayer, to the very last, be well attended. Make it your glory and your pride that this time the number of adorers before the Most Holy be greater than ever; may there be always a multitude here to repeat piously: " Blessed be the Most Holy Sacrament ! " to sing from devout hearts, "Ave Jesu! " to cry out incessantly:

"O Sacrament most holy! O Sacrament divine!
All praise and all thanksgiving be every moment Thine."

Behold then, dear brethren, three of the holy and beneficial ends which the Church had in view in establishing the Forty Hours. This beautiful feast should be a solemn thanksgiving, a means for the bestowal of grace and blessing, and a new awakening and strengthening of faith. And where the Forty Hours is such a feast, I can venture to apply to it the sublime and joyful words uttered by the inspired Apostle: " Behold now is the acceptable time; behold now is the day of salvation." For to the Christian who believes, how acceptable must this time be, how he must look forward to, and long for this most blessed time, in which an opportunity is given him to diminish the incalculable guilt that lies upon his soul, and solemnly give thanks to our dear Lord for that excessive love which makes Him dwell with us, constantly bestowing His graces, day and night, even to the end of time. How acceptable to the Christian who believes, how longed for, and antici-

pated, must be that day which the Church has ordained
and directed shall be a day of salvation, a day on which
Our Lord in the Blessed Sacrament opens wide His gentle
hand, and pours forth in excessive fulness the treasures
of the kingdom of heaven upon all; a day on which our
dear Lord puts new strength and life into the hearts of
His own who show to Him their faith in this great, mysterious Sacrament of His love. Now, beloved, greet this
time of the Forty Hours with joy, as the blessed day which
is sent to you by heaven; celebrate it also in such spirit,
and with such disposition, that it may become to you a
holy time—truly a *"day of salvation."*

Yes, beloved, a holy time must it be; perfectly holy
must be all your actions at this celebration; we have to
render the service of angels before the Most Holy, we must
hasten to come to Him, fall down before Him, "with
cherubim and seraphim raise our voices to praise God, the
God of Sabaoth" for this Bread of heaven, to solemnly
render to Our Lord the thanks due Him for remaining so
lovingly with us. It must also be a day of salvation; everything we do on this day must be productive of blessing.
Let your conviction be strong that Our Lord will dis-
tribute His graces most generously when His followers
surround Him in a great multitude, and that our faith in
the Blessed Sacrament will be enlivened and strengthened
when we are closely banded together for this solemn worship. Hence we must each of us make a strong resolution
that it shall be a sacred and inviolable duty to celebrate
the Forty Hours most zealously. Ah, my beloved, do this.

But Thou who art in this Sacrament abiding with us,
a gracious Saviour, accept this, our feeble, impotent thank-
offering; open Thy bountiful hand and fill us all with the
treasures of Thy grace, with Thy love and mercy. Above
all strengthen and enliven our faith in this Most Holy
Sacrament; grant us ever more to feel the joy, and to

profit by the great happiness of possessing Thee, our great God and our All, in the sublime Sacrament of the Altar.

Yes, dear Lord, King and Spouse of our hearts, give us the grace that as long as we live we may never weary of coming to Thee in Thy Holy Sacrament, of falling down before Thy blessed face, and praising Thee, and adoring Thee as our God truly present, as our loving Saviour and Our Redeemer. But give us also the grace to receive Thee worthily in the hour of our death, that we may pass from this vale of tears under Thy shadow and protection, and with Thee enter into eternity, to find there not an angry Judge, who shall drive us from Him, but a gentle and merciful Saviour, who will lead us into the realms of heavenly bliss, there with Mary, Thy glorious Mother, and all Thy blessed angels and saints to see Thee clearly face to face; to love, praise, and adore Thee for all eternity. Amen !

SERMON II.

ADORATION—REPARATION.

"Come, let us adore and fall down : and weep before the Lord."
—*Ps.* xciv. 6.

You know the intention of the Church in establishing the Forty Hours. She wishes that all her children, all Christians over whom she exerts a mother's right, a mother's care, should show a well-merited honor and adoration to their Lord in the Holy Eucharist; that even if it costs a sacrifice all should come to visit Him, to adore and praise Him, thanking Him, and making reparation to Him. She invites every one to do this, and gives all an opportunity to respond easily to this invitation Each hour of the whole day is consecrated to the Most Holy Sacrament, so that you can choose for yourself the time that is most convenient for you. When we reflect who invites us, and to what we are bidden, and how easily we can respond to this invitation, we must say—we, at least, who have Catholic hearts—that we cannot refuse it.

How sad it is that we can foresee with certainty that there are children whom the Church has brought up whom she will miss from the side of her Lord during the Forty Hours; but, above all, how sad it is that the Church must say that the number of her children who no longer hear her, and never again will hear her when she invites them to the Forty Hours, has grown exceedingly great. You

46

may conceive how great a grief this is to the Church; she has a mother's heart, and is anxiously careful of her children's welfare.

But, thank God, the Church has also other, and dutiful children; children who are her joy, Catholic Christians who keep the feast of the Forty Hours sacredly, and who come to their parish church, and pray devoutly to their Lord concealed in the monstrance We have Christians who do this throughout the entire year; they are found in every parish where the Forty Hours is held. We have Christians who make great sacrifices to come, whose absence might be excused, for they have no time during the day, yet who come in the early morning, and late at night when they are tired; others there are who could take a more convenient hour, but come when it is difficult to do so, choosing a time when it is hard to make a visit. There are Christians who have done this constantly for long years; who are not content with celebrating the Forty Hours, but have formed themselves into sacramental confraternities, which perpetually adore the Blessed Sacrament. Surely these faithful souls deserve great honor; theirs is a noble generosity that merits the highest praise, and the kind and loving Saviour will reward these true Christians, these dutiful children of the Catholic Church. But where are these Christians, and who are they? Beloved, they may be all of you; surely they are most of you who are found here for the opening of the Forty Hours, and my words are applicable to you. As you may conclude from what I have just said, there are two things which I wish to impress upon you to be done in the Forty Hours. I must call upon you to adore Our Lord in the Blessed Sacrament, and make reparation to Him, if not with actual tears in your eyes, at least with sorrow in your heart. Therefore, I bid you:

I. Behold Our Lord actually present in the Blessed Sacrament, and adore Him.

II. Behold Him there so little honored, and make reparation to Him.

First Point.—Behold the altar! What do you see there? The eye, as St. Cesarius says, sees something round, something without limbs, something inanimate, unable to move, something without flesh and blood, something that has not the faintest resemblance to *man*, something that has, on the other hand, not a trace of likeness to the *highest Being*, and which is to the corporeal eye totally unlike Our Lord and God: what we see is something that appears like bread. Look at the altar, and at what you see there; it is placed upon your tongue; tell me what you see and taste. Certainly no flesh, no blood, no warmth, no life. No, it tastes like bread; it looks like bread.

But now tell me, beloved, what that actually and in truth is which looks like bread, which tastes like bread? Reply candidly, just as you think; answer with conviction, saying only as much, neither more nor less, than you can assert positively. But, beloved, before you answer, allow me one word, one remark. That which we see there is something that for eighteen hundred years has been preserved in the tabernacle in costly, consecrated vessels; it is something put on the altar for homage and reverence, wherewith also benediction is given; it is something that has been held as absolutely holy, as a Thing before which every knee must bend. Now, if this is so, who can tell us, who dares tell us, what this holy Thing is that seems, and feels, and tastes like bread?

The words of St. Peter are here fulfilled: " Lord, to whom shall we go? Thou hast the words of eternal life " Speak, Lord, Thy servant heareth. No one but Our Lord can tell us this, and especially since it is He who gives us this holy Thing. You must admit this. Then, beloved, every doubt is removed; it is clear and indisputably certain what a holy Thing it is that our religion preserves upon the altar, and which appears and tastes like bread. For know that the holy, truthful, and almighty lips of Our Lord spoke an eternally memorable and efficacious word over the bread, which He took in His holy and venerable hands, blessed, and brake, and gave to His disciples, saying, " This is My body." That means: This that I hold in My hands; this that I have blessed; this that but now was bread, though outwardly it may still seem, taste, smell like bread, precisely as before, in substance is no longer bread. " It is My body." Does it not mean this ?

Hear what St. Cyril of Jerusalem says in the instructions on the Sacrament of the Altar which he gave to the newly baptized: [" When Our Lord has spoken over the bread, and said plainly and unmistakably, ' This is My body,' who will dare doubt, or be uncertain of it, much less say that it is not ? "] We must note this well. For you see, brethren, everything that may be said of the Blessed Sacrament—that it is a symbol, a sign, a memorial of the body of Jesus does not help matters; it is all false unless one say: " It is actually the body of Jesus." For all these titles you have heard deny that the Holy Eucharist is the body of Jesus, while the words spoken by those lips that are all purity, those lips that spoke so plainly to man's comprehension, and directed the hand mighty enough to perform what the lips had spoken—these words declare, " This is My body." Here, my brethren, is applicable the hymn that we sing to the Most High:

> " Christian, rouse thy faith to see
> This great work wrought here for thee."

You cannot judge this sacred Mystery of the Altar by what you see:

> " Here the senses all must fail;
> Faith alone can pierce the veil."

This holy Thing on the altar is the remembrance, the masterpiece of the wonders of God, and of the love of an incarnate God, who loved you to the end. Surely you cannot judge and estimate it by what you feel, smell, and taste, nor by any previous experience, nor by what your mind can grasp; you can only judge and estimate it by what Our Lord said in establishing this remembrance of His wonderful works. Here you will not dare to see, feel, nor taste. "No longer are our eyes of use;" "our senses cannot enter here." You will only dare confess, "Here faith alone can understand" And this faith, having heard the words, "This is My body," sees and knows:

> "From the sacred Host is fled
> All the substance of the bread."

Sees and knows that:

> "Of the bread and wine is here
> Only that which doth appear."

Sees and knows that:

> "Now the Good, supreme and best,
> On our altar deigns to rest;
> Is with flesh and blood our Guest."

Sees and knows that:

> "In the monstrance is adored
> Christ, our undivided Lord."

Sees and knows that, "God Himself is here."

Yes, beloved, we must unite ourselves to St. Cesarius, who says, "I believe the divine Word, and through it I know that that which is immolated on our altar, and is adored and received, has not merely a likeness to God, not even merely an equal value with God, but is, in truth,

actually and substantially, the divine body." And let us
add, because the true body of Jesus is living and united
with the divine majesty, so we believe that Christ is whole
and entire in the monstrance, with divinity and humanity,
with body and soul, with flesh and blood.

You are thoroughly convinced of this, brethren; it is
your strong, unalterable faith. The holy, almighty words
of the Son of God must ring forever in our ears, " This is
My body." Now, lift up your eyes and once more look
at the altar, and tell me who it is who is here with us,
before us? Who it is who is here among us, whose eyes
are turned upon us ? O my brethren ! What a great Lord,
what a mighty King and Ruler, what a magnificent Sovereign and Master, what sublime, infinite Majesty, what a
noble Guest is here! Think of it a moment. It is Christ,
the Son of the living God, adored from all eternity! Yes,
my brethren, God Himself, the thrice holy God, our great
Lord and God is here! He who created all things by a
word; He who reigns from ocean to ocean; He who sustains
the universe by a finger; He before whose breath the earth
would vanish away; He at whose touch the pillars of heaven
would crumble; He who is the King of kings, in whose
presence nothing is of value, everything is as nothing, and
dwindles away; He whom the heavens cannot contain, nor
the earth bound; He, the true, holy, eternal God is here,
with us, among us !

Surely then, beloved, our knee will bow; surely we shall
fall down before His most holy countenance and adore
Him. You know He is worthy to receive power, and divinity, and wisdom, and strength, and honor, and glory, and
benediction. You know that to your Lord hath been given
a name which is above every name; that at the name of Jesus
every knee should bow of those that are in heaven, and on
earth, and under the earth. You know that to your Lord, the
incarnate God, veneration is due from all, and that venera-

tion which is the highest of all homage, a veneration due to none other but to Him alone; it is adoration; it is the acknowledgment that· "Thou only art holy Thou only art the Lord. Thou only, O Jesus Christ, art the Most High." It is the acknowledgment: "Thou hast created us, and hast laid Thy hand upon us, and we are Thine for all eternity." And He desires this adoration. "To Me shalt thou bow the knee; the Lord thy God shalt thou adore." My brethren, I say again:

> "Now the Good, supreme and best,
> On our altar deigns to rest,
> Is with flesh and blood our Guest."

Again I say, "God Himself is here." And remember those are holy days in which the Church with her children brings solemnly and publicly to Our Lord in the Holy Eucharist the homage of adoration that is due Him, that is fitting, and that it is our duty to bring. So I call upon you to unite yourselves with the Church, and, falling down with her before Our Lord in the Blessed Sacrament, pray with deep emotion, "Blessed be the Most Holy Sacrament," and let your Lord hear from adoring hearts and lips: "Holy, holy, holy, Lord God of Sabaoth! Heaven and earth are full of Thy glory."

Now let us go a step further, and ask how you shall bring this homage of adoration to your Lord during the Forty Hours ? Look again at the altar, and see, and reflect who it is to whom you will thus pay homage. It is the Redeemer, Jesus Christ, the Son of the living God Beloved, when I repeat the name of Jesus to you, is not your heart filled with consolation and joy? And when I say that there is now a question of giving Jesus a proof of love and gratitude, is not this a message of joy to each one of us ? Do you not think, "O my Jesus, my Saviour, I have too much for which to thank Thee; of Thy fulness

have we received." He has given us the power to become
the children of God; He has filled us with grace and truth;
He has immolated Himself that we might not be lost, but
might have eternal life. He could ask us what He would,
and were it much or were it hard, we would give it to Him,
we would do it for Him, and would give and do it joyfully.
Now, brethren, keep your word; be faithful in this; do
with joyful hearts what your Lord expects of you during
these days. Yes, my brethren, we must rejoice and be
glad that we have the desired opportunity to bring publicly and solemnly to Our Lord in the Blessed Sacrament
the homage of adoration which is His due. Therefore,
beloved, say, with happy hearts, " Blessed be the Most
Holy Sacrament! " with happy hearts repeat: " Holy, holy,
holy, Lord God of Sabaoth ! Heaven and earth are full
of Thy glory." And I have still one thing to add. You
have just permitted me to say that our blessed Lord might
ask of you what He would, and you would give it to Him,
and do it for Him. Now tell me what you will do to
make the Forty Hours truly a homage of adoration which
we pay to our dear Lord ? For it depends entirely upon
you; depends on how many hours, and which hours each
of you will take, and depends especially on how the hours
of prayer in our visits are spent Before you give me your
answer look again at the altar, and tell me who it is who
is present there ? There can be but one reply:

> "In the monstrance is adored
> Christ, our undivided Lord."

You see how entirely Our Lord sacrifices Himself for
us, how much He does for us. He not merely gives us His
teaching, His commandments, His grace, His life, His
strength, His thoughts, His efforts, His time, but Himself,
as God-man, and everything that He is and has, His body
and all its members; His precious blood, and all its value;

His Heart, and all the riches of its love; His soul, with all
its virtues and merits; His divinity, with all the fulness
of its infinite perfections; all this He gives us in this Sacrament, and that is everything. There is no more to give.

Now, beloved, can it be hard for us to sacrifice something of our time, our business and gains, something of
our ease, desires and pleasures, something of our thoughts,
passions and feelings to express our love and gratitude
to Our Lord, and bear our share in making the homage of
adoration publicly paid Him in the Forty Hours a fitting
solemnity ? Oh, surely you agree with me, and I speak
for each heart here when I say that we will so arrange
that we can give a few hours to our visits, and will take
care that all hours, even to the end, many visitors shall
be here, and that we will take pains to repeat with recollection and devotion, and deep emotion, the prayer,
" Blessed be the Most Holy Sacrament!" "Holy, holy,
holy, Lord God of Sabaoth! Heaven and earth are full of
Thy glory." For this adoration is due Our Lord. But we
also owe Him reparation.

Second Point.—Not only will the Church pay Our
Lord homage by the Forty Hours; she will also make
solemn reparation to Him in the Blessed Sacrament for
all the many and great insults and offences which His ungrateful creatures have already committed, and will always
commit against Him. You well know that but little of
the honor which it is our duty to render, and is due to
Our Lord in this Most Divine Sacrament is paid Him, and
that He is even sorely dishonored. Unfortunately this is
a well-established, incontrovertible fact, and we must all
acknowledge, to our shame and our great sorrow, that we,
too, have often insulted and offended Our Lord in the
Blessed Sacrament; one more, another less. What then
remains for us to do but to unite ourselves to the Church
during the Forty Hours, sinking on our knees with hearts

full of repentance and contrition, and openly and solemnly praying, "O dearest Jesus! May Thy blessed Mother, together with all the angels and saints, bless Thee in reparation for all the insults and offences which Thy ungrateful creatures have ever committed, or ever will commit, to the end of time, against Thee, the supreme Good." But, my brethren, do you wish this to be a true reparation, restoring to Our Lord the honor of which He has been robbed, to be a solemn condemnation of the insults inflicted upon Him, and an actual reparation for them? Then this beautiful prayer of reparation must not be repeated thoughtlessly, unfeelingly, but must be said with compassion, with sorrow, with contrite and broken hearts.

Therefore, let us bring to mind the many and great outrages and insults inflicted on Our Lord in the Blessed Sacrament in the three offices—if I may so call them—which He has assumed in the Holy Eucharist. For He is in this Sacrament as our King, whom we reverence; as our Helper, to whom we pray; as the Lamb of God who taketh away our sins, perpetually with us, in order to come to us in the Holy Mass, and to enter our hearts as the nourishment of our souls in holy communion. Surely, as we repeat these words, there comes to our mind an incalculable multitude, an overwhelming flood of insults and offences that are daily poured forth and hurled at our blessed Lord.

Our Lord dwells day and night in the Holy Eucharist, waiting for His people to worship Him and pray to Him, yet most of the hours of the day He is alone, and all alone, and only now and then comes—not a great multitude of believers—but one or two faithful souls, and they not for long, but for only a few moments; yet it is the sacred duty of every one, and most profitable for him, to come often and stay long with the dear Lord. The saddest and most shocking thing is that the majority of Christians completely forget their Lord in the Blessed Sacrament, be-

cause He abides under the form of bread, and live as if
He did not dwell with them. In truth, for the majority
of Christians, Our Lord is an abandoned God! But, beloved, what contempt, what insult, what outrage for Him!
Oh, then, during the Forty Hours kneel down before your
deeply injured and dishonored Lord, and make reparation,
because He is a God forgotten and abandoned by His own.
Say to Him with compassionate, contrite and broken hearts,
" O dearest Jesus! May Thy blessed Mother, together
with all the angels and saints, bless Thee in reparation for
all the insults and offences which Thy ungrateful creatures
have committed, or ever will commit, to the end of time,
against Thee, the supreme Good."

Since Our Lord is present day and night with all His
divine majesty in the Blessed Sacrament, it is the most
sacred duty of a Christian to show the greatest possible
reverence each time and always when he enters the church.
But, brethren, how improperly most people behave then,
entering the church without the least recollection or devotion! How many Christians make no genuflection
before the Most High, and how few make an actual
genuflection, touching the ground? One frequently
sees Christians shamelessly lay aside in church all the
politeness they display in the street. For do all Christians when in church at the service of God behave as
their duty demands, or do even the majority behave
thus? Think whether people always kneel, and kneel
as long as they should; even at the consecration, the
communion, and at benediction there are many who
never fall on their knees Think whether those who kneel
at all do so decently, respectfully, and on both knees,
and whether the others who stand or sit do so decently
and respectfully. Think how carelessly, distractedly and
disrespectfully Christians pray before Our Lord! While they
repeat words of prayer, or read their prayer-books, their

thoughts are entirely on something else, their eyes wandering everywhere to see everything going on, and they even go so far as to interrupt their prayers to chatter, and amuse themselves in conversation. All this, and still more, Christians allow themselves in the presence of their Lord in the Blessed Sacrament, whom they should worship so respectfully, supplicate so earnestly. Oh, verily, Our Lord in the Blessed Sacrament is not only a God abandoned by His own; He is also a dishonored God !

But, beloved, what contempt, what offence, what insult for Him ! Therefore, during the Forty Hours, kneel down before your deeply injured and dishonored Lord, making reparation because He is a God forgotten and abandoned by His own, and is even a dishonored and disregarded God and Saviour, saying to Him with compassionate, contrite and broken hearts, " O dearest Jesus! " etc.

Our Lord is continually present in the Blessed Sacrament, and because He is King of kings, and our King, it is His due that we should honor Him there annually on the great day on which He took up His dwelling among us in the Blessed Sacrament; that we should prepare a glorious, joyful, triumphant feast, with such pomp and splendor as a virtuous, loyal people would use to celebrate the entrance among them of a benevolent king. And so the Church has established the beautiful procession of Corpus Christi in such splendor as no mere worldly feast can attain. And in this triumphal feast, as we know, all Catholic Christians must share with devout and grateful hearts; they must consider it their sacred duty to assist in it; they must be eager for the great honor of being close to their Lord, lighting His way with burning candles, bearing a banner, the triumphal sign of the religion of Christ, or carrying a statue, the figure of a hero, who was a friend and true servant of Jesus, the glory and pride of our holy Church and our model and intercessor.

But, my brethren, you know that the share of Catholics in this beautiful public solemnity has become very slight and inadequate; men of the world are conspicuously absent from it, failing out and out to bear any part therein, and the reason for this is an incredibly great indifference and insensibility toward Our Lord in the Blessed Sacrament, and, in not a few cases, that men are ashamed to do it, for you know that what is in truth the highest honor has become the least valued. To the majority, taking part in this procession seems like something humiliating and degrading, something with which their dignity, their culture and their enlightenment are not compatible, and they either omit it altogether, or do it reluctantly and against their will. You know, too, that there are those who come hither to see this holy procession who amuse themselves during it quite boldly, with no awe, never even kneeling when the dear Lord is borne past them in the Blessed Sacrament. You know, too, that they go still further; that they deliberately disturb the procession, breaking through it without necessity, out of pure rudeness, and going through the ranks with provoking and contemptuous looks. Yes, they go still further; they reach the extreme of irreverence; they look on, deriding this triumphal progress of our blessed Redeemer, scoffing and mocking it, and they do this most when the particular splendor of the procession comes, when the Most High draws near. All this and still more is done by Christians at the Corpus Christi procession; all this and still more must Our Lord endure at the moment when a solemn homage should be paid Him as King of heaven and earth; all this must He endure from Christians whose sacred duty it should be to bear their share in this worship. Truly, Our Lord in the Blessed Sacrament is not merely an abandoned God, not merely a God who is dishonored; He is also a derided God, yes, a God who is mocked ! Oh, kneel down during the Forty Hours before your deeply injured and dishonored Lord, and make reparation to Him that He is so forgotten and abandoned by His own; that He is so disregarded and neglected, so shamed and insulted; yes, even so mocked and derided, and with sorrow and compassion, with contrite and broken hearts let us say, " O dearest Jesus ! " etc.

In the Blessed Sacrament, furthermore, Our Saviour Himself praises God almighty for His great goodness, thanks Him for benefits received, atones for a guilty world, and intercedes for sinful man. In the Blessed Sacrament Our Lord Himself is the sacrifice offered to God, for this fourfold end, this fourfold duty that we owe to God; and the divine service in which this holiest work is performed is the Mass. Oh, what a sacred and salutary service is the Holy Mass. It is the most sacred and salutary of all worship of God. Since by transubstantiation Jesus conceals Himself as the incarnate God under the lifeless form of bread, He transposes His divine majesty to a condition like and equivalent to death. The God-man Jesus Christ comes, and is substantially there, but the activities and appearances of life are absent, and must be absent. Oh, how holy must be that service in which a God-man abases Himself before God, and for God's sake, even to the likeness of death. Nothing holier is conceivable, nor does it exist. And Our Lord does this to offer a fitting sacrifice of adoration, thanksgiving, reparation and prayer to God, the heavenly Father, in our stead and for our salvation How efficacious and salutary, then, is this sublime worship of God wherein we bring to Him so precious, so infinitely worthy a gift.

Now, since it is our sacred duty to worship God by means of sacrifice, and since in paying God almighty the homage that is due Him, we must choose, not the worst, in the manner of Cain, but the best of offerings, according

to the example of Abel, it follows that we Christians, possessing the most holy of all sacrifices—the Mass—are
obliged to offer it or to attend its celebration; moreover,
we ought to deem ourselves fortunate and rejoice in being
able to offer to God, our supreme Lord and Master, a worship so worthy and sublime; and we ought, in consequence,
also to find it a pleasure and a consolation to hasten to the
church and to gather in multitudes around Jesus, our
blessed Saviour, when He, for our sake, descends from
heaven, and in the sacred Host permits Himself, as the
sacrificial Lamb of God, to be laid upon the altar.

But, my brethren, many Christians no longer value
the holy sacrifice of the Mass; there is the greatest indifference and contempt toward it; there is no longer zeal and
desire to be present at it; there is the most inconceivable
lack of conscientiousness and shocking neglect in regard
to it, which has gone so far that, in order to set a break-
water check to this flood of indifference, the Church has
commanded that at least on Sundays and holy days Christians shall hear Mass with devotion. And, beloved, in
spite of this command, how incalculably great is the number of those who reject their divine Saviour as the Lamb
of sacrifice; who always, or on the slightest pretext, absent themselves from Mass, and how great is the number
of Christians who sin against Him by continual disrespect
during the holy sacrifice, while He immolates Himself for
us in the Blessed Sacrament ! All this, and still more, is
done by Christians against their blessed Saviour, when,
for love of us, He comes upon our altar as the spotless
Lamb of sacrifice of the New Law, so acceptable to God.
All this, and still more, must Our Lord endure from Christians at the time when His death is shown in an unbloody
manner, and He must suffer it from those very Christians
for whom He submitted Himself to this mysterious sacrificial death.

Oh, verily, our dear Lord in the Blessed Sacrament is not only an abandoned God, not only a God mocked and derided; He is also a God who is rejected by His own. But, my friends, what contempt, what insult, what offence this is to Him ! Oh, kneel down before your injured and dishonored Lord during these days of the Forty Hours, and make reparation to Him who is so forgotten and abandoned by His own; so dishonored and offended, so mocked and derided, and, moreover, is a God who is disowned; and with compassion and sorrow, with contrite and broken hearts say to Him, " O dearest Jesus ! " etc.

Our Lord is also present in the Blessed Sacrament in order to come into our hearts in holy communion. This is the greatest proof of the love of the Divine Heart of Jesus toward us. What an honor, beloved, and what happiness it is to receive the holy, almighty, and infinitely good King of glory, with all His graces, virtues and merits into our soul as its sustenance ! Verily, in heaven itself there is nothing more glorious for us; nothing more blessed can be conceived. And two things are certain: as pants the hart for cooling streams, so, one would imagine, the Catholic would long for this living Bread of heaven which contains in itself all sweetness, all comfort and quickening, all vigor and strength; not for the sake of the corporeal tongue and palate, but for the sake of the soul. And as we see that diamonds and precious pearls are only set in pure gold, so one would imagine each Catholic heart would take care to be perfectly spotless and adorned with virtue in order to receive this Bread of angels, to set this celestial Diamond within itself But it is not so. The great majority of Catholics feel but little longing for this heavenly Manna, this nourishment of devout souls, this food of the elect.

To them holy communion is something superfluous; it is burdensome and annoying, and they come to it but rarely and grudgingly, and are best pleased when they can stay away They have been the cause of that strange commandment of the Church that we must receive holy communion at least once a year. Truly it is sad that we Christians must be driven to Our Lord by a command, and under threat of excommunication. Oh, how such Christians thrust Our Lord from them in the Blessed Sacrament wherein His loving Heart longs to be united with them most intimately ! How contemptuously they reject Him ! What a sorrow for Him ! But it is still sadder for us ! In spite of this forcible commandment, in spite of a punishment so heavy as excommunication and being deprived of Christian burial, how great, how immense is the number of Catholic Christians who do not fulfil their duty, who do not come to receive their God even once a year, who say to Him, "There is no room for Thee," and entirely repel Him ! Oh, what sorrow for our dear Lord !

Glance now at those who do receive holy communion, and see whether they bring to Our Lord the preparation that is His due. A cursory glance suffices to recognize that a vast number of Catholics think very little about it, feel very little real desire, and make no earnest effort to thoroughly cleanse their hearts and reform their lives. It suffices most people to examine their consciences superficially, and to repent their wrong-doings rather with the lips than with the heart; to say inconsiderately that they will be better without firmly intending to be so, and then to confess these sins as trifling matters, with no thought or earnestness, say the penance and thanksgiving in the same way, and repeat the communion prayers without attention, but rather coldly and distractedly. And these people receive their great God without due respect, without emotion, without any feeling of unworthiness, without a suggestion of a good resolution, without any desire for help from their Lord. Oh, how impure, how stained, how confused everything is in such a heart, and how ,cold, and icy, and frozen it is ! It resembles a stable rather than a sanctuary, a temple, and yet they invite their Lord therein; they open their doors that He may enter into this barren place ! Verily this is a great affront to Our Saviour !

And there is yet more to follow. The crime of Judas is committed against Our Lord in the Blessed Sacrament, and all the guilt thereof is renewed. Among the Christians who come to holy communion there are those who have not on the wedding-garment; nor are they few, but many. They are still in a state of mortal sin; they harbor Satan, to whom they have sold themselves by mortal sin. Oh, what black crime against Our Lord is this ! My brethren, He sees a second Judas in these audacious Christians. Ah, this wretch delivers his Lord over to the sin that is in his heart, to the devil who reigns there, and in such a place our dear Lord is imprisoned and insulted ! It is a new crucifixion ! This, and still more, Christians do to Our Lord in the Blessed Sacrament, because He goes so far in His love as to enter personally into their hearts; all this, and still more, must He endure in this Holy Sacrament because of the superabounding love that makes Him go so far as to dwell in the hearts of men, visiting their souls and honoring them by His divine presence, drawing close to them with the fulness of His divinity. Oh, verily Our Lord in the Blessed Sacrament is not only an abandoned God, a disregarded God, not only a dishonored and derided God, not only a God mocked and rejected by His own; He is betrayed, abused, and crucified by His own ! But, O beloved, what contempt, what insult, what offence to Him ! Kneel down during the Forty Hours before your deeply injured and dishonored Saviour, and make reparation to Him for being so abandoned and forgotten by His own; so disregarded and mocked; yes, for being a God betrayed, abused and crucified, and with compassion

and sorrow, with broken and contrite hearts cry to Him,
" O dearest Jesus ! " etc.

Once more take this thought to heart: Jesus is actually
present in the Blessed Sacrament, and therefore it is our
sacred duty to bring Him the homage of *adoration*. Remember that Jesus is so little honored and is so much dishonored in this Holy Sacrament that it is our sacred duty
to bring Him the homage of *reparation*.

And this sublime feast of the Forty Hours has been
established that this well-merited double homage shall be
offered to Our Lord publicly and solemnly by all the faithful in each parish. At this time we must with special
fervor adore Our Lord in the Blessed Sacrament, and make
reparation to Him. I need not ask you to take part in
this beautiful celebration with zeal and perseverance; you
do this, and have done so before with joyful sacrifice. I
need not exhort you to make reparation to Our Lord devoutly and from your hearts, nor to adore Him, for all this
you try to do. I can lead you to Our Lord in the Blessed
Sacrament and say: See here Thy children; they love
Thee, honor and adore Thee in the Holy Eucharist, and
feel most loving compassion for the offences and insults
which are heaped upon Thee; they will fall down before
Thy holy face, and never weary throughout these hallowed
days of adoring and praising Thee in these words, " Blessed
be the Most Holy Sacrament! Holy, holy, holy, Lord God
of Sabaoth!" They will not weary of making reparation on
their knees, saying, " O dearest Jesus ! May Thy blessed
Mother, together with the angels and saints, bless Thee
in reparation for all the insults and offences which Thy
ungrateful creatures have committed, or ever will commit,
to the end of time, against Thee, the supreme Good."

Yes, my brethren, we will do this, and be assured that
while we do it the angels rejoice that the King of glory
in His lowliness on earth receives the homage of solemn,

unceasing adoration; we shall give Our Lord the greatest
joy, because we openly adore and solemnly and publicly
acknowledge and honor Him as our great God, as our loving Saviour and Redeemer under the humble veil and lifeless form of bread; and He will speak to us from the Host,
saying, "Blessed are ye who have not seen, and yet believe." To us apply the words, "Blessed are ye who in
My necessity have not rejected Me."

Oh, dear Lord, then give us through this Sacrament the
grace to live and die such true Christians that at last in
glory we may hear the salutation, "You have confessed
Me before men, and now I will confess you before My
Father who is in heaven" Yes, O beloved Jesus, O Blessed
Sacrament; be Thou in life my consolation, in death my
viaticum, in eternal glory my reward. Amen.

SERMON III.

THE ADORATION OF JESUS IN THE BLESSED SACRAMENT
OUR MOST SACRED DUTY, OUR MOST MERITORIOUS SERVICE.

"Come, let us adore and fall down. . . . For He is the Lord
our God."—*Ps.* xciv. 6, 7.

THE Catholic Church, the Spouse of Jesus, gives to
her divine Bridegroom the honor which is His due; she
pays Him divine honor, she adores Him, and renders this
divine honor to Him in the Holy Eucharist.

What the Church, our Mother, does, we also must do;
this is her desire. She is not satisfied that we should
give Him merely honor, for that is due the angels and
saints; she wishes us to give Him a special worship which
the saints cannot receive; we must bend our knee before
Him; we must adore Him. And she is not satisfied that
we should only adore Jesus in heaven, whither He has
ascended; she calls upon us to kneel before Him in the
Blessed Sacrament, and adore Him under the form of
bread. Come to the altar, so the Church says to us; let
us fall down, and adore, for He is the Lord our God. She
always calls us in these terms, but especially during the
Forty Hours.

My brethren, respond to this invitation; prostrate yourselves before the Blessed Sacrament during these three
days, and there adore your hidden Saviour. I need not
exhort you to do this, but you will rather expect me to
say something which will make your devotion marked by
recollection, fervor, and confidence. It will help us to
this end if we keep these two truths in mind:

66

I. In the Blessed Sacrament Jesus most deserves our humble adoration.

II. The adoration of Jesus in the Blessed Sacrament is most meritorious for us.

First Point.—It is in the Blessed Sacrament that Jesus merits to the utmost our adoration, and this for two reasons: First, because in the Blessed Sacrament He has drawn so close to us with His divinity and humanity, and then because His divinity and humanity are there so completely hidden.

A dutiful subject feels respect and veneration for his sovereign always, and even when he is not near him, but is ever so far away, he will say nothing, think nothing, do nothing that he would not do under the eye of his prince.

But when the prince shows himself personally, then will the true subject render him that homage which is paid a lord, and do this with profound reverence and awe. For a striking example of this, recall Moses to your mind. Wherever he might be, this servant of God was occupied with the thought of the God of his fathers, and adored Him. But when the Lord showed Himself to Moses, when He appeared in the bush burning without being consumed, and a voice resounded from this miraculous fire, speaking these words to him· "I am the God of Abraham, Isaac, and Jacob," when Moses saw that he was brought so near to the Lord, he trembled, and was awestruck, and hid his face, not daring to turn his eyes toward the flame where he knew the Lord his God was present. Now, brethren, here on the altar is more than a bush burning without being consumed; here is more than a mighty voice; here is the flesh and blood of Jesus, our supreme Good:

> "Lo, the Good, supreme and best,
> On the altar deigns to rest,
> Is with flesh and blood our Guest."

Jesus is as near to us as He was to the shepherds; as near as He was to the kings; as near as He was to St. Peter; as near as He was to Mary Magdalen. And all of us who come before Him, and adore Him, share this privilege. O then come, ye Christians, throw yourselves down and adore, for here is Our Lord and God. You, Christians, who now bend your knee when you hear His name spoken, filled with veneration, love, and gratitude, fall down before this little form of bread, for here dwells your great God, Jesus, adored from all eternity. Our Lord not only merits this adoration in the Blessed Sacrament because here He is so near us with His divinity and humanity; He also merits it because from voluntary humility He remains here with His divinity and humanity completely hidden, and that is the other motive which should strongly incite us to adore Our Lord in the form of bread.

Whoever has right and claim to exterior splendor, and to walk in greatness, but renounces it, and moves in simplicity and lowliness, deserves to be highly esteemed. Now if ever any one had a right and claim to move among us in pomp and majesty, surely it is the Son of God made man; if ever any one renounced such a claim; if ever any one walked among us in lowliness and humility, surely it was our blessed Lord. He humbled Himself, not even taking the splendor of the angels, but took the form of a servant, and in this form went about in poverty and humility, yes, and was obedient even unto the death of the cross. If ever there was any one in all the world to whom honor, glory and reverence are due, it is the Son of God made man, Jesus Christ Our Lord The words of St. Paul are just, and spoken for all Christians when he says: "Therefore hath God exalted Him, and hath given Him a name that is above all names That at the name of Jesus every knee should bow, of those that are in heaven, on earth, and under the earth. And that every tongue should confess that the Lord Jesus Christ is in the glory of God the Father."

But, beloved, look at the altar; here in the Most Holy Sacrament has the Son of God made man taken upon Himself still further humility than that which moved St. Paul, calling forth his wonder. Here He has not only concealed the magnificence of His divinity, but the splendor of His humanity also has disappeared. Here we no longer see Him in His living, moving, speaking humanity; here He is veiled under the inanimate, lifeless form of bread. How wonderful, how marvellous! Yet Jesus had a twofold right to remain with us in power and majesty, and this right is His still, not only through His birth, because He is Son of God, but also through His great merits, because He died for us upon the cross. And yet the dear Lord remains here in the lowest depths of humiliation, in the dry, poor, lifeless, impenetrable veil of the form of bread. Therefore, if ever adoration is due Our Lord, here He merits it most. For here, though He is near us with His divinity, He has shrouded its splendor, and His humanity also under the impenetrable veil of the form of bread.

Come then, O ye Christians, and adore Him, ye at least who when you hear His name are filled with love and gratitude, and whose knee bends at the sound of that name. Come, and adore Him, for here is more than His holy name; here is He Himself, with flesh and blood, our highest Good. And be assured you will not do this in vain; no, great will be your reward for having done this. For although Our Lord certainly merits our adoration in the Blessed Sacrament, yet on the other hand the adoration of Jesus in the Blessed Sacrament is most meritorious for us.

Second Point —This adoration of Jesus is most meritorious for a twofold reason: We adore that which we do not see, and even adore the contrary of what we see. The angels and the saints who have attained the bliss of heaven adore Jesus. Yes, as St John writes in the Apocalypse, they cry unceasingly with loud voices: "The Lamb that was slain is worthy to receive power, and divinity, and wisdom, and strength, and honor, and glory, and benediction." But this is not strange, for they cannot do otherwise when they look upon Him in His splendor, and in far greater radiance than was His when He was transfigured before the apostles on Mt. Thabor. It is more remarkable that the three kings from the East, in spite of the stable and the poverty of the crib, prostrated themselves before the Saviour, and by the mysterious gifts they offered Him, recognized Him as their King, and adored Him as their God. Yet even they had His blessed humanity before their eyes, and could detect, as St Jerome remarks, something superhuman, something divine revealed on all His features. But to fall down and adore where we see nothing divine, where we no longer perceive even humanity, that is to perform a sublime and meritorious act, particularly where one not even desires to see anything of that nature. Who does this ? We ourselves do this great, this incredible thing when we adore the Most Holy Sacrament; we adore without seeing, without even wishing to see. I do not say we adore without knowing, for doing which Our Lord reproached the Samaritans, oh, no, we know full well what we adore. We know full well that Jesus Our Lord and God is present here, no more subject to death and suffering, but risen from death to life; no longer capable of suffering, but immortal We know it, we are convinced of it, we believe it, but we see it not, we have no proof of it; our senses have no means of perceiving it.

What we do is this: We rely upon the clear and infallible words of the Lord, who said: " This is My body;"

we fall down, with folded hands, and are reverently silent; we pour out our hearts before Him, and adore Him. Beloved, do you not believe that Our Lord will acknowledge this faith, that He will be profoundly touched by it ? To Thomas who would see Him in order to believe He said: " Blessed are those who have not seen and yet believe," and He will also say to us: " Blessed are ye who have not seen, and yet adored."

Come then, O ye Christians, and adore; ye Christians who are filled with awe, and love, and gratitude, and bow your knee when you hear His sacred name spoken. For more than the holy name of Jesus is here:

> " Lo, the Good, supreme and best,
> On the altar deigns to rest;
> Is with flesh and blood our Guest."

And be sure your adoration is particularly meritorious, because you see not, and yet adore.

And what is still more, we actually adore the contrary of what we see. For what is it that we see ? We see all the exterior appearance of bread, and nothing more.

And that is not a false appearance; no, it has in fact the real qualities of bread and wine; no change has taken place in the appearance; it remains exactly as before; it looks like bread and wine, has the resemblance and taste of bread and wine. We have every reason to consider it truly bread and wine. And then, when our senses proclaim this so loudly, we say to them· The words of Our Lord are more potent with our hearts, and He says: " This is My body."

We have the strongest conviction that this is not bread and wine; it is the Lord God of Sabaoth, whom the heavens adore, and whom we must adore, and falling down we adore Him. O that is a glory to us, for this adoration is a victory, and we are a spectacle for angels and men, for we not only adore what we do not see, but we adore the contrary of what we see. And do you not think this is great in the eyes of God ? O my friends, Abraham was praised by Our Lord and God because he hoped even when he had every reason to hope no longer; then surely it is great in His eyes and will be reckoned meritorious in us, if we adore the Most Holy Sacrament, for were the object which we adore here perceptible to our senses, the merit of faith would not be ours

Come then, O ye Christians, fall down and adore Him, ye Christians who even bend the knee when you hear the holy name of Jesus spoken. For more than the sacred name of Jesus is here; here is the flesh and blood of Jesus, our highest Good, and be sure your adoration is the more meritorious that you not only adore what you do not see, but adore the contrary of what you see. Yes, beloved, come here to the altar during the Forty Hours, and, falling down, reverently adore your God and Saviour truly present. The invitation of the Church is too urgent to be resisted, when one reflects that in the Blessed Sacrament Jesus most deserves our adoration, and the adoration of Jesus in the Blessed Sacrament is most meritorious for us. So begin now, and do not weary, but pray without ceasing: "Blessed be the Most Holy Sacrament!" raise your voice to praise God with cherubim and seraphim for this "Bread of angels;" sing with full and inspired hearts, and let the winds re-echo your "Ave Jesu!"

This prayer and song of praise rises up to the throne of glory of the Son of God, reaches even to His ear, and sounds sweeter to Him than the "Holy" of His angels, for you sing "Ave Jesu," and pray: "Blessed be the Most Holy Sacrament" here where you see Him not, here where only the veil of the form of bread appears. Ah, this praise fills your dear Saviour with joy and admiration. And will reward you for it, reward you richly. He will say to you: " Blessed be thou who hast not seen, and yet believed," and when you have closed your faithful eyes to earth, your Saviour will open them upon the eternity into which He has called you, and you will see Jesus in all His glory. Amen.

SERMON IV.

"My delight is to be with the children of men."—*Prov.* viii. 31.

SURELY when the king himself comes to tarry among his people, it is their sacred duty to pay him the homage which is his due His subjects will do this cheerfully, joyfully, and with entire self-renunciation; it will be to them not only a sacred but also a sweet duty to pay homage to the king when they know that he loves them with all his heart. Now, my brethren, in the Forty Hours which we begin to-day the faithful pay homage to the King of their souls who has taken up His abode with them, not only silently and privately, but also publicly and solemnly. I am sure that you regard it not merely as a sacred duty, but also as a welcome and delightful obligation to adore your Lord publicly and solemnly in the Blessed Sacrament.

You must feel, and justly feel, that no one else knows what a King Our Lord is, but we, His ransomed people. This may be seen in the Blessed Sacrament. Oh, how many and what great things are here, all of which loudly proclaim: Thus Our Saviour loves His people; so great is His delight to be with the children of men ! We will consider two of these great things; two sacrifices which Our Lord made, and still makes, to be with us in the Blessed Sacrament Two hard and bitter things were re-

74

quired of Our Lord that He might be with us in the Blessed Sacrament: He must assume the most extreme poverty; He must purchase with His life the privilege of dwelling thus poor among us. Now, behold, His delight to be among us was so great that He did not shrink from these two painful requirements, but fulfilled them.

I. In order to be with us He has taken upon Himself the most extreme poverty.

II. And that He might be thus with us has cost Him His life.

First Point.—The nearer that two friends live to each other, the pleasanter it is for them and the happier they are, and they always deplore the necessity of being separated. Consequently they try to live closer together, and are prepared to make sacrifices, and very considerable sacrifices to bring this about. This is included in the idea of true friendship. Those who are really friends want to be near to one another, to see one another, and talk together, and they will not rest until they have accomplished this end. But if in order to be near his friend one had to suffer injury to his property and fortune, give up prosperity for bitter poverty, then he would prefer remaining where he was, and living apart from his friend; nor would his friend have him do otherwise. For a true friend would see this was best and that one could not expect such a sacrifice for friendship's sake.

But if you had a friend who actually would give up his prosperity, and take upon himself the most extreme poverty and need in order to be with you, what would you say? Instead of answering, you turn to me and say, Such a thing is not conceivable! But answer my question: If you did have such a friend, what would you say? Verily such a friend would seem to love me so much that he forgot himself; would seem to love me more than himself; would seem to live not for himself, but only for me. The greatest yearning of such a friend's heart would be, it seems, to be near me; he would seem to know nothing and love nothing but me. But again you think, Such love is not to be imagined, because it exceeds all comprehension. Surely such love is not felt by man, nor is it conceivable. There you are perfectly right; but with God it is not merely conceivable, it is actually true. And in the God-man you have such a friend and have Him in the Blessed Sacrament. He established this Sacrament precisely for this reason, that He might come to us, visit us, be close to us, and abide with us.

Dear friends, have you ever thought earnestly how great the poverty is in which our dear Lord has clothed Himself in order that He might be with us in the Blessed Sacrament? Ask our holy faith as to this, and do not pass quickly over what she says, but think and ponder on what she tells you. You are told by the mouth of our holy faith: In the Blessed Sacrament is Jesus Christ, whole and entire, with flesh and blood, with body and soul, with divinity and humanity, actually, really and truly present, but present under the form of bread. Therefore you sing from a believing heart:

> "In the monstrance is adored
> Christ, our undivided Lord.
> Of the bread and wine is here,
> Only that which doth appear"

If only you will not hear and speak thoughtlessly, if only you will consider a little what you say in the words, "My Lord and God dwells under the form of bread," is not the first thought that comes into your mind, and which, carried away by wonder, you utter, "What poverty! What neediness!"

O my dear Christians, if you believe this, if you hold as certain truth that, "My Lord and God dwells under

the form of bread," then understand, wondering and adoring, how poor, how abjectly poor your Lord has become ! Now it is actually true that an insignificant fragment of bread is the dwelling of my divine Saviour, that
it is all the property and riches He can call His own !

Can one have less worldly goods, can one be poorer
in possessions ? In the Blessed Sacrament Our Lord is
poorer than He was in the stable in Bethlehem. And that
is not all the poverty which Our Lord has to assume in the
Blessed Sacrament. He must not only be poor in exterior
goods; He must endure a much keener poverty. Perhaps
we can express it by saying: He must become perfectly
poor in His own Person

Yes, my brethren, if you believe, holding it for certain truth that, " My Lord and God dwells under the form
of bread," then acknowledge, wondering and adoring, how
poor, how destitute in His own Person Our Lord has become. For it is true that He has become so poor in the
Blessed Sacrament and by the Blessed Sacrament that He
does not even remain here in His own form, even His
human form.

Oh, how inexpressibly poor in His own Person has Our
Lord become in the Blessed Sacrament! Here He is
poorer than He was in the crib. For though He was very
poor in Person when, in the tiny, feeble form of a child
He lay in the hay that was His bedding, yet He was still
in His own human form, but in the Blessed Sacrament He
has not retained this form; no, He must hide both His
divinity and humanity under the veil of bread.

But the poverty with which Jesus must clothe Himself
in the Blessed Sacrament does not end with this. Not
only must Our Lord in the Blessed Sacrament become
quite poor in exterior goods and in His own Person, but
He must assume here a still greater and more striking
poverty. Perhaps we can make it clear by saying that He

must also become quite poor in what concerns the signs
and activities of life. Yes, my brethren, if you believe
and hold as certain that, " My Lord and God dwells in
the form of bread," you must also feel with adoring wonder how poor, how abjectly poor your Lord is in the Blessed
Sacrament in all that concerns and belongs to the appearances of life. For in this unfathomable mystery Jesus,
the Fulness, the Source, the Author of life is present in
a condition that resembles death and lifelessness. Life itself is there, but there is no indication of it. Oh, how poor
in all that concerns the evidences and the activities of life
has Our Lord become in the Blessed Sacrament ! Here
He is poorer than when He lay a speechless child in the
crib.

Then, by crying, by inarticulate sounds, by stretching
out His little hands, He could at least give some sign; but
in the Blessed Sacrament He cannot give even the slightest
sign of life. The worm in the dust can give a full and
complete evidence of its lowly life, but Jesus, the Fulness
of all life, cannot give the smallest indication of feeblest
life. Lifeless and motionless as is the form in which He
dwells, He must keep Himself within its limits.

How great, how inconceivably great, must this poverty appear to you, if you reflect that Our Lord must endure all the consequences that result from this apparently
lifeless condition ! He must endure our treatment of Him,
and silently and with no outward sign accept every indifference, every insult, every profanation, every rudeness,
every offence. Do you not feel, beloved, that this complete inability to resist such treatment, which the dear
Lord has assumed in the Blessed Sacrament, is the most
touching poverty which one can conceive ?   O dear
friends, how much poorer and more touching is this
poverty which makes no use of the riches it possesses than
that poverty which has nothing.

The poverty of Our Lord in the Blessed Sacrament is great beyond comprehension. Oh, how He feels the crying injustice that is done Him; how His innermost heart resists such abuse of His divine power and majesty; and yet, though in the Holy Eucharist He is in full possession of His terrible omnipotence, even that cannot give the slightest sign of His displeasure ! Oh, truly, only a little reflection on the words, " My Lord and God dwells under the form of bread," brings before us the great exterior poverty and neediness in which Our Lord remains in the Blessed Sacrament. Here He is quite poor in goods and possessions; quite poor as to His Person; quite poor as to exterior evidences of life; quite poor as to any signs of life And this extreme poverty Our Lord assumes now when the possession of His kingdom and treasures is due Him, not only because of His high descent, but because He has merited it by His death on the cross. And He does this that He may be near us, and dwell among us.

Ah, dear brethren, thus Jesus, the King of glory, loves those whom He has redeemed ! Oh, He spoke truly when He announced by the prophet the glad tidings, " My delight is to be with the children of men." How just and right, how beautiful and grateful it would be, and at the same time how necessary for themselves that it should be so, if the conduct of Christians were such that it might be said, " Behold Christians so love their hidden King, abiding with them, their Saviour and Redeemer, that it is their delight to be with Him in the Blessed Sacrament ! " Now, during the Forty Hours, we have an opportunity to give a feeble proof of our attachment to our dear Lord. You must agree with me in condemning and lamenting the conduct of so many who still call themselves Christians, but take no part in this homage; nor can you admit the excuse they offer, that they have no time; for you know that in the majority of cases this is a mere, meaningless phrase. You know the true reason is that they are ungrateful to Jesus and dead to the holy things of His religion.

But you, my hearers, keep the Forty Hours, and I am sure you rejoice that you can celebrate it, for your hearts yearn to give to your Lord in the Blessed Sacrament a little proof of gratitude and loving return for the overflowing love for us which He has shown by assuming the uttermost poverty in order to remain with us. And in this love, already so excessive, there is a point that must not be overlooked and that merits our full consideration, for it shows us that the Divine Heart of Jesus is wholly aflame with love for us. You know that Our Lord bought the privilege of being with us in this extreme poverty, and had to pay dearly for it, for He purchased and paid for it with His own life.

Second Point.—If we have a friend who, living near us, can easily come to see us, we expect and require him to come often, nor is this demand unjust. If he does not come, or comes but seldom, merely, so to speak, looking in on us in passing, then, no matter what he may say, how much he may assure us and protest he cares for us, we do not believe him, but distrust his friendship. For his whole manner of acting shows that his coming is forced, that he only comes because he must, that in his innermost heart he feels it a burden and torment, and doing too much to come to see us. It is quite otherwise when a friend lives so far from us that it is extremely hard for him to come to us, and involves so great an expense that coming is nearly impossible. In such a case we do not expect the visit, but if he should come in spite of the many and great annoyances of the long journey, not hesitating at the heavy expense, then, my brethren, we recognize him as a true and tried friend.

But what would you say if a friend should not hesitate

to stake his life for the sake of seeing us ? Instead of answering, you will exclaim, This is inconceivable ! But keep to the question and answer me: If a friend had done this, you would say: Truly such a friend would show that he loved me; that he completely forgot himself. It would show that he loved me better than himself; that he lived not for himself, but for me. Such a friend would show the strongest yearning of heart to be near me; would show he thought of nothing, loved nothing but me. You say, however, Since such love as this is beyond all comprehension, and is quite inconceivable, surely there is no such love among men. You are perfectly right in this, but such love is not only conceivable with God, but it actually exists. And in the incarnate God, in Our Saviour, you have such a friend, and have Him in the Blessed Sacrament. He has established this Blessed Sacrament precisely that by it He may come to us, visit us, abide with us Have you ever thought for a moment of what a long, hard road Our Lord had to journey; how much it must have cost Him to come to us in this extreme poverty in the Blessed Sacrament ? Ask our holy faith to tell you, and do not pass lightly over the answer, but linger over it, considering what it says. From the lips of our holy faith we learn that all the sacraments, and particularly the Most Holy Sacrament of the Altar, are the fruits of the life, sufferings and death of Jesus. In order to come to us in this excessive poverty, Jesus had to live and suffer as we know He did

Now, my brethren, if you actually believe that the Blessed Sacrament is the fruit of the life, suffering and death of Jesus Christ, then, with wondering adoration, you will perceive what a long, difficult and costly way Our Lord must have journeyed to come to us in this extreme poverty in the Blessed Sacrament; how inconceivably, dearly and painfully He must have purchased the right to dwell

among us. Leaving heaven, Our Lord entered the womb
of the Virgin, and was imprisoned there for nine long
months. That in itself was a long, burdensome and self-
sacrificing way and abiding-place. How far from each
other are God the almighty, and feeble human nature,
and how much of His divine glory the majesty of the Son
of God had to sacrifice when He became flesh !

Then came the other ways and abiding-places, each
one a little harder, more full of sacrifices, than the preced-
ing. He had to take His way to Bethlehem into a stable;
He had to go into heathen Egypt and remain there for
years. In humble, ill-requited and exhausting labor He
dwelt in Nazareth till His thirtieth year. The lonely and
awful desert served Him as an abode with the wild beasts,
where for forty days and nights He watched, and fasted,
and prayed. For full three years He went about Judea
quite poor, without shelter, enduring heat and cold, hunger and thirst, weariness and exhaustion, doing good to
all, relieving distress and bringing help wherever there
was misery, poverty, agony, and death. He gathered the
poor about Him, and preached the Gospel to them; and
He endured in return for all this only ingratitude, black
ingratitude. He had to bear being hated, calumniated, persecuted, and even that His life should be sought after.
Behold, Our Lord had to expose Himself to all this that
it might be possible for Him to come to us in this extreme
poverty. Oh, verily Our Lord is that friend who is prepared
to venture his life to come to us ! But our dear Lord is
a yet more generous, magnanimous and munificent friend;
He has done still more, sacrificed still more, that He might
come to us in the Blessed Sacrament in extreme poverty and lowliness. He has given up His life in the greatest degradation and with inexpressible agony. Thus the
Blessed Sacrament is not merely the fruit of the life
of Jesus, but is especially the fruit of His bitter

agony and death. Yes, beloved, Our Lord won it by two other cruel and painful journeys. First, He had to go in the blackness of night to the Mount of Olives, in Gethsemani; and there, utterly forsaken, with none to help Him, He had to be given over to every agony but death. He had to suffer there such torture of mind, that for hour after hour of earnest but unanswered supplication His soul was sick and sorrowful unto death. As He lay prostrate on the ground He had to feel the anguish of death, wrestling in the death struggle, till "His sweat became as drops of blood, trickling down upon the ground." Verily this road was full of anguish and suffering! And the last way that Our Saviour had to travel, the way to Golgotha, up the hill of Calvary, beloved, is heartrending; it was full to overflowing with ignominy and cruel martyrdom. There our dear Lord was engulfed by a sea of sorrows, and He had to drink the chalice of sufferings to the very dregs, even to the last drop! Before our dear Lord entered upon the way of the cross He had to pass during the night through a succession of outrages, in which He had to suffer unutterable rudeness, injustice and barbarity. He had to be seized, bound, dragged to the tribunal; at the tribunal He had to be held as a malefactor, impostor, blasphemer; He had to endure the executioners and soldiers who guarded Him outdoing themselves in abuse, mockery and cruelty. He had to endure a heavy blow from a miserable wretch in return for a meek and truthful reply. He had to bear patiently that the same judge who said, "I find no cause in Him," should give Him over to be scourged in the most inhuman manner.

Then from the sole of His foot to the crown of His head there was no soundness in Him, but wounds and bruises and swelling sores. And there was a crown of thorns pressed on His sacred head. Thus made an *Ecce*

Homo, He had to silently endure that the judge should set a notorious highwayman free, while delivering Him in whom he " found no cause " to be crucified.

And only now, after so many long, agonizing byways, could Our Lord enter upon the last sad and sorrowful way, the way to Calvary. Lamentable figure as He was, suffering from many wounds and covered with His own blood, the rude soldiers made Him drag the heavy cross from Pilate's house up the hill to Calvary. Three times He had to fall under it; three full hours He had to suffer upon this way of martyrdom. Now He had to stretch out His body, all covered with deep, gaping wounds, upon the cross, and allow His hands and feet to be nailed to it. Now the cross had to be elevated, they push and pull it into the hole prepared for it, into which it falls with a dull thud, and a heavy jar, that causes the crucified Saviour's wounds to open and bleed anew There upon the cross He was suspended between heaven and earth, in bitter anguish, for three long hours, with a thief on either side of Him, and all the while He had to endure to be insulted, cursed, mocked, reviled, and treated as the greatest malefactor. Amidst these pains of the body, in this dishonor and desolation, He had to give up His spirit, breathe out His life,—a life more precious, more valuable indeed than that of all the angels and saints together.

Behold, all this Our Lord had to undergo to make it possible that He might remain in the Blessed Sacrament, where He abides with us in the most extreme poverty. Thus is the Blessed Sacrament the fruit of the suffering and death of Jesus Now, if you will but reflect a little, you cannot wonder sufficiently at this great, this stupen dous work of your blessed Lord. We were transfixed with wonder that a God-man should assume such extreme poverty, and now we see that in order to remain here on earth in this abject poverty, He had to purchase it at so great a price and so painfully; had to secure it by humiliations, privations and sufferings from the crib in Bethlehem to the cross on Calvary. To purchase the meanest poverty at so great price—surely, this exceeds our comprehension

Behold, my brethren, thus Jesus, the King of glory, loves His ransomed people. He spoke truly when He announced by the prophet the glad tidings, "My delight is to be with the children of men." How just and right, how beautiful and grateful it would be, and at the same time how necessary for themselves that it should be so, if the conduct of Christians were such that it might be said, "Behold Christians so love their hidden King, abiding with them in the Blessed Sacrament, that it is their delight to be with Him!" Now, during the Forty Hours we have an opportunity to give a feeble proof of our attachment to our dear Lord. You must agree with me in condemning and lamenting the conduct of so many who still call themselves Christians, but take no part in this homage, nor can you hearken to the foolish excuse they offer that they have no time. You know the true reason is that they are ungrateful to Jesus, and dead to the holy things of His religion.

But you, my hearers, will keep the Forty Hours, for you yearn to give a little proof of gratitude and love in return to your Lord in the Blessed Sacrament for having purchased so dearly and painfully this extreme poverty in which He dwells here, solely that He might be with us. Yes, my dear people, I expect this of you. I have this trust in you. You have fresh proofs given you in the Blessed Sacrament by Our Lord that He is the King who is known by none else, and seems to live for none else than His ransomed people. You have heard with rejoicing hearts, and having heard, can never forget, that the longing of His Heart to be always with us is so great, so ardent, so strong, that even though

He is God-man He has not shrunk from assuming the most extreme poverty, nor has He shrunk from purchasing this poorest of all dwellings with His life; and you feel that Jesus in the Blessed Sacrament is in truth the Spouse of your soul. And you also feel that praise, honor, glory and thanksgiving are due your dear Saviour, especially in the Blessed Sacrament, where He dwells for love of us in this dearly purchased poverty. You feel that rendering homage to a king who clings to his own, who lives for his own, as Jesus does in the Blessed Sacrament for us, is not merely a sacred duty, but ought to be a most agreeable occupation for all Christians. And all ought to show an earnest endeavor to emulate one another in their efforts to avail themselves perfectly of this longed-for opportunity of adoring, thanking, honoring and making offerings to their Eucharistic King.

So we will greet the Forty Hours as the happy time in which we are permitted to give vent to our feelings of grateful veneration; we will truly sanctify the days of the Forty Hours and give a real proof that we sincerely love Our Lord in the Blessed Sacrament. O Thou God and Saviour, hidden in the Blessed Sacrament, it is Thy delight to be with us; for I see Thee nailed upon the cross that Thou mayst be with us under the appearance of bread in this poorest of dwellings. But behold, it is also our delight to be with Thee in this, Thy lowly abode; it is our delight to bring Thee, here present under the veil of bread, the public and solemn homage of our adoration; it is also our delight during these days to pray with grateful hearts, " Blessed be the Most Holy Sacrament ! " it is our delight during these days to let our " Ave Jesu ! " resound from grateful lips:

" O Sacrament most holy! O Sacrament divine!
All praise and all thanksgiving be every moment Thine."

O divine Lord, as it is Thy delight to have us with Thee, grant also that we may be with Thee in Thy glory, to adore Thee with all the angels and saints and to joyfully sing Thy praises evermore. Amen.

SERMON V.

"And the Word was made flesh, and dwelt among us."—
John i. 14.

THE various feasts which the Church celebrates from
year to year are like true apostolic messengers, annually re-
turning to announce the work of salvation. Salutary reflections are evoked by their celebration, the faith within
us quickened and strengthened, and thus our souls are prepared for the never-ending festal day in the eternal dwelling of our heavenly Father.

Now we enter upon the celebration of the Forty Hours.
It was instituted and is celebrated that we may publicly
and solemnly pay the homage due Our Lord remaining
with us ceaselessly day and night to the end of time in
the Blessed Sacrament. In what does this homage consist?
Hour after hour we praise and glorify, venerate and adore
the Most Holy Sacrament But we unite one other act to
this; we also make humble reparation to Our Lord in the
Blessed Sacrament. Why do we do this? Beloved, it is
because of the unnatural and monstrous fact that it is in
this Sacrament that innumerable and great insults and
offences are inflicted on Our Lord, and it is only just and
natural that we should be required to adore Jesus and
make reparation to Him in the Blessed Sacrament. The
Forty Hours is intended to pay Him this homage of ado-

88

ration and reparation. During these few days it is
for us to do this with the greatest possible devotion and
love.

Now we men are so constituted that we cannot refuse
a service of love to a person when it is proved that he loves
us and has suffered much for us. At all events we could not
refuse such a service of love if he plead for it from the
place and at the time in which he was ceaselessly doing
and suffering for us wonderful and superhuman things.
Thus it is in our case. For it is precisely in the Blessed
Sacrament that Our Lord—

I. Does marvellous things for us.

II. Suffers wonderful things for us.

First Point.—We judge whether or not a person loves
us, not so much from his fine words of praise and promise,
but rather from what he does for us. When some one
does me a very great service, he shows me, even without
saying a word, that he loves me dearly. But if he does
so much for me that he makes himself poor, and sheds
his blood to do it, that shows me that his love has no limit,
that his heart is on fire with love for me. Now the love
of Our Lord is a love like this, as He has proved by giving
us the Blessed Sacrament. For in doing this Our Lord does
something so great, that God as He is, He has actually shed
His blood for it, and can do nothing greater, as He Himself
avowed, "What is there that I ought to do more to My vineyard, that I have not done to it?" He does not give us there
merely many and great graces, nor even countless graces;
He not merely shares with us a marvellous number of His
heavenly treasures, but He gives us far, far more than this;
He gives us all that He has. He, the fulness, the essence,
the fountain and source of all heavenly good, gives us Himself, Himself the owner, the Lord and ruler, the beginning
and end of heavenly grace and glory; gives Himself
to us completely, with divinity and humanity, with body

and soul, with flesh and blood. This is not new to you, it is a familiar thought; you understand that

> " Lo, the Good, supreme and best,
>   On the altar deigns to rest;
>   Is with flesh and blood our Guest."

And all this Our Lord does for love of us. And now it is doubly true that the eternal God, the only Lord, so great that the heavens cannot contain Him; this only Lord, full of splendor, who dwells in unapproachable light; this only true God, the Lord of creation, dwells by means of the Blessed Sacrament within His creatures. We must say with deep emotion, "Blessed be the Most Holy Sacrament!" must sing in adoring praise, "Ave Jesu!" And now, my brethren, to understand in a measure how much Our Lord does for us in giving us the Blessed Sacrament, consider how He dwells in it among us. And when you think of it, when you behold the dwelling of your Lord, are you not overwhelmed with astonishment? For love of us He even dwells among us a prisoner, a slave.

You know how deplorably miserable is the condition of a prisoner. He is deprived of his freedom; he is a helpless man, shut up between the high and thick walls of a prison. This condition is so terrible that mankind has reserved it as a purishment for those who have rendered themselves guilty of a gross crime. And shall I find Thee, my dear Lord, in such a state as this? Hast Thou gone so far in Thy love for me as to do this? Thou canst claim the splendor of the distant heavens for Thy glorified humanity, and can it be that Thou art a prisoner; can it be that Thou art confined in a cell? Alas! freedom, and power, and joy are Thine, as they can belong to none but the Almighty, the Most High; and must I know that Thou art between high walls, under bolt and key? Alas! all help for all creatures is of Thee, and is none able to help

Thee ?   There is no spirit that knows, no intellect that
understands, no pulse that beats, no limb that stirs without
Thy action, and must I hear that Thou art a prisoner,
that Thou art feeble, impotent, helpless ?   It grieves Christian hearts to be told that Jesus is a prisoner.   And yet
it is so !   You acknowledge it when you sing:

> " In the monstrance is adored
> Christ, our undivided Lord.
> From the sacred Host is fled
> All the substance of the bread:
> Christ Himself is here instead."

When you confess that the Saviour, the infinite God,
is present under the form of bread, then you know and
acknowledge that He suffers so great a confinement that
it is much worse than any prisoner endures; that the helplessness and feebleness of your Lord in the Blessed Sacrament are greater than the impotence of a prisoner.   Was
ever prisoner locked in such a narrow cell as your Lord in
the little prison of the ciborium?   was ever helplessness
like His in the tabernacle?   was ever feebleness weaker?
The sick man confined to his bed in the hospital has more
control over himself, over his limbs, than the King of
glory, your Saviour, has under this form of bread.   Behold,
Jesus has gone so far in His love for us that He will abide
with us as a prisoner in order to gain our love, win our
hearts to Himself.   Cost Him what it may, He will have
our love.   He comes to us a prisoner only thereby to un-
lock our love.   He seems to say, " O sinful man, if thou
wilt not honor Me as thy almighty God, thou shalt at
least grieve for Me as thy helpless prisoner."

Let Him not plead so long.   Say to Him: Yes, my
most faithful Lord, Thou shalt have my love·   " Blessed
be the Most Holy Sacrament ! "   I will not weary of singing
in adoring praise, " Ave Jesu ! "   Thou hast done too much
to win my love.   Thou dwellest with us a prisoner; yes,

even more, as a slave, as a servant, Jesus dwells with us
in the Blessed Sacrament. How sadly this echoes in our
ears; again how our hearts resist hearing it ! Jesus, Our
Saviour, is in His nature a king. His name is written on
His thigh, and it is, " King of kings, and Lord of lords "
His office is to govern, and He rejoices in the immensity
of His power and His supreme majesty, for by this He is
able to multiply the opportunities of His compassion and
mercy. He sways His sceptre over eternity and the countless creatures whom He has made.

But how abject is a slave ! There is no such profound
lowliness on earth as his; he is lord over nothing, not
even himself He has no will; he is and must be
entirely submissive to another. That is a condition of
life from which every human heart recoils, and therefore we wonder at the few whom we know sold themselves voluntarily into slavery that the light of faith might
be carried to the poor slaves who were in the night
and the darkness of unbelief. What angels of mercy,
what heroes of charity, are they who acted thus ! They
did a superhuman thing in going so far as this to bring
help to the wretched. But let us see how far Our Lord
has gone in His love for us. Jesus has renounced His
throne under such humiliating circumstances as no prince
ever did, and has become a slave, a bondman, a servant
in the Blessed Sacrament. There, as you well know,
He is no longer lord over Himself; He no longer has
a will of His own, nor is it the voice of His heavenly
Father which summons Him; no, it is the voice of
a creature which calls Him forth. Nor is it the highest of intelligent beings; not a cherub nor seraph, not
even an angel; no, it is the lowliest of His rational
creatures, it is man, poor sinful man, whose word He
obeys; nor is it one man, but a multitude of men before
whose word He bows. The priest, as you know, takes

the bread, blesses it, speaks the words of consecration, "This is My body," and in the same moment, "There is no longer bread, there is but the appearance and form of bread, and what is there is Jesus Christ Himself: The Word is made flesh." Behold and feel how Jesus resigns His crown, resigns it under such humiliating circumstances. He is called forth unreservedly, unresistingly, with no conditions, by the word of His priests. And since this is so there is no depth of obedience to which He will not condescend if He is commanded. It may be that where this word is spoken there is an irreverential, sinful, unbelieving heart; it may even be that the voice which utters this word is the voice of an unworthy priest. All this puts the obedience of Our Saviour to a severe test, but only to show it more plainly. For you know that the change in the substance of the bread does not depend on the disposition of the priest who officiates.

But why has Our Lord determined to resign His crown and enter the service of a bondman? What a question! Why did Jacob serve seven years and then another seven? He wished, as you know, to obtain the hand of Rachel. And behold, O men, it is the treasure of your heart, your free heart, on which the Lord's longing is bent, for it seems that though everything else belongs to Him, your heart, because it is free, does not belong to Him; but He must serve for it. And He despises all else, for He came to win this; and would rather serve for it as a bondman than fail to have it, though His service is not of seven years, and again seven years, but shall endure even to the day of the Last Judgment.

O ye children of men, why do you not rush here in multitudes to pay the respectful homage that is due your humble Lord? O dearest Saviour! Thou shalt have from us the crown of our love. Wondering and awestruck we will not weary in repeating, "Blessed be the Most Holy

Sacrament!" of singing with touched and grateful hearts, "Ave Jesu!"

This love, my Saviour, Thou hast merited a thousand times, for marvellous are the things Thou dost for us in the Blessed Sacrament. But, dear brethren, we must also make reparation to Jesus in the Blessed Sacrament; for marvellous are the things He suffers there.

Second Point.—If we see suffering borne for love we are deeply touched, and the greater are the sufferings which the person bears for his beloved, the more are we moved But if we see that these sufferings could be avoided, that they are caused by the ingratitude and heartlessness of the one that is loved, and that the person so rudely treated does not withdraw his kindness, but continues to be as loving as ever to the ungrateful wretch, then, indeed, if we have any heart, we are struck dumb with wonder and emotion; we are overcome with feelings of grief and pity, which impel us to make compassionate reparation. Now, beloved, that is the situation in which Our Lord finds Himself in the Blessed Sacrament. He suffers bitterly, suffers inexpressibly; and the saddest part of it is that they are such stinging, unnatural sufferings; sufferings that could and should be spared Him. For the sufferings He has to endure consist in man's indifference to the Blessed Sacrament; they are due to this, that the Sacrament of His love is so much neglected, so little valued, so carelessly adored; yes, is even profaned, desecrated, dishonored. He suffers because it is not enough loved and praised, but is even hated, blasphemed, denied; because we are not grateful enough to Him in this Holy Sacrament, but are actually ungrateful, heartless to Him, causing Him thereby bitter anguish. Beloved, have you a heart? For if you have, when you hear this you cannot but pray with fervor, "O dearest Jesus! May Thy blessed Mother, together with Thy angels and saints, bless

Thee in reparation for all the insults and offences Thy un-grateful creatures have committed, or ever will commit, against Thee to the end of time."

Let us briefly consider three of the sufferings of Jesus: The first is His sorrowful loneliness, in which no one visits Him; the second is His outraged love, and the third is His derided abasement and humiliation.

His loneliness—being forsaken by His children—must fall heavily on the divine Redeemer. In heaven there are myriads of angels who never sleep day nor night, but sur-round Him in joyful and profound adoration. How natural, how desirable that men should show something akin to this around His altar-throne on earth! If the Lord of the uni-verse deigns to have a dwelling among His creatures, there at least one would expect to see a universal adoration. For one would think that the whole universe must feel that its God is near; one would think that the mountains must move and rise up to form a cordon of honor around His tabernacle-home; one would think that the wild beasts would be tamed by His presence and come to Him as they came to Adam in paradise, to beg His blessing. But Our Lord does not let this happen; nor does His Heart find comfort in being thus surrounded. To be with men, to be with His children, created after His own likeness, purchased by His blood; to be with His children sanctified by the Holy Ghost, and called to inherit the kingdom of heaven; to surround Himself with them on all sides, therein is His delight; therein is His joy; on this His Heart is set. And how easily could men respond to His wishes and spend more time with Him in the solitude of the sanctuary!

Owing to the real presence of Jesus in the tabernacle, the church should be to all a sweet abiding-place; all should frequent it as their time permits, and as their own necessities and those of their neighbor require. And yet see in what loneliness His people dare to leave Him! None of the prophets would have dared predict what has happened; that God, the uncreated Wisdom, would come and pitch His tent among men, and that they would withdraw themselves from Him and avoid Him, as if He were a homeless stranger, a trembling intruder, an offender beyond the pale of the law, an outcast condemned to death. How great, how painful the loneliness that reigns around the tabernacle! I may say it is greater than His loneliness in the desert, for there living things came and bore Him company, even though they were wild beasts. But here, in His sanctuary, one sees the feeble little light that burns before the tabernacle like a flickering star, and in many churches it is His only worshipper for many hours of the day and night. How strange, how inconceivable!

This is the same Lord who pleads here in the Blessed Sacrament with His people for their love and companionship, whom Judea would have made king without His seeking, and against His will; and this, His people, neglect Him, flee from Him! Art Thou, then, dearest Lord, no companion for Thy creatures, or only an unwelcome, a burdensome one? Ah, Thou hast laid down Thy splendor and concealed Thyself under the form of bread, amidst the greatest poverty and silence; that is Thy crime, dear Lord, and this is the reason that the seekers after pleasure, grandeur, splendor, show and pomp, call not upon Thee in Thy retirement They know not, and will not know, that it is Thy excessive love that has brought Thee into this extreme need and helplessness. Would they but acknowledge and consider this, then Thou wouldst not be so neglected, wouldst not be left in such sorrowful loneliness, for Thy ransomed people would hasten to flock hither and band themselves around Thee, glorifying and adoring Thee, and supplicating Thee in the many burdens and necessities which afflict us all. O beloved, when He has wrought so many wonders for His creatures, when He has

filled the earth with the marvels of His compassion, and
the only return He desires is to be known and loved, then
it is surely an insult to His great goodness that men do
not court His better acquaintance; that men show an utter
disregard for the memorial of His love, and leave Him in
unhonored loneliness. Oh, truly this is a great sorrow for
the loving, Eucharistic Heart of Jesus! And Thou, O
Lord, dost Thou still remain with these creatures who so
forget Thee? Why dost Thou stay? The chants of heaven
are not sung here; here the incense of its praises does not
rise, the multitude of angels and holy spirits, those worthy
creatures whose whole being is naught else than burning
love for Thee, are not here; here Thou hast but creatures
who are completely unworthy, who are all on fire with love
of gold, high station, luxurious life, but are all coldness,
forgetfulness, indifference, contempt toward Thee. Here
Thy existence is filled with grief; Thou dwellest under the
form of bread out of love and longing for Thy creatures,
and Thou art a God forgotten by them!

O my hearers, have you a heart? If you have, you
must be filled with grief in hearing this and must give
vent to your feelings by praying, " O dearest Jesus! May
Thy blessed Mother, together with all Thy angels and
saints, bless Thee in reparation for all the insults and
offences which Thy ungrateful creatures have ever committed, or ever will commit, against Thee to the end of
time." Offer up this prayer in reparation for the cruel
neglect that Jesus endures in the Blessed Sacrament; offer
it also for that other sorrow, the sorrow of His outraged
love. This sorrow is most keenly felt by Jesus, and is
especially painful to Him. When men do not love Jesus
in the Blessed Sacrament, or do not love Him enough,
these creatures who thus neglect Him deprive Him by
their cruel, heartless will of that which He has purchased
at so dear a price, at the cost of making Himself a prisoner,

a slave, in the Holy Eucharist; for He has done this to win our hearts and get our love for Himself.

Ah, if He does not obtain this, if men do not love Him, or do not love Him ardently, reverently enough, what pain this causes Him, what grief it inflicts upon Him! True, He knows that He can never be sufficiently loved; He knows that no one but Himself can love Him as He deserves; not even the archangel Michael, the cherubim and seraphim; nor even the hosts of all the angels and saints together are able to love Him with a love as great as He is worthy of receiving. This He knows, and He does not require such a love; but He knows also that the children of men who have hearts to love could give Him a little place among people, and not exclude Him from among those whom they love; it were sweet to Him if they did this, and He pleads with them to do it. The children of men could love Him most among all the people and things they love, as is indeed His due; He knows this, and how sweet were it to Him did they do this, and how they grieve Him by not doing it.

Men ought to lament that they do not love Him more; they ought to be dissatisfied with themselves, hate and abhor themselves because of their deficient love of Jesus; He knows this, and how sweet it were to Him if they did it; He would count this as love, and He pleads with them to do it, grieving that even this is not done. The children of men might take more trouble for Him; they might inflame their hearts with love for Him, they might make greater sacrifices for Him, adore Him with more childlike tenderness; this He knows, and how sweet were it to Him if they did this; what grief they inflict upon Him when they do it not. Behold, this grief so bitter, so sharp, this anguish of despised love men inflict upon Him! Some wound His love by openly blaspheming and denying His presence; others pain Him by neglecting Him and re-

fusing to come to Him when He calls them. Many come
to Him unbidden and insult Him by irreverence. Ah, what
is it that we ourselves do but wound Him by indifference,
ingratitude, coldness, too great familiarity, or wilful distractions ? Thus is the love of our divine Saviour in the
Blessed Sacrament treated ! What sorrow ! Love is the
crown of all His good qualities, and men make this love
especially the object of their insults and ill-treatment. For
among the multitude who insult the Blessed Sacrament, it
is true that for one of these who insults His *majesty*
in the Blessed Sacrament, there are a hundred who insult
His *love.*

O my Jesus, why dost Thou thus endure our sins ? Why
hast Thou not already borne away this precious Mystery
to heaven, silenced the Mass, and withdrawn the veil of
Thy abandoned tabernacles? When Thou didst choose
Judas Thou knewest that He would betray Thee; when
Thou didst go up to Calvary to drain Thy chalice of suffering to the last drop, Thou didst foresee how little the
world would care that its Creator had died for it on the
cross. But couldst Thou have foreseen on the night of the
Last Supper the return which men would make to the
end of time for this Most Blessed Sacrament, and nevertheless give Thyself forever in this Mystery ? So precious
in Thy eyes are the proofs of the poor love of the few who
take the trouble to show Thee a return of love, that for
them Thou endurest the coldness and ingratitude of the
many. Oh, how wonderful art Thou; how unfathomable
is Thy love; how inconceivable Thy longing to be loved !

Beloved, have you a heart ? Then, when you hear this,
you must be moved to sorrow, and you must long to say,
" O dearest Jesus ! " etc. Yes, offer this prayer for the
sorrow of the outraged love of Jesus in the Blessed Sacrament, and offer it also for that other sorrow, the sorrow
of His derided abasement and humiliation.

Great, inexpressibly great, is the humiliation which the ·
Saviour assumes in the Blessed Sacrament. Perfectly wonderful is the littleness in which He comes to us, and many
and unfathomably deep are the humiliations which have
accompanied and surrounded it. In this mysterious Sacrament His wisdom and power appear to be annihilated.
There He brings Himself, so to speak, to the brink of
nothingness, there He hides Himself, so to speak, in the
bosom of nothingness, therein He seems to disappear. In
this Sacrament your Saviour leads you past all the cells
of humiliation, letting you pause before the place where
He shows you that He, who is the fulness and source, the
beginning and end of all life, abides in the lifeless and motionless form of bread, and takes upon Himself the laws of
this dead substance. For the lifeless form feels not the
fulness of life so as to show it, but the Author of life
leaves this dead form its immunity, deprives all His living
members of their use, is there without the natural activities
of life; the Fulness of life dwells among us, and is as dead.

To this lowly cell you are led, and there this humiliation is shown you. Verily, Our Lord has there purposely
excluded from Himself anything that shows exteriorly the
greatness, majesty, power, dignity and splendor that He
possesses in Himself; there He has clothed Himself in the
most common and insignificant substance which the earth
can offer. But why all this humiliation, this unfathomably deep humiliation? Because herein the love of Our
Lord shows its divine wisdom. Yes, dear brethren, it is that
we may not be affrighted by the splendor of His majesty,
nor bring Him our homage in fear and trembling, but without any anxiety or terror, rather with full confidence and
love, may praise, honor, adore and supplicate Him. But certainly not that we, His creatures, should withdraw from
Him, denying to our adorable Creator the necessary adoration, thanksgiving, reparation and prayer. When men do

this to Our Lord in the Blessed Sacrament, and do it because here He is so lowly, so little, so humble, what great grief they cause the love of the divine Saviour; it is a slight, an insult, to the humiliation chosen by His love for us. And, my beloved, it is precisely this that men do inflict upon Him in this Holy Sacrament.

O my dear brethren, what scandalous behavior do we often behold in our churches, even while the Holy Mystery is celebrated ! What is done then does not spring from frivolous curiosity, but is done to show contempt for those who are worshipping, and to wound the feelings of devout believers. People take deliberate delight in standing when we kneel, in going nearer to the altar than they see we go, and taking attitudes that would be unsuitable in an ordinary lecture-room; in speaking aloud while we silently pray; staring at those who return from the communion-rail; and this is done by persons who, judging from their appearance, are well bred, and educated, and would do nothing that could wound the feelings of another. But it is not only from unbelievers, but also from believers, that our dear Lord has to endure insults and slights in consequence of His abasement in the Blessed Sacrament. His insignificant exterior appearance, the ease with which we can approach Him, the small cost of His maintenance, all these things are turned against Him, and that of which His love would make a powerful attraction, an irresistible incentive to good, the coldness and stupidity of man turn into so many opportunities to neglect, to undervalue, and insult Him. Christians, His children, thrust Him back, while He extends His arms to embrace them. They care very little that the altar should be adorned, the sacred linens and vestments should be suitable and beautiful; if it depended on them, the altar might stand there poor, bare, unadorned and dilapidated; the sacred linens and vestments might be of common, cheap and ugly material.

Although they never contribute to them, they take it upon themselves to criticise the churches as too costly, the altars as too much adorned, the linens as too expensive, the vestments as too gorgeous, and say that we spend too much on our churches and their appointments.

They neglect coming to Our Lord of their own free will, to visit Him, hear Mass, and receive holy communion; but have to be commanded to do these things, and when they do come, what disrespectful treatment must Thou endure, O Lord! Does any one make a decent genuflection to the ground, a proper sign of the cross, or beat his breast with sincere contrition? who kneels properly on both knees, even at the consecration? How many go to holy communion in a becoming manner, with hands folded on the breast, bowed head, and eyes reverently cast to the ground? We are ashamed to do all this, and the few who do it are talked about. And how is it with the hearts of men? When they are before Thee, O my Saviour, they think of everything else save of Thee. How cold, how distracted, how thoughtless, how unfeeling, how heartless they are to Thee! And all this because Our Lord abases Himself so much for us. How horrible!

At the first glance, if you weigh the matter in the scales of this world, Jesus is of all kings the one who shows outwardly the least kingly dignity. Thus would His great love for us have it. Oh, if our love were wise and enlightened, we should see that God was never so wonderful as in this debasement, never so visibly almighty as when He shows that He can bring His infinite majesty even to the dust of earthly lowliness; never so adorably spotless as when He lies beneath the feet of men. Ah, dear Lord, which will carry the day, our wickedness or Thy love? Thou usest all the artifices of lowliness that by their appeal Thou mayst win our love, and we transform it into a weapon to wound Thy Sacred Heart.

Thus is requited the humiliation which Our Lord has assumed ! What grief for His adorable Heart ! But, my Saviour, why dost Thou bear this coldness, these insults ? Why dost Thou not punish this conduct constantly, severely ? Ah, Thou wouldst disarm the wickedness of man by Thy touching patience; Thou wouldst disarm the cruelty of man by Thy gentle forbearance, and Thy fidelity so worthy of love. O Majesty, nothing can excite Thy anger; O Might, Thou hast laid aside Thy thunderbolts ! They trample Thee underfoot, and Thou utterest no complaint; they pierce Thee, and Thou dost bleed, and yet no sound ! Oh, how loudly this silence speaks to the sensitive hearts of men, and what a victory has He already won precisely because of the depth of His ignominious lowliness !

Thou wilt not battle with the pride of men and break it, Thou mighty King; rather wilt Thou imperceptibly seize and bind it, making it a reason and a means for man's loving Thee more.

Beloved, have you a heart ? Then you must be grieved by hearing this, and must wish to pray, "O dearest Jesus !" etc. Yes, offer this prayer for this excessive grief, the derided humiliation endured by Our Lord in the Blessed Sacrament. Therein He, the infinite God, comes to us personally; but He comes as a prisoner, a slave. This must incite us to pray unweariedly, "Blessed be the Most Holy Sacrament !" in singing, "Ave Jesu !"

Inexpressibly great and marvellously bitter are the sufferings of Our Lord in the Blessed Sacrament. There man inflicts upon Him, and He endures, the pangs of sorrowful loneliness, of love that is not returned, of humiliation that is despised. This must urge us to make humble reparation. Shall I now exhort you not to weary this week in bringing to your Lord the double homage due Him, the homage of *adoration* and *reparation;* to keep the Forty Hours with true zeal, perseverance and devotion ? I cannot think this will be necessary. You well know that this homage is precious to your dear Lord, your highest Good, who for thirty-three years of His life ceaselessly did so much and bore so much for you; who spent His whole life for you, and at last, in inexpressible agony, gave Himself up to martyrdom on the wood of ignominy. This Redeemer values the homage rendered Him in the Blessed Sacrament, and that is inducement enough to give it. You must feel sure that He values this homage which you bring Him in this Blessed Sacrament where He continues to do so much and bear so much for us; for He comes to us here in His own Person, and for love of us is as a prisoner, a slave, and while dwelling among us He bears with invincible patience the three sorrows which His ungrateful children inflict upon Him.

Oh, surely this is inducement enough for us to pay our homage to Our Lord in the Blessed Sacrament. And you also know that you have caused many of His sorrows. That ought to be an irresistible inducement for you to bring Him your homage this week. And you are firmly resolved to hasten to your Lord now, adoring Him, and making reparation to Him with grateful reverence and joy, praying, "Blessed be the Most Holy Sacrament!" singing, "Ave Jesu!" and with bitter sorrow sighing, "O dearest Jesus!" etc.

Now, my hearers, I congratulate you that you are to pass these days in so holy and profitable a manner; you could not easily do anything more beautiful, holy and pleasing to God. Know that when you pray, "Blessed be the Most Holy Sacrament!" or sing "Ave Jesu!" from your hearts, it not merely awakens wonder in the children of the world, but is a spectacle for the angels of heaven, though they behold the face of the heavenly Father. Heaven so desires and watches for your prayer, "O dearest Jesus!" that when it rises there is more joy than for ninety-nine

who need not say it. But how beautiful, how welcome,
how joyful, is the sight of your believing hearts, overflowing with faith and love to your Lord, the dear, silent
Prisoner of this tabernacle ! He looks upon you with joy
when He hears your " Blessed be the Most Holy Sacrament! " your " Ave Jesu! " as He looked upon St. Peter
when he confessed, " Thou art Christ, the Son of the
living God." And when He hears your prayer of reparation, " O dearest Jesus! " He looks down on you compassionately, as He looked upon Magdalen when her tears
flowed over His feet. Your adoration is like incense
wafted to His sacramental throne; your reparation like a
flame of fire illuminating His altar like the blaze of many
candles burning there.

O beloved, what pleasure, what joy, what delight, this
service of love gives Him ! In your love can the hunger of
His love be satisfied! And not in vain, dear friends, do you
show this love to your Lord; the hour will come when the
trumpet of the angel shall sound over the whole earth to
its uttermost bounds, and He will compel the cold grave
and deep sea to give up their dead. Then will your Lord
come again; He who now comes as a prisoner, a slave, in
order to win our love, who now must accept the bitter sorrow of neglect, heartlessness and insults, will come again,
but come again in power and majesty to judge the living
and the dead. Then all eyes will be turned on His radiant
face and flashing eyes, on the glowing clouds and splendor
of His throne, and there will be weeping, and moaning,
and lamentations from all those who offended this sovereign Judge when He was present in the Blessed Sacrament. But you who adored and venerated the Blessed
Sacrament, who were His friends, you will rejoice and exult.
You have confessed your Lord before the whole world, and
it is certain, for He keeps His word, that He will confess
you before His Father who is in heaven. Yes, beloved,

on that awful day, that last day that the earth shall see, He will acknowledge before the whole world to your honor, and praise, and glory what you have done here before the Blessed Sacrament, where by so many He was insulted and despised He will turn to you and speak, and the whole world will give ear and listen: " I was poor and a prisoner, a slave, and thou didst take Me in. Thy ' Blessed be the Most Holy Sacrament,' thy ' Ave Jesu,' was more to Me than riches, than freedom, than power; thou didst make My dwelling easy, endurable, sweet. I was neglected, wronged, insulted, and thou didst receive Me; thou didst come making reparation to Me, and thy prayer, ' O dearest Jesus,' was more than balsam for the many wounds of'My bleeding Heart " And He will say to you, " Come, ye blessed of My Father, possess ye the kingdom prepared for you from the foundation of the world; enter ye into the joy of your Lord."

That will be another Forty Hours, one not only of forty hours', but of perpetual, adoration. With Mary, His glorious Mother, and all the blessed saints and angels, you will see your dear Lord in His glory, and power, and majesty, and, beholding Him face to face, will love Him, adore Him, and glorify Him, chanting a *Te Deum* that shall never cease, but shall echo through all eternity. Amen.

SERMON VI.

"My delight is to be with the children of men."—*Prov.* viii. 31.

IF we examine and search closely into God's utterances
and works, one thing will strike us forcibly in both. When
God speaks it is always very briefly, and in very few words,
but each time there is very much said in these few words.
They are also very plain and simple, comprehensible to
all, but they always hold deep, many-sided, inexhaustible
and almost unfathomable meanings; they are artless and
unadorned words, but they are always convincing, impressive and penetrating, and where it is necessary, they
are beneficial, arousing, or disturbing and terrifying words.
So it is also with the works of God, and the revealed operations of His hands. In little the good God gives us much;
with small things He does great ones. He does still more;
He unites the small things with the great ones, transforming them into the great, and changing the weak into the
strong; the simple, unimportant, lowly, into the wonderful,
the heavenly, the divine We see this plainly in those
means of grace, the sacraments They are certainly the
simplest, the most ordinary, daily things that Jesus takes
for the sacraments; but what He performs with them, the
condition into which He brings them, is something so tremendous that we cannot grasp it. For such things as

107

water and oil, intended for daily household use, are, by the ordinance of Christ, endowed with strength, with unknown, marvellous strength, to penetrate the soul and completely transform and sanctify it. This, and much more, applies especially to the great and Most Holy Sacrament of the Altar.

For this, too, has Jesus taken quite ordinary things, bread and wine; but here there is something far more, far greater, than in the other sacraments   Here Our Lord changes these ordinary things into something quite extraordinary; the ordinary things are here so honored, so preferred, that Jesus, the highest Good, conceals Himself in them.   And because Jesus Himself is present in this Holy Sacrament is precisely why we adore it, not merely privately, but openly and solemnly, as in the beautiful Forty Hours.   And you are here to-day to begin the solemn adoration of our divine Saviour   It is now my task and my intention to incite you to bring this homage to your Lord in the Blessed Sacrament with pleasure, with greater love and enthusiasm.   And because love calls forth love in return, I believe that I shall better succeed if I again place before you a characteristic of the Blessed Sacrament that tends to show how Jesus has exhausted Himself in His love for us   Consider:

I   That our dear Lord is with us uninterruptedly in the Blessed Sacrament.

II. That He is here for our good.

First Point.—Our Lord likes to be with us.   He has told us so: "My delight is to be with the children of men," so run the words in which He reveals His Heart to us.   And He has also proved this by His action.   You have the strongest evidence that it is His delight to be with men in the Most Holy Sacrament, and one of the circumstances by which we recognize this is that He is with us unceasingly. For there are many things that show whether or not one likes to be with another, but it is chiefly shown by the length of time that he stays. When a person remains with us but a few minutes and seems impatient to go away again, coming but to depart, whatever he may say in excuse and explanation of his careless treatment does not convince us of his sincerity; his manner of acting shows us too plainly that he does not like to be with us, that it gives him no pleasure, nor has he any desire to be where we are. But he who abides with us long, who comes a great and wearisome distance to see us, and arranges his affairs so that he can stay with us weeks and months, likes to be with us, rejoices in seeing us, is homesick away from us; and we are sure of this whether he says anything about it or not, for his conduct proves it.

Now, beloved, if this be the case, judge, understand, and feel if you can how gladly Jesus is among us. A personage in high position shows much, very much love and condescension and kindness if he only occasionally or for a moment pays a visit to a simple, ordinary citizen. How surprised we should be at the unmerited love, condescension and friendship for man evinced by the infinite majesty of the Son of God if He had shown merely a like mindfulness of us. But that does not satisfy His love for us; He goes further, much further, in His love and condescension. That which no dignitary ever has done for his people, that which would even be taken ill of him if he had done it, as having lessened his dignity and overstepped strongly defined limits, since custom prevents dignitaries from paying such visits, this has the divine majesty of our blessed Lord done for those whom He has saved. For, beloved, not casually, not occasionally, is the dear Lord with us. Do not overlook this circumstance; consider it well; it is truly worthy of constant reflection. He dwells with us intentionally, because He had us in His mind, because He intended to dwell with us. For see, He has so established the Blessed Sacrament and so ordained it that there are in it not merely many and great graces, but He Himself, as God-man, is present therein in His own Person. Oh, verily, if the blessed Lord does this in order to dwell with us, if He works such a great miracle by His omnipotence that His whole divine majesty abides with us under the form of bread, He has proved more surely than the strongest words could express that His delight is to be with the children of men, and even were He not to remain with us long, if He were to be only a short time in this great Sacrament, you will agree with me when I say that we should not cease to praise Him, wondering at the greatness of the love, and friendship, and condescension of the dear Lord.

But you know, my brethren, that in His love for us Our Lord has gone further, much further, than this. Though it is impossible to human beings to be always without interruption with those whom they love; though even the tenderest mother does not ask to have her child whom she loves with all her heart always at her side day and night, nor could endure having it so, yet this devotion which no human being can fulfil Our Lord has shown us, and this He does forever and ever. He so comes among us that never more, even for a moment, can He withdraw from us. For behold, He has so established the Most Blessed Sacrament by which and in which He comes to us, that He is in it unceasingly, day and night; is present every hour and every moment He has so ordained it that He is present with us as long as the form of the bread that is changed into His sacred body remains incorrupt, and He has provided that the sacred species be constantly kept in existence. For in His incomprehensible—really, I might say, in His prodigal—munificence He has ordained that day after day His priests may perform the great, divine work of transforming bread anew into His sacred body, and thus bring His divine majesty under a new and fresh veil of the form of bread. If Our Lord does this that with His divine majesty He may ever dwell day and night among us in this Holy Sacrament, and by this Holy Sacrament, then in truth He has shown beyond all misconception and doubt that it is His delight to be with men, for in doing this He has gone to the utmost limits of possibility. Yes, beloved, realize this: More than the Lord has done to prove that He loves to be with us cannot be done by God Himself. There He has so completely exhausted Himself in His divine love that though He is God He must say, " What could I have done more for thee, and have not done it ? " God as He is, He must exclaim: " The zeal of thy house and for thy soul (to let thee see and feel how gladly I am with thee) has eaten Me up! "

And now you will agree with me when I say that we must not weary in praising and exalting with wonder the immeasurable greatness of the love, and friendship, and condescension of Our Lord; you will also agree with me when I add that our return of love for the love of Jesus must in some measure correspond to His, and that what we do to venerate the Blessed Sacrament must have a real likeness to our dear Lord's proof of love for us. And in the Forty Hours we have an opportunity to make this return. We should not come to Our Lord carelessly, nor, so to speak, in passing; we should come with full intention to offer Him the solemn homage of our adoration and reparation; nor should we remain with Him but a few moments; no, we will give up hours to Him, each time we come offering Him an hour of prayer. And yet to-day there are many, very many, Christians who come to Him carelessly and in passing, who do not come with the intention of making the Forty Hours, and will not remain with Him as long as they should. Because it is Sunday they come to hear Mass, but not to celebrate the Forty Hours, and therefore they do not stay even an hour, but go out the moment Mass is ended. This is certainly very wrong, and betrays either great ignorance or still greater negligence and carelessness.

No, beloved, we must not keep the Forty Hours thus. We know, and knowing value and prize, the goodness of Our Lord in coming to us intentionally and establishing this great Sacrament that He may be with us; we know and properly esteem this blessing that the dear Lord abides with us, and has so instituted this great Sacrament that He is truly present in it ceaselessly, day and night, and we desire to have in the Forty Hours a suitable opportunity to give in some measure a return of love to Our Lord for this proof of His love for us, and we come with the intention of bringing Him our homage of adoration and reparation, and as often as we can we will stay with Him an hour; each time we come we will try to give Him a whole hour of prayer. And we shall feel incited to do this if we reflect that Our Lord is in the Blessed Sacrament for our good, for our welfare.

Second Point —One can conclude whether a person likes to be with him or not by the length of time he remains. Yet he would more clearly reveal his desire if during his visit he had shown it by services to his friend.

It often happens that we require assistance from another. Now, if we should ever need help, and there were one of our kindred whose duty it was to remain with us and give us a helping hand, but who drew back, refusing his aid, no matter what he said to justify and excuse himself for so doing, we should not believe in his good-will, nor think that his excuses were not all vain pretences We should insist that the true reason for his conduct was indifference to our company, a want of friendship and sincere affection. But again, if under such circumstances we had an old friend who would not quit our side, who did not think it hard to help us, or that we needed help too long; beloved, if he said almost nothing to us in protestation of his good-will and friendship, still we should be quite sure he was our friend, for he would have shown it and would have done what became a friend in remaining with us and helping us.

We see this in the blessed Mother of God. When her cousin, St. Elizabeth, needed assistance, she hastened to her, and remained month after month with her, not leaving till she was able to help herself. In doing this she showed conclusively that she was her cousin's friend; that it was her joy to be with her. Beloved, if one can thus recognize a true friend, and his pleasure in being with us, then when one asks why and how Our Lord abides with us unceasingly, day and night, it needs no words to prove what a good, loving and kind friend Our Lord is to us. For the answer to this question is: He does this for our best good; does it to render us service at any time; it is for this that He abides with us ceaselessly, with His hands full of graces. Do not expect nor ask me to bring before you all the services of love done us by Our Lord in this Sacrament, nor count up all the graces He pours upon us here; you know that would exceed the power of man, even the mind of angels, to comprehend, and their tongues to express. It is enough for me to call your attention to one thought, and that is that here in the Blessed Sacrament Our Lord is constantly our intercessor, and this in a twofold manner; first, because He Himself prays for us ceaselessly, and then because by His mediation and recommendation He presents our prayers to the heavenly Father.

I know not, my brethren, whether you have already thought earnestly on this twofold, touching and consoling truth; but be assured it is well worth considering that in the Blessed Sacrament Our Lord Himself pleads ceaselessly for us day and night, and each time we come to Him recommends our feeble prayer. How often pious Christians ask the prayers of some servant of God, and how fortunate one counts himself, and what a great sign cf goodwill and friendship one recognizes in receiving a favorable answer to his request. But this friend can do something more for us; he can voluntarily and without asking say that he will pray to God for grace and sanctity for our souls, and when he does this we feel very much honored and exceedingly happy, recognizing the high favor in which we stand with that person, and how, beyond all expectation, he has manifested it. And even more than this can be done for us. Some one may betake himself into the deepest solitude, loneliness and retirement in order to pray for us less interruptedly and more fervently. Oh, how unspeakably fortunate, honored and comforted, and under what obligations of gratitude must he feel to whom such love as this is shown, and how inexpressibly noble and self-renunciatory is the friendship of him who does so much for another!

Now, behold, this and much more is what Our Lord does in the Blessed Sacrament. He does not do as a friend must who would pray constantly for you—go away from you. No, in order to do this He comes directly to you, close to you, in the Blessed Sacrament. Now reflect a moment, wondering, on the great retirement and seclusion, concealment and silence, in which the dear Lord places Himself. So close to us is the dear Lord, yet more hidden than any human friend who has concealed himself within cloister walls, or in the desert, for in the Blessed Sacrament Our Lord is shrouded in a veil that is never lifted; is hidden, I may say locked, in the never-opened cell of the form of bread, and there He remains uninterruptedly, each hour of the day and night.

Oh, what profound loneliness, what great concealment, what complete retirement, is that wherein your dear Lord

placed Himself when He took up His abode in the lifeless, motionless appearance of bread ! But never believe
that this husk in which the incarnate majesty of the Son
of God rests is without life, without activity, or that the
Son of God hidden there is now inactive and lifeless. Never
dare to think that. Not lifeless, not idle, not inactive, is
your blessed Lord under this motionless form, and if with
your bodily eyes you see no life, no activity, know, be
certain, for your infallible faith tells you so, that with the
entire fulness of His human and divine activity He dwells
with us in the Blessed Sacrament; dwells there with us as
God-man under the veil of the appearance of bread in
order to be Our Saviour, not afar, but right in our midst,
and for our individual needs.

By the Blessed Sacrament and in the Blessed Sacrament Our Lord exercises and unfolds for each one of us
in particular the work and the efficacy of His redemption.
Behold and wonder at all Our Lord does in the Blessed
Sacrament, for He is overladen with the work and demands
of our salvation. And among these sacred labors with
which Our Lord is thus occupied, prayer for us holds no
small place; we are not wrong, but quite exact, in saying
that Our Lord is chiefly and ceaselessly occupied in praying
for us. We may, we must, say this of Our Lord in the
Blessed Sacrament. For if He has told us by the mouth
of the Holy Spirit that in the distant heaven in His glory
He is our intercessor, and prays for us (Rom. viii. 34; 1
John ii. 1), it is more likely that here, where He has taken
up His abode with us, where He dwells so close to us in
the Blessed Sacrament, He will be what He is so far away
—our intercessor; here surely He will not cease praying for
us. And so, my brethren, it is true that in the Blessed
Sacrament your dear Lord is occupied day and night with
you, and if in the whole world there is no other heart that
thinks of you, no other heart that beats for you, one heart

is here that beats for you, that thinks of you, that is concerned for your welfare, and this heart is the Heart of
Jesus in the Blessed Sacrament. And when over the broad
universe the darkness of night enwraps everything in the
silence of the grave, and for long hours death-like sleep has
descended on all, one heart is here watching ever and watching for us; a heart that cannot sleep or be silenced ever; that
is ever occupied, and occupied with us, that ever cries out
loudly to Heaven, pleading for us, and this heart is the
Heart of Jesus in the Blessed Sacrament. Oh, if Our
Lord does this, then acknowledge and feel that it is His
delight to be with men ! What your best friend cannot do
for you, what the tenderest mother cannot offer her dearly
beloved child, the ceaseless rendering of services of love,
Our Lord does for each of us day and night, with no inter-
mission; every moment He is occupied with us, serving us
most lovingly; forever and unceasingly making His all-
powerful prayer for us—is our intercessor. And He does
still more; for He is not merely our intercessor by praying
for us, but He is our intercessor because by His mediation
and recommendation He commends our prayers to the
heavenly Father How gladly and confidently an inferior
carries his petition to his superior when he knows that it
will be recommended by him who is of all persons most
powerful with his lord ! And he who thus intercedes for
another shows him for whose benefit he exercises his valuable influence—that he is a true, good, sincere friend. One
cannot easily do more than this. For it is unusual, almost
impossible, that the potent friend would wait in the presence of the lord till the moment when the petition was to
be presented, and then, taking it in his own hand, present
it personally, improving whatever is defective or amiss in
it Surely one could not expect, could not conceive, that
such a powerful friend would never leave his own house,
but would always stay at home awaiting one there, and every

time he came, be it ever so often, listen to his petition, take it from him, and recommend it to the lord by his own effectual intercession.

Oh, surely such a friend would show that he no longer lived for himself, but only and solely for the one he helped, and that it was his joy to be with him. But, as we have said, nothing so beautiful, so noble as this could be done by man. Now this is what the dear Lord does in the Blessed Sacrament. Day and night He is continually present in the Holy Eucharist, never leaving the tabernacle for even a single moment, that you may always find Him there, and can always equally have recourse to Him. There, under the appearances of bread, He awaits you, and when you come, let it be as often as you will, He admits you, listens to your petition, and scarcely have you laid it before Him than He takes it from you and carries it straight to His heavenly Father. Your petition is now also His petition, and it stands to His heavenly Father as His own, and your deficiencies are overlooked; for Jesus' sake your petition will not be rejected. If the petition be harmful to you, He makes and shapes it suitably for you. The devotion, the earnestness, the fervor, the humility, and all other qualities wanting to the prayer Our Lord supplies, and lays your petition before His heavenly Father bettered, transformed, ennobled, glorified, by His hand in recommending it. He is your intercessor, your mediator.

All this Our Lord does for you in the Blessed Sacrament. So much and so anxiously is He occupied with you, and for precisely this end He has established His dwelling with us under the veil of the form of bread. Then it is sure and clear that Our Lord lives not for Himself in the Blessed Sacrament, but solely and entirely for us, then it is true that our dear Lord shows us in the Blessed Sacrament that it is His delight to be with men; and what no man can ever do for us He has done, for there He not merely dwells with us, but also occupies Himself ceaselessly with our welfare; is our intercessor. And, beloved, we know how to value, how to appreciate this; we rejoice that in the Forty Hours we have a suitable opportunity to give our dear Lord a feeble proof of our grateful love in return for this too great love of His, and that we are able to remain with Him hour after hour in solemn prayer, occupied with Him as He is with us.

Yes, beloved, we will rejoice in having the beautiful, sublime and fitting feast of the Forty Hours, we will rejoice that hour after hour we shall pray with devout hearts, "Blessed be the Most Holy Sacrament!" that the whole day through "Ave Jesu!" shall ceaselessly echo in the ear of Our Lord from His ransomed people, and with the greatest zeal and perseverance we will celebrate the Forty Hours. During these sacred days our dear Lord shall see that there are grateful souls, souls who desire to give to their blessed Lord in the Holy Eucharist a strong proof of love in return for His too great love for them. Yes, my dear brethren, Our Lord proves to us in the Blessed Sacrament that it is His delight to be with us, and we will prove to Him by our zealous participation in the Forty Hours that it is our delight to be with Him in the Blessed Sacrament.

But Thou who in the Blessed Sacrament art with us unceasingly, day and night, even to the end of time, Thou gracious and merciful Saviour, accept now the little we do according to our ability in praising and glorifying Thee in the Blessed Sacrament for forty hours uninterruptedly. Graciously receive the adoration and praise that we can never appropriately express in words. Accept the wish to adore Thee perpetually, when we say with sincerity of heart:

"O Sacrament most holy! O Sacrament divine!
All praise and all thanksgiving be every moment Thine."

Give us the grace of perseverance to the end in Thy service, that when life's struggles are over, we may enter into Thy heavenly kingdom, and with Mary, the glorious Mother, and all Thy blessed angels and saints, may adore Thee, love Thee, praise and glorify Thee, and rejoice in beholding Thee face to face in the splendor of Thy majesty for all eternity. Amen.

SERMON VII.

"Praise the Lord, O Jerusalem: praise thy God, O Sion."—
Ps. cxlvii. 12.

WHAT the Psalmist does in calling particularly upon
the Jewish people to praise their Lord and their God, the
Church also does, especially in the Forty Hours. She
calls upon all Christians to offer some hours to Jesus in
the Holy Eucharist in which to praise Him. She does
another thing that the Psalmist did. The royal singer
was not content with inviting God's chosen people to do
this, for he well knew it would be of little use if he did
not also set before them the motive which must irresistibly
move them to praise their Lord and God. He explains
to them the reason why they were bound in a special manner to let the praise of God resound; he showed them how
the Lord had given them directly such proofs of His love
as He had not shown to others; he showed them that
"He hath not done in like manner to every nation." And
behold, the Church also proceeds thus. Before beginning
the Forty Hours she preaches a sermon to the Christian
people on the many and great features of the love of Jesus
which they find in this Most Holy Sacrament, and which
call forth corresponding sentiments of love in their hearts.
She explains them to us, bringing one or the other of them
before us at a time, in order to incite us to celebrate the
Forty Hours with zeal and perseverance.

That you may learn to truly understand the love of
Jesus we will not fix our eyes on many things in the Blessed
Sacrament. We will on this occasion consider only two
things. I will show you:

I. How great is the gift which Our Lord bestows upon
us in the Blessed Sacrament.

II. How generously He bestows it.

First Point.—We know how great is the gift which
Our Lord bestows upon us in the Blessed Sacrament when
we consider that in this Adorable Sacrament He gives us
something of Himself, aye, of His own Person; Himself
really and substantially, whole and entire, in His humanity
and in His divinity. In the Blessed Sacrament of the Altar
Jesus has given us something of Himself, of His own Person. He announced this to us in establishing this sublime
and adorable Sacrament at the Last Supper. For then
Jesus, Our Saviour and Redeemer, did not say, " This is
bread, and that signifies My body; " nor did He say, " This
is and remains bread, and shall symbolize to you My body,"
nor did the apostles hear from His divine lips, " As this
was bread, so it remains bread, and shall be a memorial
of My body." No; those truthful, holy lips said clearly and
plainly to the apostles, " This—which I have in My hand,
which you see, which appears like bread—is My body."
And nowadays, people do violence to the words of Jesus,
twisting them at their pleasure, and say we have nothing
more in this wonderful Sacrament than in the other sacraments; they say that as in the other sacraments we
have water, oil and chrism, so in this Adorable Sacrament
we have but bread. Certainly it is true that we are purified
by water in baptism; strengthened by chrism in confirma-
tion; anointed in sickness by consecrated oils; but, O ye
who have true faith, your Lord does not nourish your soul
in holy communion by blessed bread. No, far holier, far
more divine, is this food. That which you receive here is

not really bread, but something of the Lord Himself, of
His own Person; for He said, " This is My body."

Now we will seek the reason why, in order to sanctify,
to nourish us spiritually, in order to be near us and hear
our prayers, Our Lord gives us so much and such great
things in this Most Holy Sacrament; why it is not enough
for Him to give us blessed bread; why He gives us that
which exceeds the boldest expectation, gives us something
of Himself, of His own Person. And however carefully
you consider, you can find no other reason than that given
by St. John as the motive of Jesus in establishing the Holy
Eucharist.

This beloved disciple, who in that memorable moment
rested on the breast of his divine Master, and could feel
something of His love, said: " Having loved His own who
were in the world," and given them many and great proofs
of love, in the night that He established this Sacrament,
" He loved them to the end," giving them the greatest
proof of His love. And so it is. Only the love, the incom-
prehensibly great love, of Jesus explains to us His being
present in His own Person in this Sacrament in order to
sustain us. He could have nourished our souls, sustained,
strengthened and quickened them with blessed bread, as
man's soul now is purified by water in baptism, and the
Christian is strengthened with the chrism of salvation, or
anointed with oils for the welfare of his soul. But this
would not have been sufficient to His love; He would not
have been satisfied with this. For if one has something
to do for a person whom he loves very heartily, he does
not put the task out of his own hands, nor leave it to
another to take care of, lest it were not done well enough;
no, he feels that he must do it himself; otherwise it would
not be properly done. Take the case of a mother who
loves her child tenderly, as she should; who treasures and
clings to it with all her heart; such a mother cannot con-

tent herself to allow another to support and bring up her child; no, even at the cost of great sacrifices she herself will nourish and bring up the little one. Learn in this to realize in a measure what an excessive love the dear Lord bears toward each one of His children. Behold, Our Lord cannot bring Himself to allow us to be in the hands of another. True, He has entrusted our salvation to the apostles and their successors, and they are bound to take care of our souls conscientiously, zealously and perseveringly; but He is not content with this. No; He will have us to Himself, under His own eye; He will Himself support, nourish, strengthen our souls—and therefore He has established a most holy and sublime Sacrament, in which He gives us something of Himself, of His own Person. Only love, excessive love for us has done this!

And now, my hearers, consider also how much of Himself, of His divine Person, Our Lord gives us in this Holy Sacrament of love. He gives us all of Himself, gives Himself whole and entire, really and substantially, in His humanity and in His divinity. For it is absolutely certain that He has left us His entire sacred body in this Mystery of grace. Under the form of bread we possess and receive the head, the eyes, the ears, the mouth, the tongue, the hands, the feet, the Heart of Our Lord, the Good Shepherd of our souls. He has said so Himself, for He declared, " This is My body." He did not say, " This is part of My body " Ah, no, those are not His words; His words are, " This is My body," My whole, My entire body.

Verily, if Our Lord would sustain, and strengthen, and quicken our souls by something of His sacred Person as God-man, the smallest portion of His holy, spotless flesh would have abundantly sufficed; the smallest drop of His precious blood would have been more than enough. And yet, beloved, as you see, for this end Our Lord will be present in this Sacrament with His entire holy body, with all His members and with all His senses. When we realize this, wondering we ask again: Why, then, does Our Lord give such a precious gift for this object ? Surely the answer that might be made to this question is both suitable and ingenious. It is that with these, His holy members and senses, He may sanctify the members and senses of those who receive Him; that thereby He may make the entire man healthy and holy   But true as this is, it does not cover the ground   One drop of Thy precious blood, O divine, almighty Saviour, one word from Thy creative lips, and the whole world is made sound, strong and holy to eternal life; and yet for that which Thou canst so completely attain with so little, Thou givest so much. Necessity has not led Thee, cannot ever lead Thee, to this. Is there then something else, my brethren, that could have led Our Lord to such great munificence ? Oh, yes, there is something, but only one thing, and that is love   It is part of love, it is peculiar to love to give more and greater things than is necessary for its purpose.

And as His excessive love has brought Him to us, and, in order to have us always with Him, has made Him give us the merits of His death on the cross, so to nourish our souls and sanctify all our members and senses, He has established a Most Holy Sacrament in which He has given us something of His own holy Person, and since He might have attained all this by different means, we must attribute this to His excessive love, in consequence of which He has not contented Himself with giving us of His divine Person what were more than enough—one drop of His precious blood—but has given us a Holy Sacrament in which He is present with all His senses and members

And, beloved, though all this is so much, and such a great thing to have done, I must tell you that it is not all that Our Lord gives us in this great Sacrament. You know that really great love gives up everything to the one that is loved, and makes itself poor for his sake. Parents have often done this for their children. They injure themselves, shed their blood, make themselves poor, and bring themselves to destitution in order to do good to the child that is dear to them. Now, my brethren, there is much that is precious in the sacred Person of the God-man besides His sacred body. To Him as God-man belongs also His precious blood, His blessed soul, His adorable divinity. Our Lord has all this to bestow, and surely it is not necessary, nor even reasonable, to expect that He would give us everything, for it is too much, too great, too precious, too inexpressibly holy. But He does this; He does that which love does, that knows no limit. He gives everything, even His divinity, to us He has given us this great, Adorable Sacrament, in which, with His divinity and humanity, with body and soul, with flesh and blood, He is present, whole and entire, really, truly and substantially. Then, in giving us this Most Holy Sacrament with the words, " Take and eat: this is My body," He has given us His true body, His living body, His holy body, exactly as it is and with all that it contains. Were it not so, He would never have said, " This is My body." Behold, then, how great, how precious, is that which we possess in the Most Holy Sacrament.

> " Christian, rouse thy faith to see
> This great work wrought here for thee."

O my brethren, acknowledge and believe that:

> " Now the Good, supreme and best,
> On our altar deigns to rest;
> Is with flesh and blood our Guest."

and truly realize for once what kind of love Our Lord's is, since He gives us this Sacrament in which He Himself is present entire in His own divine Person. O beloved, try to realize it; this is a love that exhausts itself, that has

loved to the end, that has given up everything. Now Our
Lord has nothing more that He could give us, for there
is nothing greater or more precious than this; now Our
Lord can say to each one of us, " What could I have done
more for thee, and have not done it ? "

Oh, how great must the gift be which is so great that
even God can give us nothing greater ! And now let us
consider how generously our dear Lord has dispensed this
gift.

Second Point.—We can understand how generously Our
Lord dispenses this gift when we think that He gives it
to all without exception, and makes it easy for every one
without exception to receive it.

Precious and valuable things are not given to many.
Such good fortune is reserved for the few, and they must
be worthy who win it, having gained distinction and
achieved illustrious things in their lives. How much more
reason had Our Lord to follow this rule in regard to this
Holy Sacrament, precisely because it is so holy, and He,
holiness itself, the Source and Author of all holiness, is
therein present.

If He had ordained that this Most Holy Sacrament
should be given only to those who had done great things
for Him, the decision would have been perfectly just; but
in that case how few would have been so highly favored !
Had He determined to bestow this Most Holy Sacrament
only on such souls as had lived purely and virtuously, it
were but a just determination, for this Most Holy Sacrament is truly the " Bread of angels," " the Food of the
elect," "the Refreshment of holy souls;" but again, how few
would then have had this high honor, this great happiness.

Yet, my beloved brethren, Our Lord has not ordained
that which seems to us so natural, and even desirable, but
has done precisely the reverse of this. Not merely for those
who have performed marvellous acts of virtue, who have

done great and heroic deeds for Him, has Our Lord ordained this Most Holy Sacrament; not merely for those
who have kept themselves in His grace and increased
therein. No, He has not excluded the sinners from it;
even they may participate in this Most Holy Sacrament.
Yes, even those sinners whose sins are as numberless
as the sands of the seashore, even those whose sins of
abomination, and inhumanity, and monstrosity, are as scarlet, are not shut off from this Most Holy Sacrament in
which Jesus, the Spouse of pure souls, is present, but they
may receive the same share as the saints; Our Lord has
ordained this exceeding gift of grace for all. Verily, do
you not marvel at this ? Surely this must make us wonder.
For however great one might have thought the love of
Our Lord, no one would ever have deemed it possible that
it would go as far as this. Already Our Lord had done
much in taking from the hearts of sinners the crimes that
cried to heaven for vengeance; and annulling and blotting
them out. It is more than we can understand that He
should give them back the precious diamond of grace in
exchange for the sugared poison of sin, and the sinner
must have rejoiced, thanking the dear Lord on his knees
that He had so much love left for him, and been perfectly
satisfied, even though he might regret it, if Our Lord
had refused him what is so great, so precious, so unspeakably holy. But oh, how great, how bountiful above all
words and thoughts, is the love of Jesus, since He has not
refused the best, the greatest, the holiest thing that there
is in heaven or on earth to them who have made themselves unworthy of such grace and worthy of all punishment—to wretched sinners ! This is surely the love of
which it is written, " Many waters cannot quench it."
And how this grace still grows in greatness and generosity
when you consider how easy the dear Lord has made it
for all to receive this great Sacrament, and how quickly one

can possess the highest Good ! One cannot so easily secure
the treasures of this world. If one would go in pursuit
of the goods of this world, and possess them, what afflic-
tions he must undergo, what perils he must encounter,
journeying into far regions, across stormy seas, enduring
many fatigues, bringing all his faculties into play to attain
his end. It certainly would not be asking too much if'
Our Lord required still more than this of us before we
came into possession of this Most Holy Sacrament. And
how little would Our Lord require of us if we were expected to do many great deeds, and had to wait long, and
conquer difficulties before we could receive this Sacrament
in which there is present not merely one grace, nor many
graces, nor precious graces, but the Fulness, the Source,
the Author of all grace, Jesus Christ Himself ! When He
comes upon the altar in the Holy Mass, when throned in
the monstrance He gives His blessing in benediction, when
every day He is present in the tabernacle, He does not exclude sinners. He never repels them. And even when
the sinner is still in sin he may, he must, come here   Certainly it grieves Jesus that He must have sinners still in
a state of sin around Him, but He endures having them,
only requiring that they shall be present piously, reverently, contritely. And if the sinner will but come thus,
he will not be present in vain. For him also Jesus opens
His treasures, and gives him not one grace, but many; not
ordinary ones, but great ones. He carries away with him
from the Holy Mass, from benediction, something that
purifies and enlivens his heart, and his prayer before the
tabernacle inclines the Heart of Jesus toward him

Ah, is not this wonderful ? Yes, beloved, it is verily
most wonderful. That Our Lord should endure near Him
at such a solemn, sacred time one who had gone over to
His enemy, who had sold himself to the enemy by sin,
and bore his shackles on his soul; that Our Lord even

should think of him in the distribution of grace; that, beloved, is truly the love which "heaps coals of fire on the heads of sinners."

And how easy it has been made for sinners to have Jesus come again into their hearts with the fulness of His graces, how little is required of them for this exceeding honor, this inexpressible happiness. My brethren, one thing obviously must be done, the omission of which will be punished with everlasting pain, and that is that the sinner must remove his sins by a good confession, for this the dear Lord requires. But how little this is, how easy this makes it for the sinner to receive the great gift, and we must marvel at the generous love of Our Saviour. Yes, verily, we must wonder at this love. It is the love of a father for his lost son. The fallen Christian confesses, "Almighty, compassionate Saviour, I have sinned," and instantly the dear Lord has forgotten everything, is ecstatic with joy. The poor, fallen wretch must confess, "I am not worthy to be called Thy child;" but he hears in reply: "It is My delight to be with thee. Receive thou also the wedding-garment." Hears, "Come thou also to My table;" hears, "I will give thee also the Bread of heaven, containing in itself all sweetness;" hears, "Take and eat: this is My body," My true body, in which flows My precious blood, in which lives and breathes My soul, in which My divinity rests and is enthroned. Oh, incomprehensible love of our divine Saviour! Yes, incomprehensible He gives us the greatest, the best, the holiest, Himself in His own Person, and gives it so bounteously.

Now, beloved, in the words, "Praise the Lord, O Jerusalem; praise thy God, O Sion," the Royal Psalmist urges the chosen people of the Old Law, the Jewish people, to take some hours from labor and spend them in praising their great and good God. He also showed the Israelites the principal reason for their doing this, that they were so richly endowed above all other people and nations, both naturally and supernaturally   And he places before them the great and special blessing that they have received, saying, " Who declareth His word to Jacob: His justices and His judgments to Israel." Other people heard not His word; they must learn to know their God through His works, but to them He had spoken. And David shows them this in the words, " He hath not done in like manner to every nation," and he urges Israel to praise her God. Beloved ! had the Psalmist known the other benefits of God, had the graces of Christianity been revealed to him, oh how would he have urged Israel to praise God! Could he have said to his people: Thou hast not only the word of God; thou hast it also from the mouth of the Son of God Himself; thou hast, moreover, the means of grace that endow thy soul with divine dignity and consecration, with beauty and nobility. Could he have said: Thou hast an altar on which is enthroned the majesty of the Son of God, actually, really and truly, with divinity and humanity, with body and soul, with flesh and blood, but concealed for thee, humiliated, debased even to the appearance of bread, and could he have told them that every one had access to this throne of God, and the access was made so easy for all, oh how would he have exclaimed: Fall down and adore, praise and glorify Him, for the Lord hath not done in like manner to other nations !

Thou art this favored people, O Catholic Christendom ! Thou chosen people of the New Law ! And to-day the invitation comes to us to spend some time during the Forty Hours in praising our dear Lord in the Blessed Sacrament. Truly, beloved, we will do this, and will do it gladly, joyfully, sincerely and heartily, with zeal and perseverance. Yes, dear Lord, Thou Spouse of our soul, we will fall down before Thy most holy face, and never weary of repeating to Thee our " Blessed be the Most Holy Sacrament ! " of intoning our " Ave Jesu ! " But do Thou, O dear Lord, we beg Thee, graciously accept our praise; receive us after this life among the number of Thy saints, that we may also praise Thee in Thy everlasting glory. Amen.

SERMON VIII.

THE LOVE OF JESUS IN THE BLESSED SACRAMENT KNOWS
NO BOUNDS AND OVERCOMES ALL OBSTACLES.

"My delight is to be with the children of men."—*Prov.* viii. 31.

THE believing Christian adores the infinite majesty of
his God under the appearance of bread. He yields himself
up to the word of Jesus, which declares positively, " This
is My body" This faith, my brethren, I must call an
heroic faith. For although the mouth of eternal Truth
has said, " This is My body," it is not without a struggle,
a mighty struggle, that the understanding submits itself
to this saying, and there is good cause for this. For when
there is question of knowledge of the truth the entire man
seeks satisfaction; not only the heart and understanding,
but the senses also demand to be taken into account And
so it is always hard to believe what we do not see, nor feel,
nor taste; it is so hard that the Lord suggests its difficulty
when He praises as blessed those who have believed without seeing But to believe the contrary of what we see,
and feel, and taste, that is a faith that costs a struggle.

Now, my brethren, do you not hear how the eyes
and mouth cry out at the words, " This is My body " ? The
eyes say: What I behold looks like bread, and can that be
the body of the Lord that shone resplendent on Mount
Thabor ? Oh, this is a hard saying; who can bear it ?

Can it be the body of the Lord, from which went out wonderful strength for healing ? The tongue exclaims: What I taste has the flavor of bread, and can it be the body of the Lord, at whose feet Magdalen wept tears of penitence, on whose breast John, the innocent, leaned ? Oh, this is a hard saying; who can bear it ? This is what the eyes and the tongue cry out; who will dare to contradict them ? The believing heart alone dares do this; it declares its own eyes and tongue to be wrong It says: The Lord has the words of eternal life, and as He says, so it is, and not as I see and taste. It says: The Lord has made everything out of nothing; has turned water into wine. He can also leave the appearance of bread, and beneath it veil His body and soul, His flesh and blood, His divinity and humanity, and the believing heart feels little surprise that infinite Wisdom has devised such a miracle, that almighty God has wrought such a work. For since the Lord said " This is My body," it knows that:

> " Here the Good, supreme and best,
> God Himself now deigns to rest;
> Is with flesh and blood our Guest."

But what makes it wonder is rather that the love of Jesus goes so far that He actually does this for poor, sinful humanity, and therefore it is inspired to exclaim, with emotion, " Ave Jesu ! "

Now, my brethren, I rejoice in having every reason to assume that Our Lord will find such a heart in you You have come here expressly to show love and gratitude to the Spouse of your soul for having established His flesh and blood in the Most Holy Sacrament for love of you and to the nourishment of your soul; you will offer Him the first fruits of your love and gratitude, and have therefore set apart for Him this hour of prayer. You have already fought a good fight with your eyes and tongue, and full of faith, you exclaim, "What the senses cannot perceive, faith teaches us." Therefore you will not expect me to say a word to show you that your faith in the Blessed Sacrament must vanquish the declaration of your senses. You would far rather hear something to enkindle still more your love of Jesus. I know it will do your hearts good if I show you that:

I. The love of Jesus in the Blessed Sacrament sacrifices all.

II. It knows no bounds and overcomes all obstacles.

First Point.—There burns in the Heart of Jesus a love that sacrifices all. He has given most convincing proof of this in leaving Himself in the Most Holy Sacrament of the Altar as a memorial. For what is the meaning of these words: Jesus has left Himself as a memorial in the Most Holy Sacrament of the Altar? It means no less than this: Jesus, the Good Shepherd, has taken care that He should be as near as possible to all His sheep, ceaselessly, in all ages and places. Have we not already seen that there burns in the Heart of Jesus a love that until it has done all in its power never says: Enough? Think a moment of a faithful friend: though he desires his friend, and cannot be without him long, he cannot make the sacrifice to remain with him always. And see a loving mother; she cleaves to her child, she yearns to have the little one with her, but the sacrifice of never being alone without her child would be too great—even a mother's love does not go as far as this. But, my brethren, the love of Our Lord can never be persuaded to seek that which the truest friend and tenderest mother must welcome; it would be the greatest grief to His Heart were He a moment away from us; He cannot bear that. No, "It is My delight to be with the children of men." He has proved this; having loved His own, He was not content till He had loved them to the end. For He had already done everything for us that we could have conceived of from His exceeding love, but He did not pause here, nor until He had done to the very last everything that He could think of in His love to us. He took care that He could be with us every day, even to the end of the world; He gave us the Most Holy Sacrament of the Altar, in truth the Sacrament of love. O beloved, unite with me in saying, "Blessed be the Most Holy Sacrament !" let your " Ave Jesu ! " resound.

And now, my brethren, direct your attention to what Jesus, the Saviour of the world, has done to be with His ransomed brothers and sisters even to the end of time. This again will show you that His Heart is completely glowing and aflame with love for us, a love sacrificing all. But first I must ask you what is your faith in this Most Holy Sacrament of the Altar ? You confess your faith when you sing and pray:

> " In the monstrance is adored
> Christ, our undivided Lord."

Yes, beloved, this is the true faith. Christ has surely said, " This is My body." But His sacred body is living, so He gives us with this sacred living body His heavenly soul also; in a word, His adorable humanity. But there also dwells in the living body of Jesus the fulness of the divinity; in the Most Holy Sacrament of the Altar Jesus also gives us His divinity and humanity. In the monstrance dwells Christ entire, everywhere, and for all time

Beloved, do you not see in this that a love is burning in the Heart of Jesus that sacrifices all ? Oh, understand then the great work which the Lord has wrought for love of you. For what does this mean: Jesus is present in the Blessed Sacrament in all places and for all time, not merely with His divinity, but also with His humanity ? It means no less than this: By a great miracle Jesus has made a new and unique law for His sacred humanity in

the Blessed Sacrament, a law applying to no other corporeal being. He has removed from His sacred body in the
Blessed Sacrament the law of space, binding all other bodies,
and which even He was under while He dwelt visibly
among men. His presence in the Blessed Sacrament is not
limited to one place; by the Blessed Sacrament He is
present in all places with His entire humanity. But for
His humanity in the Blessed Sacrament He has also removed the law of time, which binds each living being, and
which He also was under when He went about visibly
among men. He is not merely present for a few years, or a
limited time; no, He is present in the Blessed Sacrament with
His entire humanity for all time, even to the end of the
world, in order that we may come to Him, and for the sake
of our necessities. He has—oh, hear what a great thing
the Lord has done for love of you!—He has transferred
to His sacred body, in a positive and true sense, the eternal
laws of His divine nature. Two of the divine attributes,
which are so singular and peculiar to the divine majesty
that they are found in no created being, not even the
pure spirits, He has, as far as possible, transferred to His
sacred body in this Sacrament. As His divine omnipres-
ence is in all places really and entire, so in all places where
the Blessed Sacrament is found He is entirely and actually
present, not merely with His divinity, but also with His
sacred humanity, and He dwells among us in the Blessed
Sacrament always, to the end of the world, as He is present
by virtue of His eternity in all times. Truly has the Lord
" established a memorial of His wonderful works " Among
all miracles the Blessed Sacrament is the masterpiece.

And why has Our Lord done this ? My brethren, it is
His " delight to be with the children of men." And that
He may be with us everywhere completely and forever
He gives us the Most Holy Sacrament of the Altar, truly
the Sacrament of love. Beloved, unite with me in saying,

"Blessed be the Most Holy Sacrament!" let your "Ave Jesu!" resound.

But this is not yet enough; two great obstacles stand in the way of His love, so mighty that one would imagine that what the love of Jesus has in view may not be accomplished. And yet it is accomplished, for the love of Jesus is so great that it conquers everything.

Second Point.—I must once more ask you what is your belief of the presence of Jesus in the Holy Eucharist? You profess it when you pray and sing:

> "Here our God Himself we see;
> Bow the head, and bend the knee."

Yes, beloved, this is our belief. We know that the fulness of the divinity dwells in the body of Jesus and that Jesus said, "This is My body," so we believe, "Here our God Himself we see," and will seek no further. For this reason we continue to pray and sing:

> "Know'st thou not how this can be?"

And we reply you cannot wonder at this, for:

> "Here the senses all must fail,
> Faith alone can pierce the veil.
> Here our God Himself we see;
> Bow the head, and bend the knee."

Beloved, this is our belief of the presence of Jesus in the Holy Eucharist, and is it still hard to understand that only a love that overcomes all obstacles could give us this Most Holy Sacrament? Consider how He overcomes Himself in assuming the lowly form of bread, so as to find a means whereby He might remain with us everywhere and at all times! Do you not realize how the Son of God vanquished and lowered Himself by becoming man and taking upon Himself the form of a servant, albeit created

according to the likeness of His heavenly Father and des-
tined to become the instrument of many miracles and
illustrious deeds ? Witnessing this, may we not exclaim:
He hath disregarded Himself entirely ! What then does it
mean ? The Author and Fulness of life hides Himself
within a form that is utterly destitute of life; the Fountain
of all life appears possessed of less life than the worm, to
which He gives life; He appears absolutely lifeless.   O
beloved, if to assume the form of a servant by the Son
of God implies self-renunciation on His part, then dwelling
under the form of bread must mean for Him annihilation,
complete sacrifice ! Evidently nothing is too much for the
love of Jesus. His love is as strong as death. It never
relinquishes that which it has once taken in hand. Above
all things it is His delight to be with us. He did not
shrink from going into a stable in order to come to us,
and He does not hesitate to dwell with His divinity under
the lifeless form of bread that He may be with us. He
took the bread, and raised His eyes to heaven. Ah, that
look pierced the heart of His heavenly Father, and He
consented that the fulness of the divinity should dwell
under the form of bread. Jesus spake, " This is My body."
He gave us the Most Holy Sacrament of the Altar, in very
truth the Sacrament of love.

Consider how Jesus has conquered the other great obstacle placed by man in the way of His love. This obstacle was the black ingratitude with which men requite
the love of Jesus. The injuries and insults inflicted on our
dear Lord in the Most Holy Sacrament of the Altar are
numberless and terrible. Under the form of bread He
endures the greatest of all His sufferings. Only one pain
has Jesus borne that could seem to us greater, and that
is His agonizing martyrdom on the cross.

My brethren, I would not take from your conception
of the pains of Jesus on the cross, which were called great

as the sea; nor would I weaken it in the least. No, beloved, rather do I urge you to increase day by day in the knowledge of the sufferings of Jesus, which in truth are above all measure, which in truth were as great as the sea. Only I feel compelled to make one remark; it is this: We men, because of the predominance of our bodily senses, always fix our eyes on bodily pains, considering them the greatest, whence it often comes that we esteem too little, or not at all, suffering of the soul. But does not the suffering of the soul far exceed all corporeal suffering? Was it not the grief of His soul that made the agony of Jesus on the cross as great as the sea? Was it not the fact that Jesus bore His agony with a soul that was sorrowful even unto death, that which made the wounds from the soles of His feet to the crown of His head a thousand times more painful? You know that it was. His servants, the martyrs, were roasted over burning coals, torn by wild beasts, hewn by sharp axes, yet raised a song of praise to their heavenly Father in the midst of this awful anguish. For their souls tasted heavenly peace and joy, while the agony of Our Lord and Saviour Jesus Christ was so bitter because He bore it with a soul plunged in a sea of sorrow and abandonment.

Now, my brethren, if these short sufferings were so measureless, what must those in the Blessed Sacrament be? If corporeal suffering is so great, how great must be the suffering of the soul of Jesus in the Blessed Sacrament? If a few executioners left no sound spot in all His sinless flesh, and in the anguish of the vision of this His whole body was shaken and drops of blood stood upon His forehead, how He must have trembled, how His Heart must have bled when He had in view the establishment of this Most Holy Sacrament, feeling and knowing in advance as keenly and plainly as He foresaw each stroke of the scourge that the indifference and coldness of man toward

Him would be immeasurable; that numberless times He would be treated without reverence, His love repulsed; that numberless would be the times in which the treatment of Joseph by his brethren, the sons of Jacob, when they threw him in the pit, would be renewed toward Him, for He would be received by souls which were like the grave of death, souls steeped in the poison of mortal sin !

My brethren, is not His literally a measureless sorrow? And is it not an obstacle that seems insurmountable? Even a mother's heart would shrink, chilled by such treatment, and no longer love such children.

But, my dear brethren, treatment that would make a mother's heart as cold as ice and hard as stone could not in the least cool the Heart of Jesus, burning with love for us. No, be the child so sunken that even a mother must forget it, the Heart of Jesus can never forget it. He sees that man's wickedness rises even to heaven, and He lets the flame of His love ascend far, far above it; still will He be with us to the end of the world; still it were the keenest pain for Him to be away from us a moment, a pain He cannot bear; beyond all things it is His delight to be with us, and He gives us the Most Holy Sacrament, in truth the Sacrament of love.

Therefore I beg you, raise the solemn prayer of praise, " Blessed be the Most Holy Sacrament ! " let your " Ave Jesu ! " resound gratefully. For in the Blessed Sacrament you see before you a device of a love that overcomes all obstacles in order to give up everything. '

It is His delight to be with us, and He takes care that He can be with us everywhere and always. It is His delight to be with us, and it is not too much for Him to establish among us a memorial of His wonderful works, in which His holy, divine Person is entire in all places, even to the end of time. It is His delight to be with us, and therefore He does not fear annihilating Himself: the

Fulness of the Godhead dwells in the lowly form of bread. It is His delight to be with us, and He does not shrink from plunging Himself into a sea of sorrows. He gives us the Most Holy Sacrament of the Altar, in truth the Sacrament of a love that sacrifices all, that conquers all; the love that does not fail when a mother's can endure no longer; the love that still burns when a mother's heart grows cold.

And Jesus will always be so little loved, so much wounded in the Blessed Sacrament! But why? Is it a law that in His love for man God would exhaust Himself, and man should strive in emulation to out-do this love by insults and ingratitude? Beloved, these stern words may pain you; they do not apply to you, but they are intended to urge you to redouble your zeal in these few days, and show our dear Lord in the Blessed Sacrament that you reciprocate His love. Yes, beloved, we at least will praise and exalt the infinite love of Jesus in the Blessed Sacrament with grateful joy; we will lament with broken hearts all the injuries which we have been guilty of toward the Blessed Sacrament; with compassionate hearts we will also make reparation for all the offences and insults which have ever been committed against Jesus, the supreme Good, or ever will be committed, to the end of time. Beloved, in the name of Jesus we will begin the Forty Hours with living faith, sincere devotion, profound reverence and ready self-renunciation, for the adoration and glorification of our dear Eucharistic King.

But Thou, O Jesus, whose delight is to be with us, hear us now as we pray, "Blessed be the Most Holy Sacrament!" hear us, we beseech Thee, as we make reparation to Thee, crying, "We bless Thee for all the insults and offences!" hear us, we beseech Thee, when we sing and pray:

> " When the hour of death is near,
> And my soul is numb with fear,
> Jesus, Lord and Saviour, hear.
> Give this Food to be my stay;
> Lead me on my journey's way,
> Into realms of endless day."

Hear us, we beseech Thee, as we thus pray, that we also, with Mary Thy glorious Mother and all Thy blessed angels and saints may behold Thee face to face, and praise and bless Thee for all eternity. Yes, dear Lord, hear us, we beseech Thee; for it is truly Thy only joy to be with us, and our only salvation to be with Thee. Amen.

SERMON IX.

"Behold I am with you all days, even to the consummation of
the world."—*St. Matt.* xxviii. 20.

MANY of the pious and beautiful devotions which blossomed in our forefathers' day have shared the lot common to earthly things—have arisen, flourished, decreased, grown feeble and sunk at last into the grave of oblivion. The adoration of the Blessed Sacrament by the Forty Hours is also an institution of our forefathers; but it is a tree ever green and blooming, that never loses its leaves, but bears fruit always; a tree growing in the waters of immortality. Yes, my brethren, we still hold the Forty Hours in high esteem, and very many who deserve but too well the reproach of lukewarm Christianity feel themselves powerfully drawn to the Shepherd of their souls, gathering His sheep around the tabernacle—to Jesus in the Blessed Sacrament.

How is this to be explained ? Is it because the mother who bore us in her bosom and nourished us loved to come often to the altar of the Lord and tarry there ? That is probably one reason, but it is not the only one. For though what we absorb with our mother's milk is certainly strongly implanted, it can grow weak, and indeed, in many cases, it altogether disappears. I think rather that the true reason for this is to be found elsewhere; that we discover it in the Blessed Sacrament itself. For in the sacred Host

143

there burns ever a potent fire of love. No wonder that the rays of this great fire reach long distances; no wonder that these rays warm and enkindle far-off places ! But the soul of him who stands near to this fiery sea of love will glow and burn with its warmth.

Now tell me how our forefathers have kept their tender love for the Blessed Sacrament kindled and burning ? How did the beautiful and happy thought come to them that made them establish this testament of love left us in the Forty Hours, in which from early morn till darkest night the faithful gather around the tabernacle and cry ceaselessly with love and gratitude to the Spouse of their souls, " Blessed be the Most Holy Sacrament " ? This thought was given them by the glowing love of the Heart of Jesus, who abides with us constantly, day and night, to the end of time, under the veil of the form of bread.

Oh, that we were worthy children of such noble fathers ! For then this reciprocal love and gratitude to Jesus in the Blessed Sacrament which incited them to establish the Forty Hours might also induce us to celebrate it properly. O beloved, come close to the flames of love leaping out from the Blessed Sacrament, that you may be warmed into a true return of love. Understand, and feel, and see for once most clearly how the Heart of Jesus comes to us and dwells with us under the form of bread in order to continually manifest to us His love. Yes, for once consider this love more closely. It is so ardent that—

I It completely exhausts itself.

II. It cheerfully continues.

III. It patiently endures.

First Point —Love reveals itself in acts, and the more precious the gift that one receives, the greater and more ardent the love of the giver. Now behold the altar. There is the remembrance of the wonderful works of God; the infinite majesty of God dwells in the tiny, lowly form of bread: for the sacred body, the precious blood, the blessed soul pouring forth grace, and virtue, and merits, the adorable divinity of Our Lord and Saviour Jesus Christ is actually, really and truly present under the form of bread. Verily, the remembrance of the wonderful works of God is here established !

And, my brethren, you must know that this has been done for your sake. Yes, dear Christians, this is actually true; for what you see on the altar is your own. Hear your Teacher; He Himself says to you, " It is My delight "— so His words run—" to be with the children of men." Behold, His Heart is full of this; He will be with us; His love for us is so great that He yearns to dwell among us. And this longing to be with us—oh, realize how great it is ! This desire has moved Him to renounce Himself and to conceal the fulness of His divinity under the form of a servant. Yes, He had looked forward to this moment; He rejoiced in it, and, like a river that rushes on its way, He hastened His coming in the form of a servant.

But that was not yet enough for His love; His ardent desire to be with us was not satisfied that we should only see and hear Him, that He should only come in contact with us externally; He was with men thus for thirty-three years, and His longing to be with them was not assuaged The whole loving impulse of His Heart to be with us was far from satiated. His love for us had never done enough till He was with us in such a way that each one of us could taste and feel Him in his innermost being, in his very soul; till He could enter into each of us, till each of us was perfectly incorporated with Him. And in order to be with us He has not shrunk from enshrouding His humanity, which was radiant with the light of His divinity, in the poor mantle of lifeless and motionless bread. Yes, He surely waited and longed with desire, with pain, so to speak, for that moment when He could take the bread into His holy and venerable hands, and speak the mysterious and creative words, " This is My body." " With great desire," He said to His apostles that evening, " with great desire have I desired to eat this pasch with you."

I ask you, my brethren, could Jesus have given us a greater proof of His love for us than He has given us in this great, adorable Sacrament ? Surely not. For that which the love of Jesus has accomplished here is so great, that even the eternally wise and almighty God is not able to discover anything greater, nor create anything that exceeds it. Verily, it is a remembrance of the wonderful works of God. Among the miracles of God it is the masterpiece. The Source of all life truly lives in a form destitute and incapable of life, and this He does because we are so dear to His Heart that He cannot be without us; because He clings to us so that He must have us close to Him, must be within us. Because it is His delight to be with us He has established this memorial of His wonders. The love of our souls has consumed Him. His is indeed a love that has completely exhausted itself And this love for us burns continually.

Second Point.—True love proves itself by its continuance, and the longer it lasts unweakened, so much more fervent and sincere it is. Again behold the altar. See the mighty flames of love which here ceaselessly burst forth from the Heart of Jesus through the appearance of bread. Truly, does He not cry out to-day from this veil, " It is My delight to be with the children of men," and therefore I am always under this veil of the appearance of bread ?

And have you ever really considered how long this memorial of love has been among men ? Oh, do not overlook this circumstance; it shows so conclusively that the Heart of Jesus lives and beats for nothing but His creatures—for those whom He has saved ! Think a moment:

He turned water into wine, but He did it only once, only in one house; He entered the house of Zacheus and other favored souls, still it was done but once; He allowed His countenance to shine resplendent as the sun, His garments to become whiter than snow, but He did this only once, only on Mount Thabor, and before three men; but because it is His joy and delight to be among men He has changed bread into His body and wine into His precious blood daily for eighteen hundred years, in all places, and at all hours. Because it is His joy and delight to be among men, He withdraws (He the King of glory, with the fulness of His treasures of grace) into this narrow, lowly dwelling of the appearance of bread. Because it is His joy and delight to be among men, He goes, He, the eternal, luminous Sun of heaven, into the dark, rayless garment of the appearance of bread, day and night, each moment, in all places, and for all His creatures. Yes, beloved, His longing to be with us all days, even to the consummation of the world, goes so far that the perpetually binding words fall from His tongue, "Do this in commemoration of Me." With such love as this Our Lord clings to us, to each one of us. This love of our divine Saviour for each of us is so great that His Heart yearns to be with us, in the very closest proximity to us; and behold and wonder at what He does! Forever, uninterruptedly, every moment of the day and night, He dwells under the form of bread in all places on the surface of the earth!

I ask you, then, once more: Could Jesus give us a greater proof of His love than this at which we marvel in the Blessed Sacrament? Surely not. It is this love that has won from the wisdom and almighty power of God this remembrance of His wonderful works; it was this love which was never satisfied until eternal Truth bound itself to insure the continuance of this memorial of God's wonders every day and in all places before the redeemed of all nations. For He will be with them, with all of them; will be close to them all days, even to the consummation of the world Oh, this love is proved; through all this long time it has not grown cool, nor diminished; no, Jesus dwells ever in the form of bread, because His Heart has ever the same ardent desire to be with us. Although so much has been done which might have lessened this excessive love, it remains forever unchanged, for it is also a patient love.

Third Point —Love is crowned by patience, and the more enduring and unchanging the patience, the deeper rooted and stronger is the love. Now once again behold the altar. Inexpressibly great love for us has brought Jesus into this concealment Surely it must be the keenest grief to Jesus to see Himself ignored, and left without us. But this very anguish must be endured by our dear Lord, and endured in this great Sacrament of His love. For inconceivable multitudes of Christians constantly pour upon His Heart, burning with love for us in this form of bread, the icy waters of indifference, neglect, disrespect, ill treatment, derision and rejection. He yearns to be with us, and many thousands have time daily to stay with Him; but it is a burden and torment to them to be with the Blessed Sacrament, and they keep aloof from the tabernacle. Oh, the icy waters that are poured on the Heart of Jesus glowing with love for us! In His exceeding love, He has bound Himself to come every day in the Holy Mass as the Lamb of God who taketh away the sins of the world, and thousands and thousands fail to hear Mass except on those days which are of obligation. Oh, the icy waters which are poured on the glowing love of the Heart of Jesus ! The love of the dear Lord in the Blessed Sacrament for us is so great that as soon as He beholds us His eyes rest upon us, and never turn away as long as we are near Him; and yet many thousands enter the holy place, whose thoughts are guiltily wandering while they are before

Him. Oh, the icy waters that are poured over the glowing love of the Heart of Jesus ! He loves us so much that He comes to us, giving us the divine kiss of friendship, whence grace outflows, and yet who can count the number of those who allow Him to be torn and lacerated by the teeth of Satan, who is still within them ? Oh, the icy waters that are poured on the glowing love of the Heart of Jesus ! He has concealed Himself in the form of bread that He might give us all the treasures of His grace; but ah, how inconceivably great is the number of His ransomed people who repulse the warm love of His Heart, who even deride and mock Him, and insult Him because He has knocked at their door in this poor garb ! Oh, the icy waters that are poured on the Heart of Jesus glowing with love for us ! And in all places in the world these icy waters of indifference, of dishonor and contempt, have been poured out like a stream for eighteen hundred years on the Heart of Jesus burning with love for us !

But why do I say this to you ? Certainly not because I have any intention of reproaching you by these words, for this would wrong you and be unjust. For you have hastened to come here to adore your Saviour, and have thus sufficiently proved that your heart is grateful and loving to your Lord in the Blessed Sacrament. But I must say this to you, and say it so emphatically that you may see plainly how deep-seated, how patient, is the uninterrupted and self-sacrificing love of your Redeemer. For all the icy waters that for eighteen hundred years have daily been poured like a stream on the burning love of the Heart of Jesus have not been able to quench this fire of love, nor has it burned for a moment more dimly No, it still has its entire, prodigious strength; it is ever the joy and delight of our dear Lord to be with His own, and so He dwells uninterruptedly, day and night, with us in the

Blessed Sacrament, under the veil of the appearance of bread.

I have also another intention in telling you this—to make your hearts, already full of love for the Blessed Sacrament, more loving if possible, that the reciprocal love and gratitude to Jesus in the Blessed Sacrament which inspired our fathers to establish the Forty Hours may lead us to celebrate it worthily.

Yes, my brethren, the Forty Hours is the expression of a return of love to Jesus in the Blessed Sacrament corresponding to His love. In His excessive love for us He comes to us in the Holy Eucharist with all the heavenly treasures of His grace, remains there uninterruptedly with them, and waits patiently for us to give us these heavenly treasures of grace. And behold, reciprocal love finds an expression, a reply, to this. It, too, comes with all that it has; it brings body and soul to the altar, and prostrating itself before the Spouse of its soul, adores Him, praising and exalting Him, and making Him reparation. But it does not do this for a few moments, nor does it quickly tire of so doing; no, it gives a whole hour to this adoration of its Lord, and does not do so once only, but comes repeatedly during the day, not permitting business, nor pleasure, nor weariness to detain it. It longs to come and pray, " Blessed be the Most Holy Sacrament ! " to sigh, " O dearest Jesus ! Thy blessed Mother gathers all Thy angels and saints to bless Thee for all the insults and offences which Thy ungrateful creatures have ever committed, or will commit to the end of time, against Thee, the supreme Good; " and to intone " Ave Jesu ! " Oh, such adoration, praise and reparation comes from a heart filled with a generous, enduring love of Jesus !

O beloved ! during the Forty Hours give to your dear Lord in the Blessed Sacrament this proof of gratitude and reciprocal love ! Let the love and zeal with which you have begun the Forty Hours be enduring and constant to the very end. Our Lord in the Blessed Sacrament deserves this; He is worthy to receive power, and divinity, and wisdom, and strength, and honor, and glory, and benediction. To have said this to you is enough.

Yes, dear Lord, behold here before Thy most holy face children who feel how much Thou lovest them; children in whom Thou hast enkindled a return of love for Thy too great, constant, and enduring love for them; children who rejoice to know that in the Forty Hours they can in a measure return Thy love, exceeding the power of all words to describe, and therefore they are determined not to weary of publicly adoring and praising Thee during these days, and making reparation to Thee in this great Sacrament of love. O blessed Lord and compassionate Saviour, reject not our prayer and praise because we are sinners ! Behold we are sorrowful and contrite for ever having offended Thee by the slightest sin; graciously receive these few hours of prayer which we humbly offer Thee Receive also our poor souls in Thy merciful hands when they shall be cut off from our sinful bodies; lead them into the glory of Thy heavenly kingdom, and let them there celebrate the eternal, blessed Forty Hours; let us there adore Thee in perfect bliss, as we have here adored Thee with lively faith before the Blessed Sacrament. In the beauty of heaven, with all Thy angels and saints, let us adore Thee, saying, "Holy, holy, holy, Lord God of Sabaoth !" Amen.

SERMON X.

THE BLESSED SACRAMENT A SECOND BIRTH OF JESUS.

"And falling down they adored Him."—*St. Matt.* ii. 11.

THESE words are familiar to you all. They tell us what the three kings did when they came before the Child whom they found with Mary, His Mother, on entering the stable over which the star that had guided them on their journey stood still. But why do I recall this event to-day when we are beginning the Forty Hours? Beloved, no one with a taste for divine things could ask this question seriously, and I am sure you already know its answer. The reply is this: The time of these two events lies far apart; in spirit they belong together. What the swaddling-bands were to the three kings, the form of bread which hides the heavenly Treasure is to us; and what the Wise Men did as they fell down and adored the Child lying before them in the crib, we also do before the most adorable Gift exposed in the monstrance.

The Wise Men recognized that in the poor, feeble, helpless Child whom they saw before them the almighty King and Lord of heaven and earth was born; and we believe with the doctors of the Church, our fathers in the faith, that under the form of bread the consubstantial Son of the living God is, so to speak, born anew. We have come hither to adore Him, to glorify Him, to praise and supplicate Him. That we may do this with true devotion, with ardent love and strong conviction, with holy zeal and unwearying constancy, we will seek to understand in some

152

measure the sublime idea of the Blessed Sacrament which
the holy fathers had, in calling it a second birth of Jesus.
They wished to express thereby:

I. How truly,

II. How wonderfully,

III. How graciously Jesus is present in the Blessed
Sacrament.

First Point.—Because our religion is divine it contains
many truths so lofty, so sublime, so mysterious, that they
are beyond all our senses and comprehension, and even
after they are revealed to us we cannot completely grasp
and understand them. We have only a feeble presentiment
of them, and can only make to ourselves something ap-
proaching an image of them. And we thank our blessed
Lord that, as St Gregory the Great so beautifully remarks in
one of his homilies, He has condescended to liken the divine
truths He taught, and the heavenly treasures which He
brought into the world, to earthly things and temporal
goods, that thus our understanding might be enabled,
through the mundane things they know and can grasp, to
learn to comprehend in a measure, and to love and prize
the celestial truth and grace offered them by their divine
Saviour.

The entire Gospel gives evidence how well Our Lord
knew how to stoop to our necessities. There we see that
the greatest and most profound truths were laid before
man and made plain by the simplest parables, by comparisons drawn from daily life; but which, far from being
ugly, ordinary, lowly, were beautiful, noble and sublime.
And hence it comes that those who have a taste for divine
things, and have good and tender hearts, derive much
benefit from the reading of the Gospel. The least learned
gets enlightenment and understanding from it, and the
educated man and scholar also discovers there much that
enlightens him further, disclosing to him the beauty and

divinity of the truth. I will give you one example which is suitable to these circumstances, and especially applicable to holy communion. Jesus has made plain the important and profound truth of His union with the soul, and how necessary it is for each of us, when He said, "I am the vine; you are the branches." Every one knows how intimate is the union of the vine and the branches, how deeply the branch is engrafted in the vine, and how necessary it is for it to be so in order to bring forth mature fruit; and thus each Christian has a conception of how intimately he can be united with his Lord, and how necessary it is for him to be thus closely united with his Saviour if he would do anything meritorious or fruitful for his eternal salvation.

What Jesus, the divine Teacher, has done is also done by His disciples, the apostles and their successors, whom He commissioned to preach this Gospel to all the peoples of the earth, even to the end of time. They also, like their divine Master, teach the profound truths of Christianity by simple and beautiful parables, thus seeking to make them comprehensible and clear to all. And they have taken pains to make the sublime Mystery of the Holy Sacrament of the Altar loved and appreciated by presenting it to Christians in striking and beautiful comparisons. One of their favorite comparisons was to call it a second birth of Jesus. This is the language of the fathers, and of St. John Chrysostom, who says, "In the Blessed Sacrament is continued what came to pass in the stable at Bethlehem." And in his meditation, St. Augustine goes back to the house of Nazareth where the angel brought the tidings to Mary, and where that marvellous event came to pass, "The Word was made flesh," he sees this renewed upon the altar. "In the hands of the priest, and by his word, the Son of God again becomes man," he exclaims in wonder.

You will feel with me, my brethren, that this comparison expresses in an exhaustive manner what, according to the words of Christ, we are to believe of the Blessed Sacrament. Our belief in the Blessed Sacrament cannot be expressed more truly, completely and exactly than by saying that the Blessed Sacrament is a second, a new, birth of Jesus; a second, a new, incarnation of Jesus. For consider: In the Blessed Sacrament we see nothing of almightiness, nothing of divinity and humanity, nothing of body and soul, of flesh and blood; what we see, feel and taste there seems to us lifeless, seems to us like bread and wine, and yet we believe it is only the appearance of bread and wine; that under this the Son of God is present, with divinity and humanity, with body and soul, with flesh and blood, really, truly and substantially

The holy fathers say: " Yes, in truth this is so, as truly as the Son of the living God has taken flesh and blood of the blessed Virgin Mary, and has become man, so truly is He born under this veil of bread; it is a second, a new, birth of Jesus " He who thus expresses his faith believes surely that Jesus is present in the Blessed Sacrament. Because the fathers were so filled and penetrated with this faith in the actual presence of Jesus in the Blessed Sacrament you see that they did before the altar what the shepherds and kings did before the crib, there before the altar your fathers in the faith, the apostles and their successors, and all the faithful with them, falling down, adore Him.

O my brethren, join in this true and beautiful thought, receive it into your mind, make it your own, and approach the Blessed Sacrament as if you came to the crib, exclaiming with the prophet, "Thou art in truth a hidden God." Thou wert hidden in the stable, and Thou art still more hidden in this birth in the sacred Host, where Thou completely concealest Thy sacred humanity from our eyes. But hidden though Thou art, Thou art none the less the same great God who hath created heaven and earth; Thou art none the less the same God-man who sitteth at the right hand of the heavenly Father.   Yes, my Lord, I confess:

> " From the sacred Host is fled
> All the substance of the bread:"

I confess:

> " Lo, the Good, supreme and best,
> On the altar deigns to rest,
> Is with flesh and blood our Guest."

Therefore, at all times and forever, we will ceaselessly praise and exalt the Blessed Sacrament; therefore may all the angels and saints praise Thee in the Blessed Sacrament. Yes, ye blessed in heaven, join with us in adoration, saying, " Praised be the Most Holy Sacrament ! " sing with us, " Ave Jesu ! "

In calling the Blessed Sacrament a second birth of Jesus the holy fathers would not merely express how truly Jesus is present in the Holy Eucharist, they would also recognize and declare how wonderfully He is present in the Blessed Sacrament.

Second Point —The first birth of Jesus was wonderful. For therein the consubstantial Son of God had so humiliated and emptied Himself as to take the form of a servant and become man.

And He had for His Mother a virgin, who conceived and bore Him as her son, and yet remained a spotless virgin; a virgin who, when the angel brought her the tidings that she had found grace with God, and should bear the Son of the Most High, protested that she had consecrated the purity, the virginity, of her heart, her body and her soul to God, that she knew not man; a virgin upon whom the Holy Ghost descended, and who was overpowered by the shadow of the Most High.   In these things you see how wonderful was the first birth of Jesus, that birth by which He came into the world as a little child. But not less wonderful is the second birth of Jesus in the Blessed Sacrament, that birth by which He becomes present in the form of bread. And this birth is chiefly so wonderful because it comes to pass by the word of a priest.

The Holy Scriptures tell us that all things were made by the word of God. By the word of God the heavens were stretched above our heads; by the word of God has the earth been established beneath our feet; by the word of God were the waters of the deep confined; in short, by the word of God all things were called out of nothingness and created to fill the vast universe. So mighty, so powerful, is the word of God ! All this is doubtless great and worthy of wonder, admiration and adoration.

But in the holy Mystery of the body and blood of Our Lord in the Most Holy Sacrament, and in the manner and means by which it is wrought, we see something much more marvellous. For there it is not God who speaks, nor is it an angel; it is the priest, a feeble creature of God, a poor, sinful man, who speaks five little words and the greatest miracle of nature and grace comes to pass Beloved, the priest, a frail, sinful man, speaks the holy words of consecration over the bread and wine, and in the same moment, in an instant, as soon as the last syllable of the sacred words is spoken, how changed, how annihilated, is the entire substance of the bread and wine ! Under the same appearance, under the same exterior, without the slightest alteration being perceptible, bread and wine is no longer there.

> "Of the bread and wine is here,
> Only that which doth appear,"

we sing in our veneration of the Blessed Sacrament. Nor is that all: the priest, a feeble, sinful man, speaks the holy words of consecration over the bread and wine, and

in the same moment, in an instant, as soon as the last
syllable of the words is uttered, a separation occurs which
sets aside a rule, a most permanent, unalterable law of
nature, and which is and must forever be impenetrable
to created minds. The appearance of bread and wine,
namely the form, color, smell and taste of bread and wine,
are separated from their substances, from bread and wine
to which they belong, and under these circumstances continue to exist, while bread and wine cease to exist.

> " From the sacred Host is fled
> All the substance of the bread,"

again we sing in our beautiful and touching veneration of
the Blessed Sacrament.

And still more: the priest, a feeble, sinful man, speaks
the words of consecration over the bread and wine, and
the Son of God is obedient to his word. As the last syllable
ends, the Son of God, who, after His resurrection, rose
above the heaven of heavens and now sits at the right hand
of God, is here on the altar, comes into the husk of the
form of bread, and the priest holds in his hand, lays on
the altar, puts into the monstrance, Jesus, the Son of the
living God.

> " In the monstrance is adored
> Christ our undivided Lord.
> Lo, the Good, supreme and best,
> On the altar deigns to rest;
> Is with flesh and blood our Guest."

Thus we sing in our beautiful and sublime veneration of
the Most Holy Sacrament.

Oh, truly a marvellous birth is this second birth of
Our Lord in the Blessed Sacrament of the Altar! O my
hearers, take this beautiful, sublime and true thought into
your heart, and make it your own, see and feel what a
chain of the greatest miracle Jesus has wrought in giving

us the Blessed Sacrament ! Confess to Him publicly, with St. Augustine: " Yes, my Lord, I solemnly acknowledge that I do not understand how Thou canst be so completely enshrouded, Thou splendor of the divine majesty ! But I know that Thou canst do greater things than I can understand. And I believe that Thou hast done this; I believe that in Thy love for me, a sinner worthy of punishment, Thou goest so far as to forget Thyself and to work this great miracle in order to be with us "

Therefore, at all times, without ceasing, and for all eternity, we will praise and bless Thee in the Blessed Sacrament. Therefore, may all the angels and saints join us in praising Thee. O ye blessed spirits of heaven, unite with us, saying in adoration, " Blessed be the Most Holy Sacrament ! " join in our " Ave Jesu ! "

In calling the Blessed Sacrament a second birth of Jesus the holy fathers would not only show how really, actually and wonderfully Jesus is present in the Blessed Sacrament; they would also express a third idea, and that is how graciously Jesus is present here.

Third Point —" Fear not," said the angels to the shepherds when they announced the birth of Jesus to them. " Fear not; I bring you glad tidings of great joy, for unto you is born a Saviour." And this word conveys how great and innumerable would be the graces given to the barren and pining earth.

Now, beloved, Jesus is present upon our altars, and conceals Himself in this Most Holy Sacrament in the same character of Redeemer. There He holds enclosed all the infinite treasures of grace, because He is ever the Author of grace, the uncreated Source of all graces, because He is the Treasurer of all the riches of God. But He does not reserve these exceeding treasures of grace, nor keep them locked up in His Heart, but pours them out over us and shares them with us in their fulness

Therefore He has given the promise, " As I live by the Father, so He that eateth Me, the same shall also live by Me." And the Blessed Sacrament is precisely that Mystery in which these blessed words are verified in which He announced the design of His mission and coming, and we Catholic Christians are the people in relation to whom it was said, " I am come that they may have life, and have it abundantly."

Surely this is true, for the Blessed Sacrament is the Sacrament of salvation, serving especially to raise our soul to spiritual and supernatural life; to support, strengthen and uphold us in the journey to heaven. " Except you eat the flesh of the Son of man, and drink His blood, you shall not have life in you," is the explicit declaration and warning of Our Lord. Furthermore, the Blessed Eucharist cures our weakness, strengthens us against all obstacles: " Come to Me all you that labor and are burdened, and I will refresh you," is His touching invitation. It procures and provides for us the necessary help for salvation. " I am the Bread of life; he who eateth Me shall not hunger," says His consoling promise. It is a pledge of that coming life for which we sigh, and that eternal glory wherein salvation consists. " He who eateth this Bread hath eternal life, and I will raise him up on the Last Day." Thus are announced the joyful tidings, the blessed revelations of Our Lord.

Beloved, what a rich, what an inconceivably, unfathomably rich treasury and mine of grace opens here before us ! It is a pure mine of gold, so immeasurably great that one can never reach the end, nor fathom it in meditation. Thus gracious is this second birth of Jesus ! Behold why the prophet implored the Lord so yearningly, " Say to my soul: I am thy salvation " But we who possess Jesus in the Blessed Sacrament need nevermore pray thus, for already He has there anticipated all our desires. O beloved, grasp the great things that the Lord hath done for thy soul, and marvel at them! He has created thee, He has purified and washed thee from the stain of original sin, He has filled and sanctified thee with His Holy Spirit, He has Himself descended to earth from the bosom of His eternal Father, and clothed His divine majesty in our miserable flesh, in order to seek our souls, ransom them, and reconcile them to God; yes, He has not even spared His own life, but pledged it for us, sacrificed it, allowing Himself to be martyred in the deepest humiliation, and with unspeakable agony of body and soul. All this has He done, and yet it was not enough, nor satisfied His love; He wills that His most holy body should remain with us for the salvation of our souls, remain to be their inheritance; He wills that in a certain sense this adorable body should daily be born again for them, and abide with them, that thereby they may ceaselessly receive new strength and increase of grace. So gracious is this second birth of Jesus in the Blessed Sacrament! There the word of the Apostle is fulfilled anew, "He has made Himself poor that we might be rich." Therefore, dear brethren, we will show a return of love to Our Lord in the Blessed Sacrament, never wearying of praying with deep emotion, "Blessed be the Most Holy Sacrament!" of singing with our whole heart, "Ave Jesu!" And as we feel that we are weak and unable to duly praise Our Lord dwelling with us, we will turn to all the friends of God to help us praise our God and theirs in the Blessed Sacrament. Oh, yes, ye blessed spirits of heaven, ye angels and saints, unite with us in praying, "Blessed be the Most Holy Sacrament!" Join in our "Ave Jesu!"

The Blessed Sacrament, my brethren, is in truth the second birth of Jesus. For Our Lord comes to us and dwells with us by this Holy Sacrament in all reality; He works the greatest miracle in order to come and dwell with us, and He there reserves all the treasures of grace, sanctity and glory in order to share them with us.

The Blessed Sacrament is the Sacrament of salvation, of grace. And you feel that nothing but love can do all this. Therefore the Blessed Sacrament is most truly the Sacrament of love And what a love ! Oh, who can express it ? Beloved, the youth whom the Lord especially loved, who leaned on His breast in the solemn hour when He established this Sacrament of grace and love, and could feel something of the immense love burning in the Heart of Jesus, sought to explain it to us. But it is to be noted that words failed him, for he said, " Having loved His own who were in the world, He loved them to the end " But after all he could say nothing more; it could not have been expressed more strongly. A God, beloved, has loved His own to the end. Yes, my brethren, as in the work of salvation, so also and especially in this, His last legacy, Our Lord could say, " What could I have done more for thee and have not done it ? " He has gone as far as this in this Sacrament for love of us.

And what proof of love do we give, or shall we give, Our Lord in this Sacrament in return for this ? What does our heart say, or is it dumb ? Ah, if it said nothing, then we were truly insensible to this love ! But no, your heart is not silent; rather your heart bleeds at the insults and offences inflicted by Christians on your Lord, and you have come hither to show Him by your adoration a little love and gratitude, to make reparation to Him for the great indifference, neglect, and dishonor with which Christians, His ransomed people, afflict Him.

Yes, dearest Saviour, we will not weary of crying to Thee, " Blessed be the Most Holy Sacrament ! " we will not weary of singing, " Ave Jesu ! " of begging Thy blessed Mother and all Thy angels and saints to bless Thee for all the offences and insults which Thy ungrateful creatures have ever committed, or ever will commit, against Thee, to the end of time. And Thou, O dearest Jesus, we humbly beseech Thee, graciously accept these few hours of prayer, and we supplicate Thee to take us after this life into Thy kingdom, and let us behold Thee, and possess Thee, and in the possession of Thee be eternally happy. Amen.

SERMON XI.

THE BLESSED SACRAMENT A MAGNIFICENT MANIFESTATION
OF DIVINE OMNIPOTENCE.

"He hath made a remembrance of His wonderful works, being a merciful and gracious Lord."—*Ps.* cx. 4.

ALL the works of God, without exception, are wisely done; that is to say, their issue has been exactly what He willed; they attain and fulfil precisely the object for which they were created, and in this sense we must call each work of God great and perfect. None the less is it true that God calls, with a certain preference and emphasis, one of His works His great, His perfect, His memorable work. The work that God Himself calls great must then have special, preëminent qualities, extraordinary and striking. And this is the case. All works of God are a revelation of Himself; they are, if I may say so, a mirror wherein He lets us, His rational creatures, see the splendors of His invisible perfection, His hidden beauty. Now the work of God, which He Himself calls great, has with the other superiority which marks it, also the distinction of showing us, not only one of the infinite glories of our God, but many, and showing them not dimly but plainly, not feebly in faint outline, but in splendor and magnificence.

The Holy Ghost had announced the Blessed Sacrament in advance as the remembrance of the wonderful works of God. Hence it must be the masterpiece of all His wonderful works, and so it is not enough that the Blessed Sacrament should have in itself preëminent qualities, but

164

among the great works of God revealing His perfections the Blessed Sacrament must stand alone. This is a fact. Nowhere will you find or be able to cite a mystery reflecting as many divine perfections as the Blessed Sacrament, and revealing them with such astonishing clearness and accuracy, and in such overwhelming greatness.

It is no exaggeration if I say to you that the Blessed Sacrament is that unique work of God by which He manifests His divine attributes to us, showing them there most plainly, and unfolding them in their grandeur. You feel this to be so. It is the principal reason, as your heart tells you, why the Blessed Sacrament, or rather Jesus in the Blessed Sacrament, is the favorite object of your adoration; why you celebrate the Forty Hours with what I may call inspired predilection, and why you willingly listen to sermons on the Blessed Sacrament to enliven your devotion. You know that it is impossible to show in a sermon thoroughly and exhaustively how plainly the divine majesty and the glory of its attributes are unfolded to us in the Blessed Sacrament. One has plenty to do in the time allotted if he but depicts in some degree of fulness the grandeur of one or another of the divine perfections as the Blessed Sacrament gives us knowledge of them. And so, my brethren, we will content ourselves with considering how the Blessed Sacrament is a revelation of divine omnipotence.

O beloved, to a believing heart how magnificently the Blessed Sacrament reveals the divine omnipotence !

I. Consider what befalls the bread; by the consecration it is annihilated as bread.

II. Consider who is present in the place of the bread: the divine, incarnate majesty of your blessed Saviour.

First Point.—Our belief in the Blessed Sacrament, and of the Blessed Sacrament, must be the true one; we are sure of this, so sure of it that we would rather lose our lives than give up this faith. For the belief the Catholic Church has taught you is alone the right one. She does not proceed like the false religions. They have changed her teaching, her faith according to their ideas, and moreover have done violence to the words of Our Lord, distorting them, giving them a meaning not attributed to them while He lived, and which Our Lord would surely have made plain by His words had He meant that which they have taken into their heads. The Catholic Church goes to work very differently. She builds her opinions, her faith on the words of her dear Spouse; she believes exactly what the words signify and express, nor shrinks, although she sees that in His clear and simple words Our Lord unfolds a great mystery, incomprehensible to the finite mind. That this is the right method of proceeding, which must lead to the possession of the truth, each one must see, though every one will not admit it. As the mode of procedure of the Catholic Church and that of the false religions differ completely, so also the results.

In the belief of the heretical religions as regards the Blessed Sacrament, there is no mystery. All that is incomprehensible is that any one could express himself in such words as Jesus used. If the Blessed Sacrament is nothing else than bread, and that bread a remembrance of Jesus, it is easy to understand that there is no mystery here; but I cannot understand how in giving us it Jesus could say: " This is My body," or then, to speak mildly, He expressed Himself very imperfectly Nor in that case do I understand any better how the Holy Ghost could tell, as by St John, that in establishing the Holy Eucharist Our Lord loved His own to the end If a God loves us to the end, then I expect much more than that a fragment of bread will be a memorial of Him

Very different is the conclusion to which the Church comes. Here we cannot say that the mystery lies in the words Our Lord used; we cannot say in this case that it is incomprehensible that Our Lord should have used such words for such a thing; no, the words are clear, plain, perfectly comprehensible; they bear their ordinary signification, the mystery, the incomprehensibility lies rather in what I have to believe of the gift of grace left us by Our Lord as a memorial of Himself. For I must believe, and do believe, that in the Blessed Sacrament we possess the most sacred body of Our Lord and Saviour; not an ordinary, perishable thing, which is merely a symbol of the dear Lord, but something entirely supernatural, something heavenly and holy, and among all holy things the holiest; the adorable body of Our Saviour Jesus Christ, the incarnate Son of God Himself, not in the form proper to His nature and perfections, but in a new, strange, unknown form, in the lowly and lifeless form of bread. That, according to the words of Our Saviour, is the Blessed Sacrament. It is the true body of Jesus Christ, and because it is the true body so it is also His blood, His soul, His divinity; Jesus Christ entire, but veiled, hidden, even unrecognizable in the strange, the poor, the lowly form of bread. Since we believe but this we understand perfectly that the Blessed Sacrament is the work of God's hand in which His omnipotence most plainly and gloriously shines out; it is the most magnificent revelation of His omnipotence; it is the remembrance of His wonderful works; in no other work of God are wrought so many, such great and singular miracles St. Thomas of Aquinas, that profound searcher and explorer of the works of God, does not hesitate to make the significant decision that the Blessed Sacrament is the abridgement of God's miracles And in truth, my brethren, when we examine what happens, and happens in a single moment when that which was bread is changed into the true body of the Lord, through what a series of magnificent miracles we are led!

At the moment of consecration there is apparent no external change in the bread; one would suppose it to be bread still, yet what a mighty change has actually taken place in that which entirely remains unaltered! The greatest change possible or conceivable is wrought in the bread, a change so great that it can be brought about only by the omnipotence of God For what happens to the bread? Beloved, it exists no longer, it is destroyed, annihilated. Yes; this is actually true, and you confess it when during these days you sing with believing heart:

> "From the sacred Host is fled
> All the substance of the bread.
> Of the bread and wine is here
> Only that which doth appear."

This means that there is nothing left, nothing remaining of the substance of bread, that there is nothing of itself left in it; all that of which it was made is completely changed.

If this be true, then the almighty hand of God was in the bread at the moment of consecration, for the annihilation of anything is as equally, exclusively the work of God's omnipotence as creation. He was in the bread in a perfect, a wonderful and unique manner, a manner in which He is nowhere else than in the Blessed Sacrament; because He has annihilated the bread, as bread, and here the omnipotence of God acts contrary to the ordinary laws with which He sustains and rules the universe. For though individual creatures fall to ruin, decay and die, it is but dissolution, a separation of the elements to which the various qualities are united; but annihilation, the total disappearance of these elements from the universe cannot be; this action of His omnipotence God performs only in this memorial of Himself which He has established in the Blessed Sacrament: here the substance of the bread, as such, is completely changed into the most sacred body of Jesus.

Surely the Blessed Sacrament is the remembrance of
the wonderful works of God. But there is another
memorable, unique miracle wrought in this annihilation
of the bread. Although at the moment of consecration
the bread, as such, is completely annihilated, everything
by which we ordinarily perceive and recognize it to be
bread remains extant, perfectly unchanged and uninjured;
that is to say, the appearance of bread is there without
that which is in other circumstances necessary to sustain
it—the bread itself. On the altar you have the form of
bread, the color of bread, the hardness of bread, yet although in ordinary circumstances you would swear it was
bread, of bread there is no vestige. You confess this mysterious truth; from hour to hour the faithful sing:

> "Of the bread and wine is here
> Only that which doth appear."

What a great, what a mighty miracle is this, a miracle
that stands alone, a miracle never wrought elsewhere!
For consider: When a substance changes ever so slightly,
something is always changed in its appearance; this is so
true that it is precisely from the change in the appearance
that we assume, we recognize that a change has taken
place in the thing itself. And here in the Blessed Sacrament the thing itself, the bread, is quite gone,
so what were more natural, more self-evident than that
the appearance of bread would also completely disappear?
Surely, judging from our universal experience, that appears to us a necessary, an indisputably necessary result;
for throughout creation we find the appearance of a thing
in that and with that to which it belongs, and it is unknown that the appearance of a thing should subsist alone
when that to which it belonged is no longer extant. And
in the Blessed Sacrament you have precisely that unheard-of case; we should expect that where the bread is

substantially changed just because it is changed, the appearances of it would also entirely vanish; but lo ! the appearances of the bread do not vanish, they remain, nor even the slightest change befalls them; they subsist uninjured.   In the Blessed Sacrament you find this great, magnificent, unknown miracle: the appearance of bread exists, the bread itself is changed, the appearance of bread endures alone without the bread still subsisting in which, and with which the appearance should be found   Yes, beloved, the Blessed Sacrament is truly the remembrance of the wonderful works of God

And, my brethren, I can tell you still more. Not only does the appearance of bread subsist alone after the bread has completely vanished, but the mere appearance of bread, though deprived of its substance, retains the same accidents, receives the same impression, produces the same effect, is accompanied by the same qualities as if the thing to which it had belonged were not destroyed, as if it still existed.   Again, what a great, magnificent, unique miracle ! For, my brethren, ordinarily when a substance is changed, the qualities of its appearance must also change; it can no longer produce the same effect, nor receive the same impression, the same influence on itself, for the simple reason that both qualities, that of affecting something and retaining an impression, are qualities belonging less to the appearance than to the substance which has such an appearance   And here in the Blessed Sacrament the thing itself, the bread, is not merely changed, but the whole substance of bread, the bread as such, is completely gone, completely annihilated   What, then, is more natural, what more reasonable than that where bread itself no longer continues, the power to produce or receive any impression whatsoever should be altogether withdrawn from its appearance?   There is no case known in all creation where the mere appearance of a thing subsisted by itself without the thing itself; but it is absolutely unheard-of, and indeed inconceivable, that by itself alone it could have the same qualities, the same strength, the same peculiarities as the thing itself. Yet we find this very marvel, not seen elsewhere in all creation, here in the Blessed Sacrament. Here the substance of bread is quite gone, and the mere appearance becomes warm or cold, dry or damp, soft or hard, and retains all these variations; it calls forth taste, has strength to sustain, yes, even to satisfy, causes all these effects as would be the case if the thing itself, the bread, were existent, and this not merely in appearance, through delusion of the senses, but actually and truly

Those two qualities, namely, affecting other things and retaining the impression of other things, both of which are peculiar to the thing itself, and not to its appearance, are, by the power of God, in the Blessed Sacrament in a wonderful and unheard-of manner, without the thing itself, which occasions and undergoes these impressions; and though it is unknown that the mere appearance of bread should have even one of the effects belonging otherwise only to actual bread, here in the Blessed Sacrament the mere appearance of bread has all the effects and all the accidents which in every other case are peculiar to bread, and could only be peculiar to it.

Yes, beloved, surely the Blessed Sacrament is a remembrance of the wonderful works of God! What an unknown, unparalleled subversion of the laws under which the Lord our God has established His creation! What a many-sided, clear, magnificent revelation of His omnipotence! Here occurs the greatest event that has ever happened; here perfectly sound bread is annihilated; here the appearance of bread remains, although nothing of the bread exists; yes, here the appearance of bread retains all the qualities which belong to the bread alone. Oh, this surely is the greatest miracle, surpassing all others, and contrary to all the wonderful things that the Lord has hitherto wrought in nature! And yet what great, never-to-be-forgotten miracles the Lord has wrought! At His command the waters rose like a wall; the fire was cooled; the flames destroyed not the burning bush; the roaring storm was calmed in a moment; at His word the towering waves became a smooth mirror of water; he who lay in the mouldering grave was in a moment made living, healthy, vigorous. These are truly magnificent, extraordinary miracles, memorable revelations of the omnipotence of God. We see and wonder that in them things have occasionally and for a few moments qualities that are foreign to them, and against which all their strength resists. Surely these are great works, great miracles of God!

But God has but one remembrance of His wonderful works, and that is the Blessed Sacrament. Here we see not merely that a created thing has foreign and contradictory qualities, but we see more, far more; we see there to our wonder and amazement that the entire appearance of this annihilated bread remains uninjured, unaltered; we even see that the mere appearance of bread, existing by itself, has all the qualities, and only the qualities, belonging to the bread, to the thing that is no more. This is certainly far more, unspeakably more, than that a thing should remain what it is, and only once exceed itself in something ordinarily incompatible to it, and exceed itself only in one point.

And you can see this great, this unique miracle, not merely now and then, or once, nor in certain places; it is to be seen unceasingly, in every place, from the rising of the sun to the setting, even to the end of the world. Such is the Blessed Sacrament, the remembrance of the wonderful works of God And I am far from having exhausted this subject. I have not yet told you the prin-

cipal fact. For you must know that Our Lord in His
love for us is not satisfied with exerting the fulness of
His power upon His creature; ah, no, His love urges Him
to the extreme limit of possibility. In this Holy Sacrament the omnipotence of God seizes not merely one of His
creatures, but, permit me the expression, this omnipotence lays its hand on the intarnate Son of God, and applies all its force, all its fulness against Him. You will
understand this if you reflect that Jesus is in the Blessed
Sacrament in the place of bread.

Second Point.—There is nothing to be seen in the moment of consecration, and yet the most marvellous thing
occurs. An annihilation has taken place, a created thing
has ceased to exist; nor is that all; something still greater
happens at that moment; a kind of creation comes to pass.
Instead of the substance of bread there is now under the
continuing appearance of bread another substance. And
what substance is this ? O divine Lord, strengthen my
faith that I may worthily, and truly, and clearly express it;
strengthen the faith of my hearers that they may grasp it:

> " Christian, rouse thy faith to see
> This great work wrought here for thee."

And what a work ! What has happened ? O beloved,
instead of bread there is now present, really, truly and
actually present, the majesty of the Son of God Himself,
with divinity and humanity, with body and soul, with
flesh and blood. For the conversion of the whole substance of bread and wine into the body and blood of Christ,
the appearance only of the bread and wine being unchanged, is a dogma of Catholic faith. You confess this
publicly and solemnly. Oh, during these days chant as
with one mouth:

> " Lo, the Good, supreme and best,
> On the altar deigns to rest;
> Is with flesh and blood our Guest."

During these days never weary of singing:

> " Here, we know as He Himself hath said,
> Christ is present in the form of bread "

During these days let your touching hymn arise:

> " Here our God Himself we see,
> Bow the head, and bend the knee "

Beloved hearers, what a great, magnificent, unheard-of miracle; a miracle that has no like !

We wonder and are motionless with amazement at the great miracle the dear Lord wrought at the marriage in Cana. There also we see a new, marvellous creation; without a vineyard, without a vine, without branches, without sunshine or rain, without labor or time, in one moment wine takes the place of water. But great as this miracle is, yet the Lord's omnipotence remains within the compass of the laws of things; it remains within the compass of lifeless creatures; instead of one, you have another lifeless creature. But here in the Blessed Sacrament, my brethren, the Lord in the exercise of His omnipotence remains no longer within the range of things belonging to that which He has annihilated; oh, no, His omnipotence now goes far beyond this compass. He brings into the place of the annihilated, lifeless substance of bread the Being who is the King of creation. He replaces the lifeless bread with the uncreated, creative majesty of the incarnate Son of God. Here, instead of the lifeless substance, instead of bread, you have not merely a living being, not merely a sensate being, not merely a reasonable being, here you have the Fulness, the Source, the Author of all life, the infinite majesty of the incarnate Son of God Himself. Acknowledge that:

> " From the sacred Host is fled
> All the substance of the bread;
> Christ Himself is here instead."

You see into what He converts the lifeless bread. In the place of the lowliest substance there comes into the Blessed Sacrament the highest Being we know, the highest that exists, there comes the adorable, incarnate Son of God. " The Word was made flesh, and dwelt among us," and this is renewed in the moment of consecration. Verily, beloved, the Blessed Sacrament is the remembrance of the wonderful works of God. I must still ask you to remark another memorable characteristic in it. It is that in the Blessed Sacrament the infinite, adorable majesty of the Son of God abides in the appearance of bread, notwithstanding the bread is gone. This is, and must be, your belief in the Blessed Sacrament. You acknowledge this publicly, and during these three days one can hear every hour the confession of this faith. For Catholic Christians sing:

> " In the monstrance is adored
> Christ, our undivided Lord.
> Of the bread and wine is here,
> Only that which doth appear."

What a great, magnificent, unique miracle ! The majesty of your God now dwells in the poor, lowly, lifeless form of bread. It is a great, an incomprehensible miracle, a tremendous work of omnipotence, that the divine Word became flesh, the infinite majesty took the form of a servant, and in this form of a servant has been made like to us, His miserable creatures, in all save sin. And it is a great work of omnipotence that the incarnate majesty of the Son of God has endured death, and even the death of the cross; that a God was slain, that a God bled, that the life of a God was at the last extremity, that the life of a God should be breathed out, should end, and be no more.

What great, magnificent miracles are all these ! But how these wonders are surpassed, how they sink into the

background beside the miracle of humiliation wrought by
the omnipotence of God in the Blessed Sacrament! Here
it never rests until, so to speak, the infinite majesty of
God has hidden itself in the bosom of nothingness. Who
could have anticipated that such a sublime majesty as
makes the columns of heaven tremble would enclose itself and dwell in such a narrow prison as the sacred Host?
The appearance of the lowest substance, the lifeless and
powerless form of bread incloses all that is included in the
Blessed Trinity. He who fills the heavens and the earth
with His immensity is now locked and hidden in the tiny
round Host. He who clothes all creatures with their
splendor is now clad in the feeble, needy form of bread,
instead of with royal purple. A God in a tabernacle of
worm-eaten wood; a God in a drinking-chalice, in a monstrance of paltry metal; a God under a canopy of a substance that is the food of worms; a God humiliated even
till He is completely unrecognizable! Yes, my brethren,
the Blessed Sacrament is verily a remembrance of the wonderful works of God!

On the other hand Our Lord works in the Blessed
Sacrament an extraordinary, ceaseless miracle by which
His sacred body receives the greatest glory. But first re-
call your belief. You confess it when you sing: " The
Word of God has changed bread into His flesh, wine into
His blood." And we sing also in the beautiful hymn
" Lauda Sion " :

> " This faith to Christian men is given—
> Bread is made flesh by words from heaven;
> Into His blood the wine is turned."

You believe that the true, most sacred body of Our
Lord, with all its corporeal substance, with all its corporeal
qualities, with all its members, is actually present under
the little, insignificant form of bread, and equally under

the whole form of bread, and under each portion thereof. What a great, magnificent, unique miracle! What an overpowering revelation of the omnipotence of God! Beloved hearer, when on Mount Thabor the face of the Lord shone as the sun, and the garments covering His body became whiter than snow; when once He came among His apostles through closed doors; when He walked dryshod over the waters of the sea; when on Mount Olivet His glorified body of itself rose up from the earth, and ascended through space into the heights of heaven, then we must say that creation felt the nearness of its Creator, and bowed down before Him; we must say that Our Lord revealed in His holy body a little of the splendor, and glory, and power of His divinity dwelling in it. Magnificent as are these wonders, and greatly as the body of the Lord is glorified by them, yet they are far inferior to the miracles of glorification which Our Lord performs in the Blessed Sacrament to honor His adorable body. For on all these occasions the body of Our Lord retained that characteristic which we find in all substances without exception which are made up of parts, and that is that where one part of His sacred body was there would not be also any other part at the same time; each part being only in that place proper to it. Where His hand was, His foot was not; where His eyes were, His ears were not also. And His sacred body did not then possess that great characteristic commonly found in a simple being—that is, one not composed of parts, a spirit; namely, the quality of having in the place where there is one part, where one limb is, also another, or all others equally present.

To be thus present, as we have said, is the characteristic of substances that are indivisible, which do not exist in parts; and this is easily understood, for precisely because they are indivisible, because they do not exist in parts, they must be entire in the place, and that part of a place where they are. But hitherto we have held this to be an inalienable, exclusive trait of indivisible, spiritual beings, for we understand thoroughly that in the case of a complex being where one part is another cannot be also. And it would be an unheard-of thing, something that never has been, and a great mystery to us if it were otherwise, if we were to find in the case of a substance made up of different portions of various limbs, that where one portion was there was also another at the same time. It is quite inconceivable to us that all portions of a corporeal substance, and consequently the entire corporeal substance, should be found in one and the same place. That is contrary to all experience.

Now behold, my brethren, this unheard-of, this inconceivable case is precisely that of the Blessed Sacrament. Our Lord does not rest until He has shared with His sacred body the quality, the splendid quality which is a characteristic of spiritual, indivisible beings, of substances not composed of united parts, and hitherto and otherwise an exclusive and inalienable characteristic of them. Although His adorable body exists in parts and has limbs, it is yet entire under the smallest form of bread, under the tiniest fragment thereof, and in the same place where there is one member of His sacred body there is not merely one other limb, but all its limbs: the entire body of the Lord. If this be so, then you understand that the body of your Lord in the Blessed Sacrament is raised above the condition of a body, and, if I may say so, is placed in the ranks of spiritual beings, whose characteristic it shares

It retains, as we see, the ability to be present corporeally, in the manner belonging properly only to the nature of spiritual beings; the most sacred body of your Lord is present entire and with all its members at once under the form of bread, and is wholly under each portion of the bread. What a great, what a unique miracle ! It is perhaps the most marvellous of the resplendent circle of miracles surrounding the Blessed Sacrament, and it has not its like outside the Blessed Sacrament. Yes, beloved, the Blessed Sacrament is verily the remembrance of the wonderful works of God.

Yet more, beloved. This characteristic of being entire in the sacred Host, and under each portion of it, the body of Our Lord possesses in higher excellence than even the spiritual, the indivisible, beings to whom this distinction is peculiar But what do I mean by this ? I mean by this that mysterious, unfathomable truth which the hymn I have just quoted celebrates. In the " Lauda Sion " we sing:

> " We break the sacred Host: but bold
> And firm thy faith shall keep its hold;
> Deem not the whole doth more enfold
> Than in the fractured part resides."

Let us throw some light upon this. What was formerly bread is now the body of the Lord. If you divide bread, it is, and remains under each new portion, still bread; and here also in the Blessed Sacrament instead of bread there is now under each newly formed portion of the appearance of bread the true body of Our Lord. And that is a prerogative not even possessed by a spiritual being. And why ? My brethren, our soul is in our body and in each portion of it, but in a very imperfect manner. In order for it to be so it is requisite that the individual parts of our body should be united to one another. Should a limb be taken from the body it necessarily follows that the soul is gone from the limb thus separated, and it very often happens that the soul departs from the mutilated body. The presence of our soul in a part of our body is entirely and completely dependent, not merely on the presence of the adjoining parts, but also on each part remaining united to the entire body

Now, my brethren, the body of Our Lord is not contained in each portion of the form of bread in this imperfect manner. You may divide the form of bread as often as you will, and how you will, the sacred body of Our Lord is truly present in each fragment thus formed. That is the inviolable, strongly established teaching of our holy faith But do you know, Christian soul, who is present in this substance for which the law does not hold that a portion must be united to the whole; who it is that can be present in these fragments taken from one another? This prerogative belongs only to the uncreated, infinitely perfect Spirit—to the Spirit of God.

You see, also, that in the Blessed Sacrament the body of Our Lord has something of His divine attributes; you see that to glorify His body in the Blessed Sacrament it was not enough for Our Lord to raise it so high that it was among the ranks of created spiritual beings; oh, no, He does not rest until He has raised it so high that it shares something of His divine attributes: His sacred body is entire in each portion of the form of bread, be these portions separate or united And it would have been more than enough, an overwhelming miracle, if He had given His sacred body only once in a complete form But the body of Our Lord is in each portion, and in the tiniest portion of the form of bread What a miracle is this! Oh, this is perhaps the most marvellous of the splendid circle of miracles surrounding the Blessed Sacrament, and outside the mystery of the Holy Eucharist this miracle has not its like. Yes, beloved, the Blessed Sacrament is truly the remembrance of the wonderful works of God.

The Blessed Sacrament is the remembrance of the wonderful works of God; it is the most magnificent and overwhelming revelation and disclosure of the omnipotence of God; therein is wrought the most tremendous, resplendent miracle. On the one hand is the bread, as

such, completely changed, and yet retaining the form
of the bread which is no longer there; yes, and this remaining appearance has all the qualities, and only the
qualities, which belong to bread: on the other hand this
bread is replaced by the infinite majesty of the incarnate
Son of God, who takes upon Himself the deepest humiliation, abiding there under the lifeless and powerless form
of bread, yet prepares here the greatest glorification for
His sacred body, in that this body, composed of different
members is present in each portion of the Host; yes, when
this form is divided, is present entire under each fragment.
Therefore is the Blessed Sacrament a remembrance of the
wonderful works of God.

My brethren, I have not set forth a pious, disputable
opinion of the Blessed Sacrament. No; what I have said
to you has the strongest truth to warrant it; I have not
set forth groundless assertions. No; all I have said to you
are but so many dogmas which the Church teaches of the
Blessed Sacrament. I have announced nothing but what
the study of the Catechism gives you. And how great,
how sublime the Blessed Sacrament appears to you; how
magnificent a revelation of the omnipotence of God is all
that occurs in the moment when the Blessed Sacrament is
called into being!

To sum it up once more briefly, and in other words:
Annihilation and creation, those two opposite poles of
omnipotence, with other actions containing and uniting
the nature and characteristics of annihilation and creation; then a collection of special miracles, the most beautiful and rarest of their kind, with quite new miracles
peculiar to this Mystery, having nowhere else their like;
moreover the ingenious love of the divine incarnate Word,
humiliating Himself ever deeper and deeper in His own
creation, till He approaches even to the verge of nothingness, till He can almost conceal Himself in the bosom of

nothingness, and thus annihilates Himself daily thousands and thousands of times; the human flesh of Jesus, not merely adorned with the qualities of His soul, but, so to speak, raised above His soul, and glorified with the attributes of God, by drawing near to His divinity and the Holy Trinity, surrounding, I may say, this sacred body with the retinue and court of heaven—this is the glorious, the splendid picture of the Blessed Sacrament which our holy faith unrolls before us and offers to our wondering eyes. And here if ever the words of Tertullian applied when he said: "Nothing gives us such a worthy idea of God, such a noble conception of His majesty, as the impossibility of grasping Him His eternal perfections reveal Him to men, and conceal Him from them at one and the same time."

Now you know, my brethren, that Our Lord has established this remembrance of His wonderful works in order to be close to us, and to offer Himself in sacrifice for our sins and necessities, in order to pour upon us the treasures of His grace; in a word, in order to reveal all the love of His Heart. You also know that love calls forth a return of love. And if the love of Jesus is, and has proved itself to be, superabundant, one would imagine that the love of Christians for Jesus in the Blessed Sacrament would be unlimited in return; one would imagine that we priests, when preaching on the Blessed Sacrament, would have to exhort Christians to moderate a little their zeal and devotion towards the Blessed Sacrament, but that it would never be necessary to urge them to be zealous, to love and venerate the Blessed Sacrament. There have been such souls. Such an exhortation was suitable to an Aloysius. Whenever he was with Our Lord in the Blessed Sacrament he could not contain himself, and when duty led him from the tabernacle he prayed to his Lord: "Lord, do not hold me so fast; I pray Thee let me go." Such

souls, souls like his, there are still; oh, that all were
such! But alas, dear Lord, what a confession we have to
make ! A'h, Lord, the earth has no standard wherewith
to measure this miracle of Thy love, but to our shame we
must confess that men can approach it; yes, can even exceed it, I will not say by their unbelief, for that could
almost be forgiven, Thou art so inconceivably good, but
by their coldness toward this gift of the tenderest, most
burning love, wherein Thou Thyself givest us Thy dearest,
most divine life. You know this, my friends. But tell me,
do you not shudder, and do not cold chills run through all
your frame when you consider this and reflect upon it ?
Do you not feel penetrated and overwhelmed with the
sense of obligation of giving a proof of love in return to
your blessed Lord for His unlimited love for you ? Does
it not urge you to make reparation for the coldness of so
many, such innumerable Christians who so little value
and reverence the Blessed Sacrament ?

Then, my brethren, I exhort you not to weary these
days in showing your Lord the veneration and adoration
due Him; do not weary of bringing Him this homage
with warmth, with emotion and with joy. Beloved, I exhort you to let your hearts be inflamed with love when
you pray: " Blessed be the Most Holy Sacrament ! " when
you say:

> "From the sacred Host is fled
> All the substance of the bread."

Be overwhelmed with wonder when you sing:

> 'Of the bread and wine is here
> Only that which doth appear."

Let your heart leap up and beat with joy when you confess:

> "Lo, the Good, supreme and best,
> On our altar deigns to rest;
> Is with flesh and blood our Guest."

Sink down in deepest adoration when you hear the words:

> " Here our God Himself we see;
> Bow the head, and bend the knee."

Let your heart be broken with pain and bitter contrition when you pray: " O dearest Jesus ! May Thy blessed Mother, together with all Thy angels and saints, bless Thee for all the insults and offences which Thy ungrateful creatures have ever committed, or ever will commit to the end of time, against Thee, the supreme Good." Let your heart be dissolved and melted with longing for heaven when you sing:

> " When the hour of death is near,
> And my soul is numb with fear,
> Jesus, Lord and Saviour, hear.
> Give this food to be my stay;
> Lead me on my journey's way
> Into realms of endless day."

And as often as you repeat your " Ave Jesu ! " do so with such emotion that it may reveal the fervor of your heart.

Yes, beloved, so be it. We will give this proof of love to our dear Lord, the Spouse of our soul, and oh, that we might do so in such a way that Our Lord might have joy and satisfaction therein ! O Thou dear Saviour, Thou givest here in the Blessed Sacrament something that is so great that we must wonder at it; oh, that our proof of reciprocal love could be such that Thou couldst wonder at it ! Will you have it so ? O then, beloved, bring such faith as the centurion in the Gospel had, whose faith made Jesus wonder ! Bring Him such love as Mary Magdalen had, for this love evoked the praise and admiration of Jesus. Do what lies in your power; you cannot do too much. Beloved, say with me, and let it be spoken from the heart (O Lord, hear and rejoice now when we pray !): " Blessed be the Most Holy Sacrament ! " Amen.

SERMON XII.

THE EXCESS OF THE LOVE OF JESUS IN THE BLESSED SAC-
RAMENT EXPRESSED BY THE GRANTING OF THE SACERDO-
TAL POWER.

"Do this for a commemoration of Me."—*St. Luke* xxii. 19.

OUR Lord loves us with divine love, and therefore He
has made us so many and such great gifts of the riches
of His supernatural, His heavenly treasures. But precisely
because love leads Him to bestow on us His celestial treasures, He presents them to us in the simplest, shortest, and
plainest language.

Consider how precious is the gift that we receive in
holy Baptism. There in a moment we are raised and
changed from the children of wrath, which we were, into
children of God; we are elevated to the high dignity of
friends of God, fellow citizens of the saints and of the
household of God.

And yet, beloved, with what simple words has Our
Lord given the commission to bestow this gift which so
far exceeds all expectation ! " Going, therefore," He said
to His apostles, " teach ye all nations, baptizing them in
the name of the Father, and of the Son, and of the Holy
Ghost." And how great beyond all conception is the gift
that He made us in the Sacrament of Penance. The unhappy sinner who has the high treason on his soul of offence against his great God; who is guilty of sacrificing
the heavenly treasures of his Lord to sin, and therefore
is worthy of the eternal punishment of fire, is there ab-

185

solved from the whole unpayable debt, freed from such an
eternal, frightful, yet well-merited punishment. Nor is
that enough; in a moment he is established, raised up, elevated—do you know where ?—even into the ranks of the
true servants and friends of God; even into the ranks of
those clad in the glory of grace, and to be blessed with
the celestial glory belonging to the children of God.

But again, my brethren, with what simple words did
Our Lord ordain that this inexpressibly great gift should
be poured upon poor sinners! "Receive ye the Holy
Ghost: whose sins ye shall forgive they are forgiven them;
and whose sins ye shall retain they are retained." Buthow
great among all the great gifts of His divine love is that
gift of grace which He gives us in the Holy Sacrament of
the Altar! There it is not merely one or another great
grace, not merely many, not merely innumerable graces,
not merely extraordinary, not merely all graces which we
receive in this gift; it is He Himself, the Fulness, the
Source, the Author of all graces, whom we receive from
His own hand. And do you know in what words He has
ordained that we should come into possession of this excessive Gift of grace ? It was with the words, "Do this for a
commemoration of Me."

Truly these are simple words! Yes, I may add they
are so simple, so plain, that there is danger that many
will not notice them, but heedlessly pass them by. My
brethren, we will not do this; rather will we pause over
these simple words in order to enkindle and strengthen
our souls for the solemn adoration which this week we are
to pay Our Lord in the Blessed Sacrament. We will consider them and see how significant they are; what a glorious revelation of His love they express; what a great and
marvellous miracle of His love they present to us. We
shall understand this in some measure if we answer the
two questions that present themselves to us:

I. Whom has Our Lord commissioned to transmit this great gift ?

II. To how many has He given this charge ?

First Point.—The first and most important considera-tion which suggests itself in these words of Our Lord, " Do this for a commemoration of Me," is certainly this: We ask ourselves what kind of a commission Our Lord has given in these words, with what kind of power, what kind of ability, has He invested those to whom He spoke these words ? We have seen that the Blessed Sacrament is a remembrance of the wonderful works of God; for therein is at once the greatest, the most magnificent, overwhelm-ing miracle. Annihilation and creation, these two opposite poles of omnipotence, with a complete chain of special miracles, both beautiful and unique, there are made mani-fest. The bread is substantially changed, completely dis-appears from existence, and under the form of bread comes the infinite majesty of the Son of God. If one knew that such a wondrous miracle were to be wrought once, such a gracious sacrament to be called into existence, one would desire to know whose work it was to perform this sacred task, who was called to this divine, marvellous office.

Now, my brethren, we know and know precisely, for our holy faith teaches us, who it is. Our Lord has ap-pointed another, His creature, to produce this great Sacra-ment, this remembrance of His wonderful works; and of His creatures it is actually miserable man, made from the dust of the earth, whom He has Himself chosen for this office. For He spoke, and spoke to His apostles, saying, " Do this for a commemoration of Me "

If we reflect even briefly on this it must call forth the most intense surprise in us, and if we are not dumb with wonder we must exclaim: What is this ? Is it possible, my Lord, that Thou in Thy love for creatures, and such

creatures as these, such as men are, canst go so far, canst
so forget Thyself ?

Beloved, only think that one who has the power to call
the Blessed Sacrament into existence has actually power over
a mysterious world; namely, over a wonderful annihilation,
and still more wonderful creation; for it lies in his power
to actually change the bread into the flesh of the Lord Now,
beloved, this great power belongs naturally to your Saviour;
that we understand perfectly well, and when He had the
goodness to give us the Blessed Sacrament He had to use
this power which was His alone. But, my brethren, could
He do such a thing as to let this awful power of bringing
forth His sacred body, and making it present under the
appearance of bread go out of His hands, surrender it, and
present it to one of His creatures ? Verily, beloved, if
we did not know what has happened, and such a thought
had occurred to any one, we should not only have declared
with all confidence that it would be going much too far,
be altogether too audacious and bordering on presumption
to expect such a thing of the goodness of Jesus; but we
should never have hesitated a moment to declare with
perfect certainty that it could not happen, would be absolutely impossible; that this power of bringing forth the
body of Jesus, and making it present under the appearance of bread, would be an inalienable, incommunicable
power belonging to the divine Saviour, and to Him alone.

Then, my brethren, realize how far Jesus has gone in
His love for us in establishing the Blessed Sacrament
What would never have come to our mind, what we should
have considered impossible had the thought come to us,
what we should have declared a prerogative requiring His
grandeur and majesty, and therefore not transmitable even
had we recognized it as possible, the power, the divine
power of bringing forth His sacred body for us under the
appearance of bread, He gives out of His hand, entirely out

of His hand, and will never more exercise it, for He has given it away completely to one of His creatures. For we hear Him say, "Do this for a commemoration of Me;" do the same as I have done; you have the power to change the bread into My sacred body.

And it was not enough for Our Lord that in the Blessed Sacrament He gave us Himself in His whole divine majesty —and what a generous love that was—but He has also resigned to us, His own creatures, the power to produce the Most Holy Sacrament; of giving His most sacred body to the poor children of Adam.

But, my Saviour, can one of Thy creatures be pure, and holy, and high, and perfect enough in Thy eyes for Thee to submit Thyself to him; that Thou givest him power over Thy most sacred body; that Thou art present at his command, in the form of bread, and abidest with us? To which of Thy creatures, then, wilt Thou give this high commission? Oh, permit me to say to Thee, dear Lord, if Thou hadst ordained this for the highest of Thy creatures, if Thou hadst ordained this for those who dwell in the highest heavens, and are close to Thy throne, and therefore are of all heavenly spirits most filled with Thy love and knowledge; if it had been the cherubim shining next to Thee in glory to whom Thou gavest the commission, "Do this for a commemoration of Me," they must have trembled and been afraid. They would feel that they were not high enough, not pure enough to exercise this divine power, to speak this most holy, creative word which calls down the Lord of the universe, the God of majesty, upon the earth.

But surely you feel, my brethren, that if Jesus would go so far in His love for us as to bestow upon a creature the power of calling this Sacrament into being, it would be given to no one else than the cherubim and seraphim, the most holy creatures that have come from His hand.

We should have expected Him to say to this choir of
blessed spirits, " Do this for a commemoration of Me."
Nevertheless it is not the chosen dwellers of heaven, not
the pure angels and saints, to whom the words were addressed, " Do this for a commemoration of Me " We
should have imagined that this commission would have
been given to the cherubim and seraphim; that cherubim
and seraphim would have appeared at our altars and called
down for us into the form of bread the God whom in heaven
they beheld, adoring, and yet it was His apostles to whom
He said the words that gave them such wondrous power,
" Do this for a commemoration of Me." And behold, it
is such as we, it is infirm men who stand at our altars armed
with this great power, and call down for themselves and
their fellow-men the Saviour of the world under the appearance of bread.

O beloved, what a love is that of our divine Saviour,
that in order to come to us in the Blessed Sacrament He
abases Himself to one of His human creatures, endowing
his imperfection with such power ! We wonder, and
rightly wonder, when we see that for one day Josue had
power to make the sun stand still; but, my brethren, what
a power is that which the Lord has given to us that we
can call down from heaven into the form of bread the
Creator of this sun ! What love for us has the Lord revealed thereby ! How shall I describe this love ? It overpowered the blessed youth who rested on the breast of Our
Lord, and could feel something of His love. He knew
nothing else to say than this, " Having loved His own who
were in the world, He loved them to the end." And beloved, this love has still another feature. We can ask,
To how many men has He given this power ?

Second Point.—When one knows what kind of power
was imparted, and to whom it was given by the words, " Do
this for a commemoration of Me," one must also take into

consideration the number of men to whom Our Lord has given this power. For, as you know, dear brethren, precious and valuable gifts are shared by only a few; and as soon as one sees that many are enabled to perform a work, there is danger that because of our pettiness and weakness we men will not value it as highly as it deserves.

Now, my brethren, I have already mentioned that in the Old Law Josue had power to make the sun stand still. But among all men he was the only one to whom God had given this power, and he did not have it forever, nor even many times, nor often; no, beloved, in his entire life he had this power but one single time.

Now Our Lord has endowed man with the power to change bread into His sacred body, that humanity may possess Him in the Blessed Sacrament, and therefore He rejected the plan which we should have found natural and fitting, that of all the men in the whole earth only one should have the power, and he but once, to perform this immeasurably great work of calling down to earth his God under the appearance of bread.

No, beloved, Our Lord's intention to be with man in the Blessed Sacrament prevented this manner of leaving it, and more than one man must be chosen to perform this inexpressibly great work, and more than once must this greatest of all works be fulfilled on earth. If but once one man had power over that great work of God, the resplendent sun, it would seem that power over the Creator of the sun Himself, of controlling the awful majesty of the Son of God, and calling Him forth under the appearance of bread, and making Him present among us, that this power, I say, would be shared by few, extremely few, and that these few would certainly dare use this power but seldom. And therefore, if Our Lord had ordained that a mere handful of men should share this power; that in each city there should be but one priest who only once a year, or once each month, should perform this amazing work, beloved, we must then have said that the Lord had been generous in the bestowal of this power which is great beyond our comprehension; we must have said that the Lord had extended beyond all expectation a power so sublime that even the angels do not possess it. And we must have said further that Our Lord had taken care, at least in a measure, that this Most Holy Sacrament would not be so likely to become something to which we miserable men were indifferent, but rather that it would seem to us as it really is, something very holy, the holiest of holies, precisely because we should see that few possessed the power to celebrate this mystery which should make us mortals tremble; and these few dared use it but seldom, celebrating it in certain appointed places, and at appointed times. But we know that it is not as we should think it would be; in truth it is very different, and as it has been ordained by Jesus, Our Saviour, we must confess that Our Lord has distributed this great gift in lavish extravagance. For consider He has conferred this awful power on an inconceivable number, on a whole multitude of priests; has conferred it not merely for one day, month, or year, but forever, for every day of their life; they can never lose it, and He has conferred it on them in such manner that they may exercise it, not merely at one or another time in the year, not merely in some special church; no, beloved, His many priests may and should call forth daily His sacred body in the Blessed Sacrament for themselves and for the faithful, and this not merely under the distant domes of stately cathedrals, but within the narrow walls of lowly chapels; not merely at costly altars, but also at the poorest altars He allows Himself to be called forth by His priests for the faithful under the appearance of bread

Yes, beloved, and still more. There is no power on earth that can take this sublime right from those who have once had it, and he who is lawfully consecrated a priest can always truly change bread into the real body of the Lord; nor is this all. Even, beloved—for this is always possible, and has happened—even if he who has this power degenerates, if he give himself up to a life of sin, if he load himself with crime, if he fall from the true faith, even then he cannot lose this power; even then nothing on earth can take it from him. Of course the Church can and must forbid such a wretched being using his awful power for which he is accountable; but if he still ventured to use it, beloved, he could call down the dear Lord on the altar. My brethren, since each individual priest has this power, and retains it, it can happen, and already has happened, that criminals, blasphemers, heretics, traitors, have called down our Lord upon the altar. What crime ! What black crime ! What sacrilege ! Lips which are an abomination to the Lord call Him here ! Hands stained with sin, reeking with crime, touch Him, and hold Him ! Ah, beloved, what outrage and ignominy can be inflicted and already has been inflicted on Our Lord because of this ordinance; what desecration and profanation of His most holy presence can occur, and has already occurred ! Oh, here the bloody scene of His bitter agony is renewed ! For, my dear Christians, do you not find resemblance, do you not find perfect likeness here to that which your Lord endured in falling into the hands of executioners ? And when He gave this loving commission Our Lord knew all the horrible outrages which the wickedness and ingratitude of men would inflict on Him because of it, and it would have been easy for Him to have escaped all these insults, to have guarded Himself from these sacrileges which men would pour on Him; He had but to make some condition in which this power would be quickly annulled, and He has not done so. He gives power to His priests by which they can always, and everywhere call Him forth for the faithful into the form of bread. He made no exception; He said simply and comprehensively, " Do this for a commemoration of Me."

How is this possible ? We are face to face with a great, and to us, an insoluble enigma. For it almost seems as though it grieved our dear Lord but slightly, as though He concerned Himself little, nor thought it mattered much that such contemptuous treatment, or better, such rude abuse, should be given Him. Beloved, what shall we say to this ? Dare we say that any treatment from us is the same to Our Lord ? We dare not think this for a moment. No, my brethren, He cannot do otherwise than require, and He does require, that we, His creatures, serve Him in holiness and righteousness. But as in the other sacraments, so in this, and I might almost say especially in this Most Holy Sacrament, He sees what is for our good, and if He does not consider that solely and exclusively, at least He considers it principally, and orders everything as is best for us. By this Sacrament He will be everywhere; He will always hear us; He will be with us entirely, as His love for us urges Him to be.

The adorable sacrifice in which He gives Himself anew for the salvation of the world, and in which the Most Holy Sacrament is called into being, must be easily accessible and ready for all; the opportunities for holy communion, that wonderful, gracious union of Christians with their Lord, the Good Shepherd, must be for all as free, as common as the air we breathe. For behold, He says, and says without restriction, " Do this for a commemoration of Me." He determines that so many shall have this sublime power forever and inalienably, in order that they can always make a valid use of it, and offer for the faithful Him, the incarnate God adored by angels, and call Him forth in the form of bread, and give Him to the faithful in holy communion. Therefore He does not shrink, although in taking this generous determination there is not only opportunity and possibility of His being dishonored anew, but certainty that because of the perversity and wickedness of human hearts there will come a Judas to inflict on Him great outrages and affronts; and that not once, but many times, the sacrilege of the improper use of this power will be committed. Even the thought that this might happen, even the knowledge that it would happen, could not withhold Him from taking such a determination, a determination so gracious and benevolent to us that now we can always and everywhere come to Him, our dear Lord, and have Him with us. Yes, beloved, this is really the reason why He thus determined; He sees that this Blessed Sacrament in which we have with us our dear, good Lord is for us the best, the most precious, most beautiful and sweetest Gift, and as our welfare is the rule of conduct for His divine goodness, He said without restriction, "Do this for a commemoration of Me" He would make it easy for us at all times and everywhere to have Him with us.

What a love is this! We should have expected that if the dear Lord would have given this great power to man He would have shared it among a few of the noblest; we should have expected that these few would but seldom have dared use their awful power; that this power would not always have remained in man; we should have expected it to have been withdrawn, invariably have been withdrawn from the unworthy, the sinner, the heretic Yet we seem to hear Our Lord say. But, my children, I must make it easy for you to possess the precious Gift, the pearl of all graces, and so I ordain that, from the rising of the sun even to its setting, many shall have this power; I ordain that often, and I prefer it to be daily, my priests over the whole earth shall exercise this sublime power for you; I ordain that they shall never lose this most holy power. I call upon them to serve Me, their God, in holiness, not profaning My name: but I ordain that for love of you if one is unhappy enough to wear his consecration unworthily, still he may effectually use his power. I will be with you, and I would rather that godless lips called Me forth, rather that sinful hands should touch and carry Me, than that you, my faithful people, should be deprived of your Good Shepherd because of the hireling   Behold, I say without reservation, " Do this for a commemoration of Me," and say it at the risk of many of you, My people, no longer valuing this Most Holy Sacrament, of your forgetting, neglecting, and even despising your Lord and God under the appearance of bread, because I have made it so easy for you to possess Him. I must be with you; I love you; you shall see that I love you; I must be with you though I gain nothing for Myself but only being with you. How great, then, is this love ! How shall I describe it ?

O beloved, once more we will turn to the apostle who was allowed to rest on the Lord's breast in the solemn moment when He instituted this Most Holy Sacrament, to the beloved youth, St. John; he could feel, he could breathe in something of this excessive love; he can tell us how great it is. And he exclaims, " Having loved His own who were in the world, He loved them to the end "; not merely to the end of His life, but to the end of the possibilities of His divine bounty, even to the extremest limit that love can reach, though that love was at once God's and man's. Ah, yes, this is true, and it is spoken directly to our hearts.

" Do this for a commemoration of Me." How simple are these words, and what an indescribably great thing they express ! They declare that Our Lord has renounced the immeasurably great power of calling forth Himself under the form of bread, has given it to His creatures, and surely to the most miserable of His rational creatures, to wretched man; they announce that He has not given this

power to certain men, nor for rare occasions, but that He
has bestowed this power upon a great multitude of priests,
irrevocably, in all places, and for all times, so that they
can and shall exercise it daily; they announce that He has
ordained it thus, although He foresaw that in the hands of
base men the Holiest of holies would no longer be holily
nor worthily treated because of this excessive facility; they
announce that He has ordained to come to us in such
abundant fulness, and in so simple a manner, that He might
be of easy access to each of His own.

All this these words express, and consequently they
declare: So far has Jesus gone in His love ! For the love
of Jesus has exhausted itself in the Blessed Sacrament,
and God that He is, He must say of this, as of many
things that He has given us, " What could I have done
more for thee and have not done it ? " These memorable
words express also a wish, a request, a claim which He sets
before us What is this wish, this request, this claim of
Our Lord ? Before I speak of it, first tell me what your
feeling is on this point ? Surely I express your conviction
when I say: Whatever Our Lord should require of us in
return, whatever He desires to obtain from us in this
Blessed Sacrament, were it ever so great, or difficult, it
could not be too much, nor too difficult. Listen, then, for
I can tell you what He desires of us, and what He would
accomplish in us by giving us this Most Holy Sacrament.
It is this: That we should keep Him in vivid remembrance, that we should not forget Him. " Do this for a
commemoration of Me "

What do you say to this ? Did you expect it ? Surely
this seems very little to you. We must then only do for
Him what He has done for us. Ah, who could forget the
dear Lord who for love of us has emptied Himself, and has
taken the form of a servant, and lain in the crib; who
for love of us was obedient in the poor house of Nazareth

for the long term of thirty years, and earned His bread
by the sweat of His brow in exhausting labor ?   Who could
forget the dear Lord who went about Judea preaching the
Gospel untiringly for three years, who breathed out His
life for us on the cross; in brief, who could forget the
dear Lord who employed His life solely for our welfare,
and then delivered this life, more precious than the lives
of all the saints and angels, to deepest humiliations and
nameless pains ?

Surely these are such great actions and works that they
must maintain Him in everlasting remembrance; surely
He has erected in our hearts by these sublime and loving
works a perpetual memorial of Himself   Each one of these
actions calls upon us and forces us to keep Him in constant
memory.   He need not plead with us to do this.   It is
our sacred duty.   Surely He need not perfect it by giving
us a new, still greater proof of His love for us !   We had
enough in what He had already done not for one proof,
nor many, but for countless proofs of His love for us   And
yet, in order to secure from us a vivid remembrance of
Himself and of all that He had done for us, He gave us
a new proof of His love, and the greatest proof that lay
within the compass of His wisdom and omnipotence; He
loved His own to the end   He gave us a Gift which is
the remembrance, the crown, the masterpiece of all His
wonderful works.   He gave us the Blessed Sacrament, He
gave us His divine majesty under the appearance of bread,
for all time, and in all places   He gave to us, to a great multitude of us, the immeasurable power of calling down His
most sacred body, with all His divine majesty, into the
form of bread.   " Do this," He said, as He relinquished
this power over Himself, " do this for a remembrance of
Me."   You see what He desired, for what He pleaded; then
what you must do is to keep Him in constant remembrance.
" Do this "—I beg thee—" in remembrance of Me."

– Verily Our Lord forces me to say: This is too much that Thou dost for me; too little that Thou askest of me in return.

Now, beloved, we will give an answer to this plea of Our Lord by which we shall honor ourselves and which shall be worthy of such a plea and will rejoice His sacred, loving Heart. We will say to Him: Yes, dear Lord, Thou shalt have from us that for which Thou remainest with us, and for which Thou hast established this Most Holy Sacrament; we will not forget Thee; Thou shalt be to us in constant remembrance; what Thou hast said to us shall be sacred to us, what Thou hast commanded us we will do; what Thou hast forbidden us we will avoid, what Thou praisest we will prize; against that concerning which Thou warnest us we will guard ourselves; for that to which Thou urgest us we will strive. This shall be the fruit of Thy great Sacrament. Hear, O Lord, how each heart sighs to Thee, each tongue cries to Thee: "Jesus, 1 live in Thee; I die in Thee; Thine I am; to Thee I belong in life and death!" This Thou shalt have, dear Lord, we protest to Thee; not in vain shalt Thou have said, "Do this for a commemoration of Me" Surely I speak for each heart here when I say to Our Lord in your name: Thou shalt have more from us, O dearest Jesus, for this great Sacrament, and in this great Sacrament; Thou shalt have more from us. Again this week we will bring our homage to Thee in the Blessed Sacrament; bring it openly, publicly, and solemnly. We will prostrate ourselves, before Thee, the Spouse of our soul, and pay Thee our tribute of adoration, thanksgiving, reparation and prayer We will not weary of gratefully praying, "Blessed be the Most Holy Sacrament!" we will not weary of blessing Thee with contrite and broken hearts with Mary, Thy sweetest Mother, and all Thy angels and saints, for all the insults that have been committed against Thee; we will not weary of singing with adoring wonder:

> " From the sacred Host is fled
> All the substance of the bread.
> Lo, the Good, supreme and best,
> On the altar deigns to rest;
> Is with flesh and blood our Guest."

Ceaselessly shall the walls of this church reverberate with our jubilant, exultant, " Ave Jesu ! " This shalt Thou receive from us; this is our response to all Thou hast given us, and the little Thou askest from us in saying, " Do this for a commemoration of Me."

And now have but the goodness to receive these few hours of prayer which we humbly offer Thee. Hear also, we beseech Thee, the plea which we make to Thee. As we are allowed to spend these days in the sunshine and warmth of Thy love, let us be truly warmed by it; enkindle in us a love for this Most Holy Sacrament which shall never grow cold; be Thou in this life in the Blessed Sacrament our consolation; reject us not when now we so often pray to Thee:

> " When the hour of death is near,
> And my soul is numb with fear,
> Jesus, Lord and Saviour, hear.
> Give this food to be my stay;
> Lead me on my journey's way
> Into realms of endless day."

Ah, yes; be Thou in death my Viaticum, and in eternal glory, O my Saviour, be Thou my reward. I pray Thee let me see Thee with Mary, Thy glorious Mother, and all Thy blessed angels and saints, face to face, from one glory to another, eternally to love, praise, and glorify Thee. Amen.

SERMON XIII.

THE EXERCISE OF THE SACERDOTAL POWER A NEW PROOF OF THE SUPERABUNDANT LOVE OF JESUS.

"Do this for a commemoration of Me."—*St. Luke* xxii. 19.

WE can best judge, or rather we can only judge, the regard in which a person holds a thing, how highly he values it, by the way he treats it, by the honor he gives it.

Now, my brethren, you have assembled here at this hour, you have given up your time, and have done it gladly, have made a willing, a joyful sacrifice. Why have you done this? To give yourselves pleasure, distraction, amusement? By no means; on the contrary the fulfilment of a sacred duty, the accomplishment of a pious, fatiguing work has led you to make this sacrifice; you have come here to celebrate the Forty Hours, to bring publicly and solemnly to your Lord, graciously abiding with us in the Blessed Sacrament the humble and devout homage of adoration and reparation due Him

Hence I may conclude, I must conclude, that you value the Blessed Sacrament highly, that it is holy to you, it is to you the Most Holy; you believe:

> "Lo, the Good, supreme and best,
> On the altar deigns to rest,
> Is with flesh and blood our Guest."

And I congratulate you on your great faith. Yes, beloved, if to the question: What do you believe of the Blessed Sacrament ? you reply:

> "From the sacred Host is fled
> All the substance of the bread; "

if you reply,

> "Christ Himself is here instead,"

then will apply to you the "Blessed art thou" which Our Lord said to Peter, when to the question: "Whom do you say I am ? " he solemnly confessed· "Thou art Christ, the Son of the living God."

Yes, even more than to Peter these words apply to you, for Peter had before him the living, wonder-working Son of man, while you only see the lifeless, powerless form of bread. Every one knows how difficult it is to have this faith, and best of all Jesus, your Master and Teacher, knows how hard it is to say:

> "In the monstrance is adored
> Christ, our undivided Lord.
> Of the bread and wine is here
> Only that which doth appear "

And this faith, this difficult faith, this strong faith, is yours. Then you can be sure that as the Lord said to Peter, and more than as He said to Peter those words of commendation, He will say to you: "Blessed art thou who thus believest, for flesh and blood hath not revealed it to thee, but My Father, who is in heaven."

Surely this is true, and here, beloved, apply also the words of the Holy Ghost: "He hath not done in like manner to every nation." Not to all is it given to know what you believe of the Blessed Sacrament, and not all who have known it glorify the Blessed Sacrament. This must be a new motive to us, a greater inducement to celebrate the Forty Hours this week with fervent, unremitting zeal, with unflagging, conscientious perseverance, and correspondence to the invitation contained in the words: "Do this for a commemoration of Me." And, beloved, how forcible, how irresistible is this invitation, precisely for the reason that Our Lord expresses it in these very words. For you must know, my brethren, the words "Do this for a commemoration of Me" are really not only an invitation to us, but they express the immeasurable love of our divine Lord, a love that has no limit, a love that goes to extremes, and these words of invitation are, so to speak, the veil under which He hides this singular love Raise this veil a moment, and what do you see? You see that Christ has contrived a marvellous, new, and tremendous means in order not to be separated from us For in these words Our Lord ordained for man, and for a great multitude of men, the divine power of changing bread and wine into His flesh and blood, and these words also teach what these chosen men are to do to exercise this power, exceeding all the power of angels And I can show you, my brethren, that the love of Jesus for you, His people, goes so far that He has made the exercise of this power easy—

I Beyond all expectation.

II. Even contrary to all expectation.

First Point.—If one would understand in a measure all the mysteries of love expressed by the memorable words of Our Lord: "Do this for a commemoration of Me," he must answer several questions The first question suggested to us by these words is this: What kind of a commission, and consequently what kind of a power, does Our Lord give to those to whom these words were addressed? You know that He gave them the awful power to work, not one great, marvellous miracle, but to make the memorial, the monument of all the wonders of God; for He gave them the unheard-of power of changing

the lifeless bread into the most living and holiest thing
that exists, into His holy, living body. When one knows
this, and has sufficiently considered it, then one must in-
quire who they are to whom Our Lord gave this high
commission, this awful power ? And we know that they
are His creatures whom He has thus honored. Now one
asks further, What kind of beings, in what range of creation are those who have this high power ? And one learns
that, in giving this most honorable commission, Our Lord
has completely passed over the highest and holiest of
His creatures; that He has not entrusted His angels, nor
a single choir of angels, nor the princes among the angels
with this distinguishing service. We learn that the most
miserable, the poorest of His rational creatures are they
to whom He has entrusted this work belonging to the
majesty of God: to those like us, beloved, to ordinary
men the Lord of heaven and earth has said, " Do this for
a commemoration of Me."

Then if one asks further to how many men, and for
how long, and how often He has given this sublime power,
we learn what one would never have ventured to antici-
pate; we learn that the dear Lord has irrevocably relinquished this power to a countless multitude of priests, so
that in all places and for all time His priests can daily
bring the Lord of heaven and earth down into the sacred
Host for the faithful. All this is included in the simple
words, " Do this for a commemoration of Me " One must
reflect on this in order in some measure to fathom the
love expressed by them.

I have dwelt on these thoughts with you in another
sermon, but this is not enough In considering these
words, " Do this for a commemoration of Me," when one
knows to what kind of creatures, and to how many the
dear Lord has given this excessive power, one must ask
one more question in order to have a complete image, a

full conception of the loving and bountiful goodness that He showed us in this last legacy. We must ask what the dear Lord desired, what He has ordained that His priests should do to perform this great work, and call down Him, the infinite Lord of heaven and earth for His chosen people on the altar under the form of bread. And one would imagine that it must be something very great, very difficult that our High Priest according to the order of Melchisedech, Jesus Our Saviour, prescribed for His priests in the solemn moment when they should perform this awful work. Would you not imagine so ? Now listen ! The working of miracles was, and is, and shall be, generally only a matter for saints, and we must consider and weigh this thoroughly. The working of miracles speaks to us of long years of prayer, struggle, mortification; of long years of splendid combat for virtue; of long years of heroic sacrifices and suffering for righteousness, which heroes of goodness concealed in humility and modesty. Now here in the Blessed Sacrament there is not question of performing a simple, ordinary, frequently recurring miracle; there is not even question of performing merely a great, rare, unknown miracle; no, there is question of working a whole series of extraordinary miracles—theology reckons them twelve—miracles which are of all miracles the most beautiful and rarest, which are new and peculiar to this Most Holy Mystery; there is question of annihilating bread, as bread, and in the place of the annihilated bread calling forth the incarnate God who sitteth at the right hand of the heavenly Father, with His flesh and blood, body and soul, divinity and humanity, actually, really and truly under the appearance of bread still remaining after the bread is changed.

If one must be a saint to be chosen by God as the instrument of an ordinary miracle, does it not seem that the Lord must have ordained that he who was chosen to work this miracle of miracles must have done something superhuman before he would dare undertake it ? O beloved, if Our Lord had ordained that it must be preceded by long-continued and severe fasts, by long years of victorious struggles against temptation; that it must be preceded by long years of recollected, concentrated prayer, by unbroken, silent vigils, by profound and suitable erudition; that it must be preceded by pain and labor, the exercise of this power of consecration were not too dearly purchased when one considers the marvellous dignity of the work. But no; five little words, and it is done, the remembrance of the wonders of God is consummated; the whole series of these miracles is at once, in a moment, wrought; the Word is made flesh, the incarnate Son of God is called down from heaven to earth, is hidden under the appearance of bread, dwells among us. And what has done all this ? Five little words. What is easier ?

Oh, it is easy beyond all expectation; it is astonishingly easy; it is so easy that when one hears of it for the first time he is tempted to doubt it, and when one hears it for the thousandth time he must exclaim with surprise: What is this ? Is this possible ? Yes, beloved, it is possible. Only five little words are spoken by the lips of a miserable man, a frail, sinful man, and the remembrance of the wonderful works of God is finished before us !

Yes, beloved, this is true; this is really the ordinance, the intention of Our Lord. " Do this," He says—that which I have done—" for a commemoration of Me." And our dear Lord had just spoken these five little words, and the remembrance of all the wonders of God was in His hand. Nor can this seem strange to us: it is Our Lord. But, my brethren, if it would seem to us desirable, on account of the sublimity of the majesty coming into the form of bread that Our Lord should make it a sacred duty for His priests not to dare to attempt the exercise of their invested power until they had performed in the exercise of all virtues great, heroic and superhuman actions, until they had struggled upward to the heights of Christian perfection, and become heroes of virtue; why does He not at least require one single, extraordinary, superhuman achievement; why has He made the exercise of a power that is actually divine, which even the cherubim and seraphim do not possess, so very easy to them, so unexpectedly easy; why does He require but the utterance of five little words ?

O beloved, hear, and wonder, and rejoice ! Our Lord has done this for love of you, that you may have Him among you always and everywhere the more surely and quickly and easily. It is truly His delight, it is His yearning to be with us And He sees were He to require that before His priests called forth the remembrance of His wonderful works, before they called down their God into the form of bread, they were obliged to attain such distinction, such preëminence in virtue and sanctity, His people must pine and wait year after year till they could have their Good Shepherd among them; and that would delay Him too long, much too long. Yes; it would be too long to Him if He had to be absent from His own till His priests had accomplished even one extraordinary, superhuman act of virtue ! And what does He do ? Yes, beloved, what does He do ? In His love for us, and in order to be with us, He goes so far that He renounces all the claims of His divine majesty, even refraining from demanding one work of virtue that is its due, because even one would retard His coming among us. That He may always, and surely, and quickly be with us, He has ordained that the five little words which He spoke, His priests should speak over the bread, and the remembrance of the wonderful works of God should be wrought.

Verily, beloved, this is love, this is great love ! How shall we describe it ? Oh, we will let the apostle who rested on Jesus' breast at the solemn moment when Our Lord instituted the Most Holy Sacrament describe it for us. We will turn to the beloved youth, St. John; he could feel and breathe in something of this excessive love; he can tell us how great it is. And he exclaims: " Having loved His own who were in the world, He loved them to the end," not merely to the end of His life, but to the end of the possibilities of a divine generosity, even to the extreme limit which love can attain, though it was the love that was at once God's and man's. Ah, yes, this is true; this appeals to our hearts, for Our Lord has certainly made it easy, easy beyond all expectation for His priests to exercise this divine power. Yes, when we examine it a little more closely we must say that He has made it easy, contrary to all expectation.

Second Point.—Our Lord has said almost nothing of what His priests had to do when they celebrated this Most Holy Mystery, how they should celebrate it, nor has He said anything to show how the faithful who had the happiness to be present were to conduct themselves. Therefore we understand that Our Lord requires nothing extraordinary, nothing superhuman either from the priests or the people.

But, beloved, since it is written once for all by the Holy Ghost, and Our Lord has repeatedly impressed upon us that we are to treat holy things sacredly, then it is self-evident that Our Lord wills, and must will, that we treat most sacredly the Most Holy Hence the Church has taken all imaginable pains, and made every effort for this end, having it sincerely at heart. Consider this: What has not our Church done and ordained in order to fill the faithful with the true spirit of veneration and adoration in celebrating this Most Holy Mystery, and worthily re-

ceiving the Saviour descended under the form of bread ?
With what celestial splendor, with what impressive
majesty, with what grandeur her lofty, spiritual, reverent,
overwhelming rites surround the five little words which
call down Our Lord to earth ! All her ceremonies cry
out, one ever louder than the other: Thy God comes to
fulfil the work of redemption, salvation, thy God is here;
the work of salvation is fulfilled. With a spirit that
I may truly call angelic, and which she expresses in
her rites, she raises us above earth, above ourselves,
envelops us in a luminous cloud of deep emotion and
mysterious sweetness, so that I may say almost without
any effort on our part we experience in ourselves an impression that earth cannot give us, and which has something of the charm of heavenly ecstasy. Reflect a moment
how everything that is done and said by the priest
from the Preface to the solemn moment of consecration inspires us to devotion and clearly proclaims the coming of the
Lord. He confesses that it is meet and just, right and
salutary, to praise Our Lord and God always and everywhere, that the angels and archangels, cherubim and
seraphim, and all the heavenly spirits, never weary of
praising Him, and singing to Him their " Holy," and he
beseeches God to permit that our voices also be raised in
suppliant confession, saying: " Holy, Lord God of Sabaoth.
Heaven and earth are full of Thy glory. Hosanna in the
highest. Blessed is He that cometh in the name of the
Lord. Hosanna in the highest."

And now follows the holy silence of the priest; he
extends his hands wide and high towards heaven, bows
profoundly and kisses the altar, raises himself, praying
with outstretched arms in deeper, greater silence. Thus
already everything speaks of holy reverence, already announces that something great, something holy is to happen. Suddenly a signal is given with the bell; profound

and sacred silence reigns in the church; the soft, adoring tones of the organ which had penetrated the ear are hushed, and all Christians fall prostrate on their knees, nor raise their eyes longer towards the altar because of That which descends upon it. Then with his two anointed fingers, which he has already washed, the priest brushes the white corporal that not even a particle of dust may cling to it, takes the bread in both fingers, raises his eyes suppliantly with holy awe to heaven, towards the crucifix before him, bows his head low, and in a moment, a little moment, he makes a deep genuflection to the ground. What has happened ? O beloved, he has spoken the five little words which call down to earth the Lord of heaven and earth under the appearance of bread; the Word is made flesh, the work of salvation is accomplished; your God is there, the supreme Good; God Himself reposes here with flesh and blood. He holds in his hand his God and yours; he shows Him to you, raises Him on high, and you bow your head and beat your breast, remembering your own unworthiness and guilt.

O verily, the Church has surrounded these five little words with such a vesture of reverence that we must see that she has guarded us from irreverence, and defended Our Lord from dishonor, proving herself, if I may say so, a loving mother to us, and to Our Lord in His daily birth. Certainly she urgently impresses upon priests and people to do all that human nature can do to treat the Holy of holies sacredly above all sacred things Since the priest has to perform this sacred task, the Church bids him occupy himself throughout his day with prayer, study of the Holy Scriptures, giving Christian instruction, visiting and consoling the sick and suffering, and by earnest meditation inflaming his heart to ardent devotion before he goes up to the altar to celebrate this Most Holy Mystery. And the Church calls upon the faithful to be present

at its celebration wherein the work of our salvation is renewed, with the same sentiments as those of Mary, the
blessed Mother of God; John, the virgin youth; Magdalen,
the contrite penitent, when they stood on the hill of Calvary
beneath the cross on which the precious life of the Saviour
was sacrificed for the sins of the world, beneath the cross
of the Lamb who taketh away the sins of the world.

The conscientious priest will do what the Church desires. All his occupations during the day will be holy,
and he will not attempt to celebrate the great and holy
Mystery without first meditating on the wonderful things
accomplished by the grandeur, majesty, goodness, love
and condescension of his God. And the conscientious
Christian will take pains to prepare his heart so that, in
the moment when these five little but creative words are
spoken, he will adore with holy awe his God concealed and
sacrificed under the appearance of bread, praying to Him
with profound contrition for forgiveness, and invoking
Him with gratitude and confidence. But, beloved, on the
other hand it is true that we are ungrateful, wandering,
distracted, in a word, miserable, fallen men, unfitted for
heavenly things, and the priests also—yes, beloved, the
priests also—are men, miserable and frail in body and
soul.

And so, beloved, what may happen ? Alas, what may
happen ? Because Our Lord has made it so unexpectedly
easy to call Him, the God of heaven and earth, down upon
the altar in the form of bread, it may happen that the
priest, relying upon his own strength, may omit to make
proper preparation, may fail to fill his day with holy occupations, and inflame his heart by prayer and meditation, to devotion, zeal and love, and beloved, it may happen that the priest will perform the awful ceremonies with
distraction and thoughtlessness, and the faithful be present
in the same manner. Yes, beloved, because the dear Lord

has made it unexpectedly easy to bring the Most Holy among us, it may happen, and has happened, that a priest will celebrate this Holy Mystery with none of the earnestness due it, nor with the required fervor or holiness, and that the faithful are present at its celebration without the necessary reverence, attention and devotion; it may happen that Our Lord comes, and no heart salutes Him with " Hosanna in the highest," nor " I adore Thee," nor " Be merciful to me; " it may happen that Our Lord comes, and the heart of him who holds Him in his hand, and the hearts of those around Him, are cold, distracted, ungrateful; it may happen that He comes to His own, and His own receive Him not, it may happen that He comes into the world, and the world He made knows Him not; in short, it may happen, and has happened, that our dear Lord comes, and many of His people do not honor Him; yes, even among His priests there are many who hold Him in their hand without due reflection, and Our Lord is robbed of the honor that is His. Because He has made it easy beyond all expectation for us to call Him down upon our altars; because He has renounced the honors He could have claimed for His sublime majesty, it happens that when He appears we do not show Him even the reverence which it is in our power to pay Him. He must endure that the Most Holy, which He gives us in His excessive love, should not be treated as holy, even in the moment when He gives it. One would have imagined that Our Lord would have guarded Himself from this; that this abuse of His too great love would have caused Him to set some slight limit to His goodness to us, at least as far as was necessary to prevent these insults And how easy it would have been for Our Lord to have taken Himself out of this condition, and protected Himself from irreverence at His coming ! He had but to ordain that He would not come upon the altar if the priest and faithful had not at

least done what belonged to them to do, and taken pains
to be devout and reverent.

But, beloved, He has not done this, although He foresaw how many irreverences would be inflicted upon Him.
Thus He has not only made it easy to bring Him among
us, but has actually made it easy beyond all expectation.
And why this facility in calling Him forth which is so
dangerous to us ? For the same reason, my brethren, that
He has given us the great multitude of priests. He acts
thus for our sake, for our best good; it is His joy to be
with us, and hence He makes it in every way possible to
come to us, not only by giving the sacerdotal power to a
multitude of priests, but by making it so easy, so incredibly easy for them to exercise this power: this is the
work of His love. Oh, how great this love is ! How shall
we describe it ? My brethren, once more we will allow
that apostle who rested on Jesus' breast in the solemn
moment when Our Lord instituted the Blessed Sacrament to tell us of it; we will go to the beloved youth, St.
John, for he could feel something of this marvellous love,
he can tell us how excessive this love is. And he exclaims: "Having loved His own who were in the world,
He loved them to the end," not merely to the end of His
life, but even to the end of the possibilities of divine
generosity, even to the extreme limit which love could attain, the love indeed of one who is both God and man.
Ah, yes, we feel this to be true; it appeals to our hearts,
for Our Lord has made it easy for His priests to exercise
this power, not merely beyond all expectation, but contrary to all expectation.

"Do this for a commemoration." What simple words,
and yet what unfathomably great things they express !
They tell us that our divine Saviour has resigned to His
creatures His immeasurably great power of producing
Himself under the form of bread, and has resigned it to

the most miserable of His rational creatures, to wretched man; they tell us that He has not merely given this power to just a few men, and to be used now and then only, but that He has bestowed this mighty power upon a great multitude of priests in all places, and for all time, so that they can, and shall exercise it daily; they tell us that He has made it perfectly easy for His priests to use this power, too holy for angelic hosts, has made it easy beyond all expectation and contrary to all expectation; they tell us that He has ordained everything thus even though He foresaw that because of this excessive facility the Holiest of holies would be unworthily treated at the hands of impious men; they tell us that He has ordained to come to us in so plentiful and in so easy a manner, that thereby He might be perfectly accessible to His people. All this these words express. So far has Jesus gone in His love for us !

Now, my beloved, where one sees love, and such great love, one expects to see love in return Shall I ask you, and plead with you to show Our Lord that reciprocal love we owe Him, and which it is our turn to render this week by celebrating the Forty Hours ? You know what we have in view in this solemn veneration of the Blessed Sacrament, or at least you should know. Through these continuous, solemn hours of prayer we will show a little recognition of this great love of Our Lord, for His abiding with us unceasingly day and night, even to the end of the world, in this Most Holy Sacrament.

I do not exhort you, beloved, to celebrate the Forty Hours this week with zeal and perseverance; if that were necessary for any of us it would be disgraceful, for it would show that the person who required it was devoid of human feeling. For, my brethren, when we see that a person loves us, and especially that he loves us magnanimously, generously, heroically, disinterestedly, then there is no need of any one telling us that we should love that person. No; we do so spontaneously, we are irresistibly moved to do so, and could not endure being prevented showing that person love in return. Therefore, beloved, I should blush for myself if at the close of this sermon I should even say to you: Bear your share in the Forty Hours zealously and perseveringly. Ah, no; I have another request to make. What I do beg of you is this: Do what you have to do this week in bringing to your dear Lord in the Blessed Sacrament the homage of your adoration and reparation in such a manner that it may resemble what Our Lord Himself does in the Blessed Sacrament; do it so that you too can say· " What could I have done more, and have not done it ?" So celebrate the Forty Hours that you may become a spectacle for angels and men. My brethren, when you come before the Blessed Sacrament bring with you a living faith, be penetrated, convinced, filled with the thought that the infinite God, before whom the beings higher, nobler, mightier, richer in intelligence and grace than we, the angels, archangels, cherubim and seraphim fall upon their faces, adoring, and crying without ceasing: "Holy, holy, holy,"— this great Lord and God is ceaselessly present day and night with us, and for love of us, sinners deserving of punishment. And wondering at this thought our hearts cry out: Is this possible ? And we hear and see nothing else; everything is uninteresting to us, and is to us as nothing; we are completely submerged in the Blessed Sacrament, and never weary of joining in the hymn of praise: " Blessed be the Most Holy Sacrament !" never tire of singing again and again with pious inspiration the " Ave Jesu !" and adoring chant: " Holy, holy, holy, Lord God of Sabaoth !"

Let us consider that this infinite God, to whom the highest princes among the angels bring the homage of their adoration in the deepest reverence, receives from us miserable, wretched creatures so little honor, and reverence, and even receives dishonor and insult, is slightly esteemed, is not considered, is neglected, derided, mocked and scorned, and let us be pierced with profound pain and terror, be filled with bitter grief and sorrow, realizing that we are not able to expiate such crime, such sacrilege, such ingratitude, and let us turn to Mary and all the saints entreating: " O dearest Jesus, may Thy august Mother, together with all Thy angels and saints, bless Thee for all the insults and outrages which Thy ungrateful creatures have committed, or ever will commit to the end of time, against Thee, the supreme Good." My brethren, if with such sentiments, with such sincere devotion, you observe the hours of prayer, you do something that resembles what your Lord does in the Blessed Sacrament; you can then say: " What could I have done more, and have not done it ? " Then you will be a spectacle for angels and men; Jesus will be adored by men on earth, as He is by angels in heaven. Beloved, I call upon you to celebrate the Forty Hours thus, and I hope I shall not do so in vain. If you do this you are to be congratulated. Then you can offer your dear Lord your hours of adoration to His honor and glory, and He will accept them with pleasure and delight

Then, beloved, you can confidently ask for three great graces in regard to the Blessed Sacrament. You can be sure that you will not ask in vain that Our Lord will give you grace that this Blessed Sacrament shall be " in this life " your consolation; that this Blessed Sacrament may be your Viaticum " in death," and your sustenance on your journey to heaven, so that with Jesus in your heart you may enter into eternity, and there meet Him, not as your Judge, but as your Saviour; that this Blessed Sacrament may be " in eternal glory " your reward, and you may be-

hold in His splendor Him whom here you adore in concealment, and that you may ceaselessly cry: "Holy God,
we praise Thy name!" Therefore, beloved, "Blessed forever be the Most Holy Sacrament!" Amen.

SERMON XIV.

THE BLESSED SACRAMENT THE DEEPEST SELF-ABASEMENT AND CONDESCENSION OF JESUS.

"He humbled Himself . . . For which cause God also hath exalted Him."—*Philip.* ii. 8, 9.

THESE words of St Paul refer on the one hand to the extreme self-abasement of the Son of God in the mystery of His incarnation and death for our salvation, and on the other hand to the great exaltation which this has won for Him.

In full, the words of the Apostle are as follows: " Who, being in the form of God, thought it not robbery to be equal to God, but emptied Himself, taking the form of a servant, being made in the likeness of men, and in habit found as a man. He humbled Himself, becoming obedient unto death, even to the death of the cross. For which cause God also hath exalted Him, and hath given Him a name which is above all names: That in the name of Jesus every knee should bow, of those that are in heaven, on earth, and under the earth And every tongue should confess that the Lord Jesus Christ is in the glory of the Father."

Surely, however, I make no mistake in using these words when I would speak to you of that great work by which the Son of God in the last hours of His life made provision for remaining with us forever in eternal remembrance; when I speak of the Blessed Sacrament of the Altar. For, beloved, in this work of love in which He loved His own even to the end not merely of His life, but also to the end of the possibilities of His divine bounty, to the most extreme limit love can reach, though it be the love that is both God's and man's,—in this greatest work of the love of Our Lord there are found the two characteristics which St. Paul mentions of the work of salvation: on the one hand is the great self-abasement of Jesus, who stoops even to the appearance of bread in the real presence, and on the other hand is the great exaltation which for this reason becomes His portion. We bring our homage to the Blessed Sacrament in significant and manifold ways, and we find in this greatest work of the love of our divine Saviour precisely the two characteristics distinguished by St Paul in the work of salvation. The fact that in this Sacrament Our Lord is so much humiliated is exactly the reason why the faithful exalt Him by this solemn homage; and the more we realize how deep the condescension of the God-man is in assuming in His real presence the appearances of bread, the more we will contribute by our solemn homage to the honor of Our Lord in the Blessed Sacrament. These two characteristics are in this greatest work of the love of Jesus, because it is in the highest degree the work of a God-man; the humiliation, the condescension, the abasement, the self-abnegation are there at their greatest; and there also the homage, the exaltation, the glorifying must be the most magnificent, lofty, solemn, majestic, that can be conceived by hearts overflowing with gratitude.

Now, beloved, this week Our Lord is to receive one of these solemn, touching tributes appointed by the Church for us to pay Him: We are to adore Our Lord in the Blessed Sacrament publicly and openly; to unite in repeating: "Blessed be the Most Holy Sacrament!" and "Ave Jesu!" Surely it will be a noble homage to Our Lord if for these three days from early morning to darkest night the faithful come to Him and in deepest gratitude repeat to Him:

" Blessed be the Most Holy Sacrament ! " and the walls resound with their " Ave Jesu ! "

If it be true that we honor and glorify Our Lord in the Blessed Sacrament more, the better we know how deeply He has humiliated Himself for us, how completely He has renounced Himself, then, in order to make our zeal for this great festival of prayer lively and fitting, we will try to see and to measure a little of this great depth of the self-abasement of Jesus, and learn how profound it is. Beloved, I assure you that in the Blessed Sacrament we behold the deepest condescension and self-abasement of the Son of God. Such it is—

I. In itself;

II. In its circumstances.

First Point —When we venture to assert that among all the works of the love and omnipotence of God His greatest work is the institution of the Blessed Sacrament, at first sight our action may have the appearance of being somewhat presumptuous, as though we would take it upon ourselves to sit in judgment on the works of God; and who can have such insight into the decrees of God as to be able to judge His works correctly ? This He seems to try to do who has the boldness to say that of all the works of God the greatest is the Most Holy Sacrament. I admit, my brethren, that a person may act thus; one may attempt to judge the works of God, declaring one to be the greatest, the masterwork, and holding another as less because it seems less to his senses. And such conduct is indeed wrong and presumptuous. If there were no other way of saying that the Blessed Sacrament was the greatest of God's works, we could not have asserted it; we must have kept silence, for this would be wrong and sacrilegious for a twofold reason: first, because one would assume to know all God's intentions and all that He had in view in performing these works as they are, and not otherwise; and second, because one would then venture to think that one work of God had not resulted as well as another.

But, my brethren, there is another way by which we can determine that the Blessed Sacrament is especially and particularly that work of God which is to be called great, and how it is so. I may ask whether of all His perfect works God Himself has not given the preference to one above another, calling one great and memorable with special predilection; and I may ask in what sense and for what reason He calls but one of His works great and memorable, when all the works of His hand are great and masterly, since they perfectly attain the end for which He willed them. You see, beloved, that sounds very different. Here there is no trace of presumption, it is a modest, honest endeavor to learn to know better, and therefore value more highly, the works and great achievements of God. And to these two questions we receive an answer that is clear and satisfactory.

In the first place one thing is certain, and that is that God makes a distinction in His works, and gives one a preference over another. The saints are works of God, yet St. Paul says of them: "For star differeth from star in glory One is the glory of the sun, and another the glory of the moon, and another the glory of the stars." And even in the Old Law God revealed to us that the Blessed Sacrament was the remembrance of the wonderful works of God, and in the New Law God announces to us by the lips of His beloved apostle, St. John, that in this Blessed Sacrament, having loved His own who were in the world, He loved them to the end.

Beloved, you see this is clear, and therefore we do not hesitate a moment to declare the Blessed Sacrament to be the greatest work of the love of God. In saying this we are certain that we are guilty of no presumption, but rather are full of faith, for the Holy Ghost has so declared.

But, my brethren, we can also discover by the light of faith why the Blessed Sacrament is the greatest work of God. There are defined rules in human knowledge whereby inquiries are conducted and judgments determined. And so in considering the works of God there are rules specified by Himself which disclose to us for what reason and in what sense God, the Lord Himself, gives preference to one work over all the others performed by His hand, calling it His great, His noble work, His masterpiece, and even the remembrance of all His wonderful works.

If, then, God, the Lord, calls one of His works great above all others, the reason is surely that the work is of such nature that there is greater condescension of God in it than in the others. For you must know that in each of His works, and by each of His works, God reveals to us His condescension. That is an essential characteristic of all God's works, and if we reflect we must pronounce St. Ephrem perfectly right when he makes the remarkable observation: " God has made Himself infinitely small in order to create the world which to us seems so large " Is not this true ? Consider, my brethren: we were not necessary to God, nor was any created being, however holy, wise or beautiful it might be. Creation was not necessary, neither for His honor, nor for His happiness, nor, strictly speaking, for His bounty. We know this much of the infinite majesty of God, and know it with all certainty: He is infinite majesty in Himself, and would be had He created nothing outside Himself. That He has created a world, and such a great, such a magnificent, such a perfect world, is a profound condescension of God's infinite majesty, He has made Himself infinitely small to create a world that seems to us so large; thus creation is a great work of God.

You will understand that this condescension of God, which is and must be found in each of His works, is not found in all of them to the same degree. Oh, no; this condescension of God has its gradations, and He can descend a step deeper in condescension in one of His works than in another. And the lower the great God descends in His works the greater we must call that work. God Himself calls our attention to this, for the Holy Ghost, by the mouth of the apostles of the Gentiles, calls the incarnation of the Son of God an emptying of self, such a profound condescension is it. It is well worth our while to do what the first Christians did—descend in spirit the various steps that led the infinite splendor of the majesty of the Son of God into this incarnation—that we can, at least in a degree, better see and understand the abyss of condescension in which we find ourselves when we come to the mystery of the incarnation of the Son of God. The first step in condescension is this: The Son of God might have taken the nature of the heavenly spirits. Had the eternal Word done this, had He united His divine Person to the nature of angels, it would have been a work far greater than the prodigious work of creation, in that it would have been more condescending than the magnificent work of creation, for then the infinite majesty of God would have approached closely to a creature, uniting itself intimately with him Had the consubstantial Son of the heavenly Father passed by the angels, had He rather preferred to unite His divine Person to human nature, surely it would not have been merely a step in His condescension, but would have been descending a deep, unfathomable abyss; for of all rational creatures man is least, the most insignificant, the lowliest, and it would then be true that infinite, supreme Majesty had set aside the noblest and most perfect of His creatures, and in His condescension had gone so far as to look upon the meanest of His rational creatures and come to him in the closest, most intimate relation. But note well that this would have been true in case humanity had not fallen, or

if the Son of God had vouchsafed to assume human nature
ere man had sinned, and had taken the nature of sinless
man, free from suffering, and had then dwelt with us and
been like to us. But it has been very different from this:
Our Lord waited until man had fallen; until humanity, by
inconceivable sins of ingratitude, by audacious sacrilege,
had destroyed, slain its stainless, noble nature, created in
the likeness of the divine; until the greatest work of God
on earth had been utterly destroyed, as far as its own power
could destroy it. After mankind had committed this trans-
gression, this crime, then the Son of God passed by the
angels and looked on man so disgraced and fallen, and
deigned to take his nature. Not even a nature free from
suffering, assuming this nature with all its miseries,
sin only excepted, suffering in this nature, not only
fully enduring all kinds of bodily and mental agony of humanity, but exhausting Himself; and this He has done, not
only in spite of our sins, but to save us from them, and
make us kings, and co-heirs of heaven. What can you say
of this condescension of God ? Surely, you think, here
the abyss of God's abasement is at its deepest, and in this
divine work of the infinite majesty of the Son of God for a
fallen race, when for full thirty-three years He bore not
only unimaginable but incredible humiliation, abasement and pain, the divine condescension had reached the
extremest limit, for it certainly seems impossible for it to
be more profound.

Now, beloved, we can in some measure estimate what
was done. For a still greater work of condescension has
Our Lord wrought In this human nature the consubstantial Son of God approached the end of His life, and
in the solemn moment when for the last time He was with
His own in this inferior nature He performed this work,—
a work of which His beloved apostle, John, who then leaned
on His breast and felt the beating of the Heart of Jesus,

said: " Having loved His own who were in the world, He loved them to the end "—meaning not merely to the end of His life, but to the end of the possibilities of divine bounty and goodness.

But, I ask myself, what happened then; what did Jesus do in that last evening of His life ? That evening, my brethren, according to the law, Our Lord had eaten the paschal lamb with His disciples. When they had finished He arose, but not yet to go out; no, He remained standing, and this time He did not, as in other years, observe the prohibition of the Jewish law to touch other food, but did exactly the contrary. He took bread, while the apostles in speechless wonder tried to guess what their Master intended doing, and they saw Him bless the bread. Then they understood that it was not to give them more to eat, not to satisfy their bodily hunger, that Jesus took the bread, nor would the law be transgressed, for He took the bread to make over it a holy sign. " He took the bread into His holy and venerable hands, and blessed it." Thereupon their wonder increased; they eagerly awaited what was coming next. Then Jesus broke the bread, and divided it. Then they saw that this holy thing that was to be formed from the bread was for them. Then their wonder was very great; they were eager to know what sacred thing their divine Lord was to give them. And they heard the eternal words, " Take and eat;" they heard plainly that they could receive it: " Take and eat; this is My body." Behold, beloved, this is the work, the great work wrought by Our Lord at the close of His life, whereby He bequeathed to us the legacy in which He will abide with us in everlasting remembrance.

And do you ask what it was that had happened then, what Our Lord had done ? Then was fulfilled the greatest work of Our Saviour's condescension. Do you not understand this ? Perhaps it seems to you exaggerated. But,

my brethren, reflect: all the divine majesty of the Son of
God is now hidden, and hidden under a morsel of bread.
A little while ago you thought that you had reached the
deepest abyss of condescension, the extreme limit for a
God and sovereign Lord, when you learned that the infinite
majesty was hidden under the feeble, impenetrable form
of a child. And truly, that the Fulness and Source, the
Author of all life, should be hidden under the form of a
child, having such a slight, feeble hold on life, is an abyss
of condescension; it is an abyss of condescension that the
Fulness, the Source, the Author of all wisdom should be
hidden in the form of a child, allowing Himself to be gov-
erned, guided and taught by the word and example of His
creatures   Most surely it is an abyss of condescension that
the infinite, almighty, creative power is hidden in the
feeble and impotent little hands of a child. Nevertheless
that was a form not only capable of life, it was a living
form; not merely a form capable of reason, but endowed
with reason; not only capable of strength, but to a certain
extent filled with strength—in a word, since it was a human form, it was a form in which Jesus could give proof
before men's eyes of His divinity. But here in the Blessed
Sacrament you find condescension, humiliation, self-abasement in a yet deeper abyss.

Here the incarnate Son of God dwells in the form of
bread, a form not only dead, lifeless, but also absolutely
incapable of life; a form not merely destitute of understanding and intelligence, but completely incapable of giving the slightest sign of life. In this form your Lord and
God is now hidden, and, what is the most amazing, has
yielded the victory to the lifeless form of bread; it remains
unchanged even after the divine majesty has concealed
Himself within it. Here Jesus, the incarnate, divine majesty, has become completely unrecognizable.

Behold here, beloved, the real abyss of condescension;

this is the deepest condescension; here has it reached the utmost limit; Jesus has emptied Himself that He might be humbled even to the appearance of bread. But there are other circumstances which show this condescension, already proved so deep, to be still more profound.

Second Point.—Verily it is worthy of wonder and consideration that in the human nature which He assumed for love of us Our Lord withheld from Himself everything that could have brought Him pleasure, veneration, power and greatness, but chose, on the contrary, everything that was humiliating, self-sacrificing and difficult. It is a true, a significant saying of St. Paul's: "Who having joy set before Him endured the cross." For, beloved, because of His origin, because of His high descent, because His was and is the infinite majesty of the Son of God, all splendor, all glory, all power was His due. There can be nothing less conceivable than that Our Lord should have done as He did. Nevertheless we find it comprehensible in a measure that He acted thus. For then He was among us to fulfil the work of our salvation, and it is not strange that He rejected all the honor that was His and assumed humiliation and suffering. But now this work of redemption is finished; now He has consummated it; now is fulfilled what St. Paul said, "He endured the cross." He has "emptied Himself," and now has God raised Him up, and to Him is given a name that is above every name, and every knee bends at the name of Jesus; and yet it is now that His condescension goes so far as to dwell in the form of bread; it is now that He reaches the extreme limits of the abyss of His condescension. Yes, beloved, this is one of the circumstances that make this condescension in the Blessed Sacrament the greatest, and proves it so to us Now we come to a second circumstance. It is this: Jesus takes this deep condescension upon Himself in the Blessed Sacrament without betraying even the least little sign of His divine majesty, while during the humiliations of His earthly life He gave many proofs of it. See and consider what happened at the birth of Jesus. As a feeble, helpless, poor little child, the infinite majesty of the Son of God lay in a crib. Oh, what a humiliation, what lowliness, what condescension ! But the inhabitants of heaven could not rest, nor behold it in silence; the heavens opened, and the angels of heaven came forth and announced to earth— to earth which had robbed God of His honor and was not able to restore it, and from which, therefore, all joy had fled—announced to earth great joy: " To you is born a Saviour " (who will restore to God His honor, and to you your joy), and burst forth into the significant hymn of praise and jubilation: " Glory to God in the highest, and peace on earth to men of good will " You see that here, in the midst of this great humiliation, the splendor of His divinity shone forth.

Again Jesus took upon Himself a great humiliation; it was in the solemn moment when His thirty years of hidden life ended and His public life began.   Then Jesus went down into the Jordan to be baptized by His forerunner, St. John the Baptist.   St. John knew who He was who asked baptism, and, feeling his own unworthiness, he cried out: " I ought to be baptized by Thee, and comest Thou to me ? " But Jesus said to him: " Suffer it to be so now. For so it becometh us to fulfil all justice; " and He actually was baptized, baptized by John. What humiliation, what abasement, what condescension this was for Jesus ! He submitted to His creature; allowed Himself to receive the same treatment as sinful man must undergo. But scarcely had the blessed Lord come out of the water than the heavens opened, the Spirit of God descended upon Him, and the voice of the heavenly Father was heard from heaven making public acknowledgment: " This is My beloved Son, in whom I am well pleased," whereby was announced that

Jesus is the only-begotten Son of God. You see here again that in this great humiliation of Our Lord there was not lacking a magnificent proof that the divine power, majesty and glory dwelt in Him.

And, beloved, still another great humiliation, abasement and condescension was Our Lord's portion. It was in the eternally memorable day when He fulfilled the great work of redemption, the last day of His life. Oh, what an inconceivably deep humiliation Our Lord then endured! Then, as you know, the sacred body of Our Saviour from the crown of His head to the sole of His foot was one wound on another; there was not one sound spot in His whole body; our dear Lord's entire body was literally one great wound, and this one great wound was nailed fast by three gaping wounds to a rough tree-trunk in the form of a cross. Oh, He seemed no longer to be a man, but a worm trodden under foot, as He hung there between heaven and earth, held fast by three great nails! Thus must Jesus end His life; such a death as this must He die, die longing for His people. Verily, unspeakably, inconceivably profound was this abasement. The Sun of divine justice was obscured. But, my brethren, as when in a frightful storm the black clouds seem to lie on the earth, and it grows so dark one would fancy the sun to have disappeared, suddenly its dazzling rays flash through the darkness like flames of fire. So on Good Friday, when the Son of the living God was so profoundly humiliated that the human form, like a downtrodden worm, writhed in a thousand wounds, the sun-ray of His divine majesty shone through in beams of dazzling light. For behold, beloved, as Our Lord hung there, crushed like a worm, as His thousand wounds gaped painfully, suddenly how awful, how frightful the whole earth became! The birds flying affrighted here and there, the terror-stricken animals trembling, crying and wailing, and men filled with horror, hurrying hither and thither to reach shelter; the hill of Calvary and the streets deserted and desolate For suddenly the whole earth trembled, the ancient rocks were burst asunder, the graves opened and gave up their dead, over the whole earth the sun was obscured, and at noontide—at twelve o'clock —there lay upon the earth such black night as was never over the earth before. It was a sight so frightfully magnificent, so awfully majestic, that at Athens the great scholar Dionysius, still a heathen, cried out: "Either a God is dead, or the whole earth is to be destroyed." Again you see that in this profound abasement of the divine Saviour a magnificent miracle announced that the divine majesty dwelt within Him   And this always was the case while Jesus wrought the work of redemption; the great humiliations which He underwent were each time accompanied by proofs, great, remarkable proofs of His divine majesty. And now, my brethren, now when this work of salvation, combined with so many and such great miracles, is accomplished; now when God the Father has glorified Him, His beloved Son, now when a name is given Him above every name, now He humiliates Himself so deeply that He makes Himself unrecognizable; He assumes the form of bread, and what happens ? What proof of His divine grandeur and majesty will be given ? My brethren, hear, and wonder Absolutely nothing perceptible happens, either in the place, or the vessels, or the servant by whom this most adorable mystery is wrought. At this most solemn moment the altar is not bathed with radiance; no flames of fire burst forth from the candles, nor is the light of the sun in the church or on the altar different in this awful moment, never do rays of light surround the hands of the priest, the highly honored priest, who holds in his hand, in the insignificant form of bread, the infinite majesty of the Son of God; there are no rays of splendor surrounding the poor form of bread in which the grandeur of the infinite majesty now dwells. No, in this solemn moment, everything, everything remains unchanged in the whole church as if nothing had happened there. And yet what a change, what a great, awe-inspiring change has taken place ! The Lord our God is present in the tiny, insignificant form of bread. Yes, beloved, this is what makes this condescension of Our Lord in the Blessed Sacrament the greatest condescension; He goes into the form of bread, and although He does so now when for a twofold reason the highest glory is due Him, yet He does it in such a way that He gives not the slightest sign of His divine majesty. Now the words of St. Paul appeal to us in their fullest truth: "He emptied Himself" But therefore He is exalted. Oh, the Church does not leave Our Lord lonely and neglected in this deep concealment which He has assumed; the Church does not reject her Lord because in this Sacrament He reveals such profound condescension. No, she brings to Him her homage of adoration due Him especially while hidden in the form of bread. She keeps the Forty Hours, the beautiful, solemn, touching Forty Hours. And this week it is our turn to celebrate it, and bring to Our Lord this solemn tribute of adoration, thanksgiving, reparation and prayer. Shall I urge you to bear your share in this homage zealously and perseveringly ? No, beloved, I will not do this; I tell you frankly that I should be ashamed for you and myself were it necessary. We will rather begin our veneration at once and with earnestness. To this intention we will first let Our Lord in the Blessed Sacrament give us His blessing; we will bear Him in solemn procession through the church, that He may pour forth His almighty benediction in every part of the house of God, and with deep emotion we will sing the "Pange Lingua," and gratefully pray, "Blessed be the Most Holy Sacrament !" while our "Ave Jesu !" still resounds. We will chant with full hearts the Te

Deum at the close of the Forty Hours. Thus we will keep this solemn devotion. And may our dear Lord grant us all to truly love the Blessed Sacrament throughout our life, to venerate it and to profit by it ! May He also grant it to be our last Food, so that we may pass from this temporal life into the eternal, uniting our voice with the heavenly hosts, and singing for all eternity: " We praise Thee, O God; we acknowledge Thee to be the Lord " ! Amen.

SERMON XV.

THE VOLUNTARY AND INVOLUNTARY HUMILIATIONS OF
JESUS IN THE BLESSED SACRAMENT.

"I will sacrifice to Thee the sacrifice of praise."—*Ps.* cxv. 7.

OUR holy religion makes every effort, yes, we may say
that it is indefatigable and inexhaustible in its efforts to
glorify the Blessed Sacrament. We can say with all truth
that our holy religion has taken care that the Blessed Sacrament should be ceaselessly honored, and that this homage
should be rich in variety and full of sublimity. This is a
fact beyond denial. And the Forty Hours, so dear and
precious to Catholics, which we shall celebrate this week,
is truly a magnificent, sublime and touching tribute by
which to glorify the Blessed Sacrament. But how is it
that the Church is so insatiable in her desires, so full of
devices to honor, praise and glorify the Blessed Sacrament? What a question! You know that in proportion
to the measure in which one sees that he is loved by
another he feels drawn to show gratitude and love in return. Now it is precisely by the Most Holy Sacrament of
the Altar that Our Lord has shown and proved His love
for us, which is so great that language fails to describe it,
and our Church understands this perfectly. No wonder,
therefore, that the Church is indefatigable in her efforts
to show the greatest possible veneration to the Blessed
Sacrament!

That I may say everything to you on this subject I

233

must add that the Church has insight into and understands and feels this inexhaustible love of Jesus in the Blessed Sacrament, because she properly investigates this mysterious Sacrament. Not that the Church examines or seeks to determine how it is possible for the infinite majesty of God to be enthroned in the form of bread; she believes this strongly and steadfastly, and thinks, with St. Augustine, that God can do more than we can understand. But what she does strive to learn by investigation is what it is, and what it means, that a God has determined to abide with His creatures in all places, and to all time. And she finds a whole series of actions worthy of meditation, having their seat and source in the Heart of Jesus consumed with love for His own.

And now, my brethren, we also will do this. We will leave to others the aimless and useless inquiries arising from unbelieving hearts, as to how it is possible that a God can be present under these lowly appearances; we will unreservedly believe this, because He has said that this is His body, but we will not stop here; we will rather take pains to fix our eyes on the many wonderful things contained in the Blessed Sacrament, the rays of which burst forth and enlighten us who watch them closely.

Jesus shrank not from confining Himself in the Blessed Sacrament in order to be with us, although He knew that there He must undergo the greatest humiliations. For these humiliations are more than great when you consider—

I   How Jesus is present in the Blessed Sacrament.

II. How He is treated there by His creatures.

First Point.—Truly it sounds incredible when one says that in His love for us whom He has saved, Jesus has gone so far, has made us a gift of grace so great and precious, that though He is almighty He can never do or create anything more wonderful Yet this is true, and, beloved, he who truly believes, as every Christian should believe, that Jesus is present, actually and really present in the Blessed Sacrament for love of us, believes that it did not satisfy His love for us to give us the treasures of grace contained in the other sacraments, and that He was not content till He had given us Himself in His sacred humanity and divinity. Thus has Our Lord truly exhausted Himself in His love for us, thus, as St. John so beautifully tells us, He has loved us to the end. For now there remains nothing that He has withheld, or that we have not received

Great love has another characteristic It does not shrink from bearing suffering, fatigue, humiliation for its beloved. The Holy Ghost tells us this when He says: "Love is as strong as death." He whom death once seizes it never releases; no power on earth is strong enough to snatch him from its jaws; so with love: what love has undertaken it seeks to carry through, and to attain. No obstacles are able to move it and make it relinquish its hold Yes, this characteristic of endurance is so peculiar to that conception of love which is the Holy Spirit's—and that alone is the true one—that the Apostle of the Gentiles cannot cease repeating and insisting that this endurance is a mark of love. He says simply and beautifully: "Love is patient;" that were enough, but he adds: "It beareth all things;" that were more than enough, but again he adds: "It endureth all things." And, beloved, though we men may not always act thus, still we think thus. With truth and justice we call only that real friendship which like pure gold the fire has tried. As gold is not pure which cannot stand the heat of fire, so that is not true love which cools or diminishes when there is a question of making a sacrifice for a friend, and the proverb says· "In necessity our friends flee by the hundreds;" and "A friend in need is a friend indeed."

Now, my brethren, if the love of Jesus proves itself
so unspeakably great in establishing the Blessed Sacrament, by giving us the greatest, and best, and holiest thing
that there is in heaven or on earth, then this love, already
shown to be great beyond all words, proves itself far
greater, since in order to make us this excessive Gift Our
Lord did not shrink from inexpressible humiliations
Consider as you will, you can find no word strong enough
to express how great the humiliation, the self-denial of
Our Lord has been in bringing Himself to confer on mankind this greatest benefit precisely at the time when humanity had determined to commit the greatest sacrilege
against Him. Never, I might say, has the love of Jesus
shown itself more burning, glowing and brilliant than
when He performed His greatest work of love for the
human race, and man overwhelmed Him with the flood of
blackest crime. "In the night that He was betrayed,"
the Holy Ghost says so significantly, He gave us this
Most Holy Sacrament ! So great, so unconquerable, so
far-reaching is this love ! Never, my brethren, is a flame
of fire more magnificent than when it is fanned by the
rushing gusts of wind which should extinguish it, and in
the night when the greatest crime that the world has ever
seen was concocted and arranged against the sovereign
Lord of the world, Jesus wrought the greatest work of
love that has ever been wrought on earth for degenerate
humanity The many icy waters of more than human
cruelty could not quench His burning love for us.

But, my brethren, these humiliations did not endure
long; they ended with that black night. Yet, in giving
us this Most Holy Sacrament, He could not have overlooked the fact that He would undergo other humiliations,
which, although not so excessive, would continue always,
continue even to the end of the world. This Blessed
Sacrament shall be a remembrance and renewal of His

death on the cross for love of us, and the long-continued humiliation and abasement which our dear Lord ceaselessly, voluntarily assumes seem to us greater than those in the incarnation, and in a certain sense even greater than the humiliation of His death on the cross. In the Blessed Sacrament Our Lord humiliates Himself even to the form of bread ! How inexpressibly deep is this humiliation ! Reflect a moment. That humiliation in which the Son of God took upon Himself the form of a servant, and became man, was so deep that St. Paul called it an " emptying of self." And the Church exclaims amazed· " Having taken upon Thee to deliver man, Thou didst not abhor the Virgin's womb " If it was such a great humiliation for the Son of God, for the Person of the divine Word to assume flesh and dwell among us that He could truthfully say: " The Father is greater than I," " I am less than the Father," how great must be the humiliation which our dear Lord took upon Himself in the Blessed Sacrament, for here He seems still smaller and more insignificant than we miserable men ! He even places Himself below all irrational, living creatures; the Fulness of life, the Source of life, Life itself, takes the lifeless form of bread, the form of a dead substance.

Verily, this is not merely to renew the humiliations of the incarnation, it is to exceed them, and this humiliation is also in a certain sense greater than the humiliations of the cross. For though as He hung on the cross Our Lord's whole body was disfigured, and at last dead, yet He was still in the human form proper to Him. But in the Blessed Sacrament He is in a form strange to all the world, a lowly form, and so far from belonging to Our Lord that He is perfectly unrecognizable as He dwells among us under the inactive, the lifeless appearance of bread. " God only on the cross lay hid from view," sings first the inspired St. Thomas of Aquinas, and with him the whole Church. " But here lies hid at once the manhood too." Oh, verily, more than great is the humiliation that our dear Lord takes upon Himself in the Blessed Sacrament, where He abides in such an unworthy, lowly form, under the veil of bread.

And, beloved, keep constantly before your eyes the fact that this great humiliation is not to end soon, it endures long, it is unceasing, it has no end, it lasts even to the end of time. Yet our dear Lord does not shrink from assuming this great and long-enduring humiliation in order to give us the greatest gift that heaven or earth has to bestow, the Most Holy Sacrament of the Altar. Oh, it is indeed true that the love shown us by Our Lord in the Blessed Sacrament is great beyond all words !

Nor, my beloved, have I yet shown you the depth of humiliation into which Our Lord has descended in the Blessed Sacrament. This humiliation of our dear Lord to the form of bread is not merely a humiliation to the poorest and most miserable dwelling; it is a humiliation even unto death. We can say with perfect justice, that in the Blessed Sacrament, and by the Blessed Sacrament, Jesus in a certain sense dies anew. The glorified body of our dear Lord is present in the form of bread in the same manner as the soul is in the body. We have learned this in our Catechism, and we must believe surely and unfalteringly that Our Lord is present entire in the whole Host, and in each particle of the Host. How this can be no one can understand; that it is so every one must believe, believe because Jesus has plainly said that He is present in the form of bread. It is evident that whether the form of bread be large or small, whether it be left entire or divided, it is always the form of bread, and so it is evident that Our Saviour is present not only in the whole Host, but in each portion of it. Now what does this mean ? On the one hand this is a glorification, an inconceivably great glorification of the body of Jesus. Thereby Our Lord has given, as far as lay in His power, His glorified body the qualities of a spirit. For, my brethren, in like manner is our soul in our body; it is at once in the entire body, and in each limb thereof.

On the other hand, beloved, why is this great miracle worked ? Certainly also that He may be humiliated even unto death, if not solely for this reason. For with its greater glorification His sacred body is brought into a condition that is like to death Now His whole sacred body, with all its members, is restrained in the narrow, tiny space of a little piece of bread, now there is nothing to be seen of a human being's limbs, now are all His members, if I may say so, sentenced not to exercise their proper energy, the requisite space is lacking to them; though they have life, yet they are as the dead, devoid of life, since for this they must have freedom and liberty to move.

These are great things, and for the ordinary understanding they are perfectly inscrutable and mysterious, but precisely because they are so they give us a deep insight into the Divine Heart of Jesus, allowing us to better understand the divine source from which they spring. This is the invincible love of Jesus for us, which hesitates at no sacrifice, and conquers all obstacles; a love that goes so far as to work the miracle, the great, unparalleled miracle, of bringing itself into the deepest humility that we may be honored and enriched. And though ordinarily medicine is only bitter to those who take it, and not to him who prepares it, here the case is reversed. Our Lord died on the cross to merit for us this celestial gift And surely, my brethren, it is sweet indeed for us to have Jesus with us; to see Him sacrificed on the altar in the Holy Mass; to receive Jesus into our hearts in holy communion; but, that we might possess this fountain of grace,

Jesus puts His members into the condition of death after they actually had died painfully on the cross to purchase the right to do this.

Verily, beloved, the humiliations which Jesus has taken upon Himself in the Blessed Sacrament are more than great when we consider how He is present there. Nevertheless, my brethren, great as are these humiliations, Our Lord Himself has chosen them. But He also has to endure in the Blessed Sacrament even greater humiliations; they re the humiliations inflicted on Him by His creatures.

Second Point.—If a man had made himself poor, lowly, insignificant in order to help, advance and ennoble his fellow men, the consequence would not be that he would be made little of by those who knew of his action, that they would care nothing about him, and permit themselves all sorts of liberties in his presence and to his person; but on the contrary every one knowing of it would behave in a manner exactly the reverse of this, though they derived no personal benefit from his action. It would be enough to know that he had acted so nobly, and we should consider it an honor to meet him, and we should strive to show how highly we valued and honored him, taking pains to behave with the utmost reverence, and show him the greatest attention when in his presence. We should consider this our duty, and call those rude who failed in it.

Now, beloved, Our Lord has made Himself poor and little in the Blessed Sacrament in order to help and raise up His ransomed people. And Catholic Christendom knows this. Catholics know how miserably poor and insignificant Our Lord has made Himself in the Blessed Sacrament; Catholics know that the many who do not hear the true Church do not know the great Sacrament of the Altar; that because they are separated from the Church of Jesus they are deprived of all the blessings of this grace-giving Sacrament; that they cannot receive it. But how highly all Catholics must prize this great Sacrament, because they possess in it Jesus, Our Saviour, the Fulness, the Source and the Author of all grace, how our value of Jesus in the Blessed Sacrament must increase when we see how poor and little Our Lord has become in this remembrance of His wonderful works, that we might be rich and great in grace, how all Catholics must feel it to be their sacred duty to show Our Lord how highly they prize it; what love and reverence toward it fill their hearts; what an honor they must esteem it to adore Him in this Sacrament, and show Him the greatest attention and reverence, and when they are about to receive this Bread of angels, with what scrupulous care they must try to bring Him a heart pure, sanctified and well prepared.

But if none of these things were so, if the contrary were true, and in this Most Holy Sacrament where He has made Himself poor for the sake of His people Our Lord lost much of the honor and reverence due Him because He dwelt with His divine majesty in the insignificant form of bread, and nothing was to be perceived here where God had hidden Himself but a fragment of bread; if, I say, this great Sacrament, and the infinite God concealed in it, were rather despised than esteemed, if because of the veil under which Jesus dwelt, men allowed themselves all sorts of liberties in His presence, even those Catholic Christians for whom He had thus humiliated and emptied Himself, and they were not few but many, yes, very many, who thus treated Jesus in the Blessed Sacrament, then what I have hinted is certain: since the beginning of Christianity there has been no more awful sacrilege, no greater crime, no blacker ingratitude It is the greatest contempt, dishonor, outrage to Jesus; it is certain, and we should reflect earnestly upon it, that this humiliation and abasement inflicted on Our Lord in His

Sacrament of love by His ungrateful, inhuman people is the great, apparently insurmountable obstacle that stood in the way of the establishment of this Sacrament of His most sacred body.

Yes, my brethren, this circumstance deserves to be well considered and meditated upon, that the base treatment to which Our Lord would be subjected in the Blessed Sacrament by His own people was an inexpressibly great obstacle to the establishment of this Sacrament of the love of a God-man, which was to continue to the end For it was not possible for Our Lord to be ignorant like we poor men from whom the future lies hidden in darkness, in that solemn moment when He ordained to dwell in the form of bread, of how basely Christendom would treat Him when He dwelt among His people, or that all these many and great humiliations came upon Him unexpectedly; oh, no, my brethren, all the future, even to the end of time, lies open and clear before Our Lord, and on this most holy, eternally memorable night when He stood in the upper room in Jerusalem, intending to make for all time the legacy of His most precious body and blood, there lay before Him in clearest light the treatment which He must undergo in this Sacrament of love; there were present before His soul, there were felt in their multitude and keenness the humiliation and abasement, swelling to an ocean, which Christians in general would inflict on His divine majesty, abiding truly present under the form of bread.

He saw and felt in their exact number and magnitude all the insults and offences which each individual Christian has committed against Him in the Blessed Sacrament from the day that he attained the use of reason even to the hour of his death; Our Lord then saw everything, all the liberties that would be taken in His presence, and even with His sacred Person. How shocking to the eyes of Jesus and to His Sacred Heart must have been what He saw then !

Ah, my brethren, the positions and attitudes of most Christians in the church before the Most Holy are neither fitting nor what one would expect to see, nor what we should wish them to be when one is before his great God; they are not even such as one would assume before a human being whom he respected; they are unbecoming, indecent, rude, and one would never dare sit or stand thus in the presence of a mere man of whom he stood in awe.

I repeat, my brethren, this behavior is not fitting the presence of the majesty of God; it is not even such as is shown a respected human being. One should kneel here silently, occupied in earnest prayer, and instead of that he looks all around as if he were on the street; yes, as well-bred people never do on the street, chattering, amusing himself, actually relating stories, laughing and diverting himself.

All this and more is done in church before the incarnate God dwelling in the form of bread You can see what Catholics allow themselves to do in the presence of their Saviour abiding with them in the Holy Eucharist. And surely such behavior is in your eyes gross contempt, insult, humiliation heaped on Our Lord in the Blessed Sacrament But we will defer that thought till later, for I have yet something to tell you; for men do still more than this to offend their Lord. Reflect a moment on all the liberty people allow themselves in thoughts, words and actions in His presence, and even to His Sacred Person.

What do most Christians think of at Mass and at holy communion ? Both are the holiest things, not only that there are on earth but that there are in heaven. Nothing can be more holy than the sacrifice of the Mass and holy communion. Even in heaven there is nothing more holy, for in the Mass the thrice holy God who is enthroned in heaven comes on the altar as the Lamb of sacrifice, and in holy communion comes into our soul as manna containing in itself all strength and sweetness. Oh, then they must be the holiest of all things to Christians; they must prize the Mass and holy communion as the most sacred, most worthy of reverence and love of all things, holding them in adoring respect. But the great God is present under the appearance of bread, and since most people form their opinions solely by that which they see, they cannot raise themselves to the height of having a just appreciation of the Blessed Sacrament. Alas, they do not love, they do not value the Holy Mass and holy communion ! How many nowadays care very little for these two treasures of grace, and make little of them ! How great the number of those to whom these celestial gems are trifles or burdens ! Yes, there are those to whom they are contemptible ! And what expressions Christians permit themselves toward their infinite God, abiding with them in the form of bread !

My brethren, the place in which I stand is too holy for me to dare to quote in it the devilish, the infernal speeches against the Blessed Sacrament which bad Christians in their godlessness have poured forth. It is sufficient for me to hint at the insults, the sneers, the mockery, the unbelief directed against Our Lord dwelling under the sacramental veils by these wicked tongues. And they are tongues that have been taught to pray, and which once said: "Blessed be the Most Holy Sacrament !"

But how horrible, how frightful is the humiliation, the injury, the ignominy inflicted by Christians on the Person of Our Lord in the Blessed Sacrament by unworthy communions. By this sacrilegious act Christians profane the Person of Our Lord and render themselves guilty of the body and blood of Jesus Shall I faintly illustrate this horrible crime, crying to heaven for ven-

geance, by means of an inadequate image ? Then listen.
What an outrage it would be, how degraded, disgraced,
and at the same time how tortured and pained a king
would be were one of his subjects to put him in a grave
with a loathsome corpse, already decaying and putrid.
But greater, greater beyond all comprehension or comparison is the insult and martyrdom which Our Lord must
endure each time that a Christian communicates with mortal sin in his heart. For it must be more degrading, more
insulting, more horrible than any grave can be to Our
Lord to be obliged to enter a heart which is a den of
thieves, because it is the shelter and abode of sin and the
author of sin, the devil. It must be more degrading and
dishonorable, more horrible to our dear Lord to be domi-
ciled with sin, and the author of sin, the devil, in one and
the same heart, than for the noblest of temporal kings to lie
beside a decaying body. And, my brethren, it is not seldom,
nor by a few people, that this great outrage and insult is
done Our Lord. It happens often, and the number of those
who commit this sacrilege is greater than you imagine.

Reflect on the many who no longer receive holy communion. In all of these cases one has well-founded reason to believe that before they reached this condition the
crime of one, or even more, unworthy communions was
on their soul. And there is one time in the year, the Eas-
tertide, when one is forced to fear that a great number of
Christians inflict this vile affront on their loving Lord,
receiving the Bread of angels with sin on their souls, receiving the living Bread that cometh down from heaven,
not distinguishing it from ordinary food, and that the
number of those who dare receive this Food of the soul
with sin and the devil in their heart constantly increases.

I say one is forced to fear this. For when the Apostle
says: " Therefore are there many infirm and weak among
you, and many sleep; " when the Holy Ghost Himself de-

clares as a consequence and as characteristic of unworthy communions that the increasing weakness, the infirmity and the sleep of sin is found among men, we can but fear it. How can we help fearing that very many Easter communions are unworthy ones—ay, sacrileges—when we have before our eyes the painful fact that the majority of Christians show absolutely no improvement after having made their Easter communion ? That after, and notwithstanding the reception of Our Lord, no real strength nor health of soul can be seen in them, that they are precisely as weak and infirm of soul, if not more so than before; that they are like a man overcome and drunken with sleep, who after he has been violently and with difficulty awakened lies back again to sleep fast and deep ? For after they have been brought to themselves by Our Lord, the thrice holy God, they quietly sink back into the sleep of sin, and once more resume their sinful life. And they who inflict this great outrage on their Lord, year in and year out, committing the incredible crime of uniting Him with sin in their hearts, and the author of sin, the devil, dwelling there, are not few but many, very many, perhaps the majority of Christians.

Now, beloved, in that solemn night, when for love of us, and that He might be always and everywhere with us, Our Lord determined to give Himself to us in the form of bread, He saw and felt this profane treatment, He saw and felt these sacrileges and their incalculable number and guilt which Christians would commit in His presence and inflict on His Person. Surely you feel that what Our Lord saw then was an obstacle standing in the way of His giving this multitude of ungrateful, irreverent Christians this testament of love; an obstacle to our minds insurmountable, and which demanded of Him the abandonment of the plan He had formed of bequeathing His most sacred living body, and therefore Himself as God-man, under the appearance of bread. And you feel, too, that this humiliation and abasement inflicted on Our Lord by Christians were far more deterrent and more horrible than that which He chose in the night in which He was betrayed when He wrought for humanity His greatest work of love and humbled Himself to the form of bread.

Now, my brethren, marvel at and adore the immeasurable greatness, the unfathomable depth, the insurmountable height of the love of Jesus! Beloved, that has happened which no one can understand; the icy waters of contempt, of dishonor, of humiliation, of abasement which Our Lord saw that Christendom would pour upon Him could not make Him shrink nor withhold Him from giving us this Sacrament of love; could not quench the love that burned in His Heart. He knew, and felt, and saw how badly and irreverently He would be treated when He concealed Himself under the form of bread. Yet He then determined to be with us here under this form of bread even to the end of time. He consented to be so little honored, so sorely dishonored by Christians in order to dwell under the form of bread and be with them. The love of Jesus goes so far that He will be poor and dishonored if only He can dwell among us.

Oh, this love is inconceivable! Certainly it is, but you must reflect that it is a divine love, and a divine love that has loved us to the end, a love which can say: " What could I have done more for thee, and have not done it?" The love of Jesus proves itself great beyond all words and conception when we fix our eyes on the fact that He did not shrink from being with us in the Blessed Sacrament, although He saw that He must undergo great and unknown humiliations, although He saw how poor He must dwell among us in the form of bread, and how badly on that very account He would be treated by His people.

Now, beloved, love always calls forth love in return,

and as you have just heard, and are sure that in His divine love Our Saviour has completely exhausted Himself, and gone to the extreme limit of possibility,—there can be no necessity for me to call upon you to unite yourself to the Church, and with her bring to your dear Lord in the Blessed Sacrament the homage of the Forty Hours. Rather I look to see you welcome this festival, and feel it is the desire of your hearts to pray ceaselessly: "Blessed be the Most Holy Sacrament!" sighing sorrowfully: "O dearest Jesus! May Thy blessed Mother, together with all Thy angels and saints, bless Thee for all the insults and offences which Thy ungrateful creatures have committed, or ever will commit to the end of time, against Thee the supreme Good," and unwearyingly let your "Ave Jesu!" resound.

Yes, my brethren, be worthy successors of your pious forefathers, to whom the days of the Forty Hours were so dear and sacred, who turned night into day in this feast, going without sleep like the dwellers of heaven, who sleep not, and bringing their sacrifice of praise during the night to their Lord in the Blessed Sacrament. Let these days be dear and sacred to you also, make it your duty to celebrate them faithfully, affrighted at the thought of being like to those who esteem Our Lord in the Blessed Sacrament lightly, because He has humbled Himself to the form of bread. Remember more honor, praise, glory and adoration are due Our Lord in the Blessed Sacrament the poorer and smaller He has made Himself for love of us. Bring Him there the praise-offering of the Forty Hours.

But Thou, dear Lord, let us praise Thee in the Blessed Sacrament; receive us when full of wonder and admiration we pray: "Blessed be the Most Holy Sacrament!" accept us when rejoicing we sing: "Ave Jesu!" Let us make reparation to Thee, and graciously receive our prayer when with sorrowing hearts we say: "O dearest Jesus!

May Thy blessed Mother, together with all Thy angels and saints, bless Thee for all the insults and offences which Thy ungrateful creatures have ever committed, or ever will commit to the end of time, against Thee the supreme Good." Hear us, we beseech Thee, when we sincerely and heartily pray to Thee: " O loving Jesus ! O Blessed Sacrament ! Be Thou in this life my consolation, in death my Viaticum, in eternal glory my reward, where, with Mary, Thy glorious Mother, and all Thy blessed angels and saints, I may behold Thee face to face, and love, praise and glorify Thee for all eternity. Amen."

SERMON XVI.

THE HEROIC OBEDIENCE OF JESUS IN THE BLESSED SACRA-
MENT.

"And He was subject to them."—*St. Luke* ii. 51.

THAT is the life history of an incarnate God as it has
been told us, not by human lips, nor by an angel, but by
the uncreated, infinite Spirit of God Himself, the Spirit of
truth. He considers it especially noteworthy and wonderful in the life of the incarnate Son of God that "He was
subject" to His parents. God as He was, and is, He led
a life of obedience

Yes, my brethren, this is the greatest fact in the life
of our divine Saviour. In His nature He is royal, because
He is God; His name is written on His garment, and on
His thigh, and it is, "King of kings, and Lord of lords";
and yet in the house of Nazareth God the Creator, the
King, the Lord of the universe, was obedient to His creatures, to the work of His hands. This is such a stupendous
truth that you, and I, and all human beings are not able
to grasp it; it is and must be a mystery, a sublime mystery.

Now, my brethren, I can tell you something more.
Jesus, the King of kings, whose right it is to command, has
continued this great mystery—He still practises obedience
on earth. He now practises heroic obedience, and does
so in the Blessed Sacrament. As we are beginning the
Forty Hours to-day, as this week we are to pay the homage

of adoration and reparation to Our Lord in the Blessed
Sacrament, we should do well to place before ourselves, and
try to see and feel, how Our Lord practises heroic obedience
in the Blessed Sacrament. It would be most profitable to
our soul were we to fill our mind and heart with this
truth Then we should take pains to offer this solemn
homage to our dear Lord sincerely and devoutly, making
Him reparation and adoring Him perseveringly. The heroic obedience of our dear Lord should be the subject of
our meditation We must call the obedience of Our Lord
in the Blessed Sacrament heroic for two reasons:

I Because of the matter in which Jesus is obedient;

II. Because of the manner in which He is obedient.

First Point—It certainly depends above all things on
the matter in which one obeys as to how great the obedience is to be called. The harder, the more self-sacrificing,
the more humiliating an affair is in which we see a person
obedient, the greater is the obedience. And why is this ?
Because then it is harder, and costs many and great pains,
and struggles, and self-conquest to accomplish it. Reflect
a moment on what the story of King David shows us.
After his crime of adultery and murder the prophet Na-
than came to him, at God's command, warning him of the
anger of God, and demanding of him a very severe penance. When he had to flee from his degenerate son
Absalom, David went up Mount Olivet, clothed in sack-
cloth, barefooted, his face veiled. Yet David was a king,
clothed in purple and gold, the crown on his head, ruling
from his throne, and giving commandment to his people.
Now which seems to you greater, David in royal pomp,
giving commandment, or David doing severe penance out
of obedience ? You call that David great who, in obedience to God's command, climbed Mount Olivet in peniten-
tial garments; and you are right, for doing this would cost
a mighty ruler a great struggle. But, my brethren, what

is this action really which we call great ? What has this king actually done that was so remarkable ? Looking into his action carefully, we discover only this: for a few days the king took upon himself humiliating employment; he did such things as were a little derogatory to his royal dignity. It was nothing more than this, and yet it seems so great to us ! But were a king to announce the tidings that he would completely and forever give up his throne for the sake of his subjects, and henceforth lead a life of severe penance, should he announce that he would deliver up his life for love of them, beloved, that would cost a violent struggle, for even the worm in the road turns when one would take away its life, though it knows not what life is. It would be heroic obedience to consent to such a requirement.

Now, my hearers, you understand thoroughly that if the Son of God were but once, and in one trifling matter, to lay aside His majesty and obey in one insignificant affair, it would not merely seem too humiliating, too debasing to the majesty of God, it would seem to us incompatible with the grandeur of the divine Majesty, would seem like self-renunciation, self-annihilation. For to demand that God should even once cease to command, and only once obey, would seem equivalent to a demand that He should cease to be God. Is this, then, the obedience practised by Jesus in the Blessed Sacrament ? That were indeed heroic obedience. But no, my brethren, this is not yet the obedience of your Lord in the Blessed Sacrament; this is but the first obedience of the Son of God in the incarnation. For His heavenly Father desired Him to renounce His natural right, and live under obedience like ordinary men, and do so not only in one matter, but in everything; and His life was so ordered that He must forego pleasure, bearing a life of bitterness: and this was not to be for a few days, weeks, months, years; it was to be for all the time of His earthly life; and this life lasted full three and thirty years.

This obedience of the Son of God is so great, so amazing, that one's mind is unable to grasp it, much less can one express it in words; and the Apostle of the Gentiles, striving for the right terms for this obedience of the Son of God, fails to find them. He restricts himself to the most comprehensive, strongest expression there is. He says: "He emptied Himself, taking the form of a servant, being made in the likeness of men, and in habit found as a man." Oh, this is heroic obedience ! But though this is truly wonderful, marvellous, it is not yet the obedience of Jesus in the Blessed Sacrament. What, then, is His obedience in the Blessed Sacrament ? Is there a greater obedience than the obedience of the Son of God to His earthly parents ?

Yes, my brethren, there is a still greater obedience than this, as you must know. Jesus, Our Saviour, has practised it; it is the obedience of the cross. In the obedience of the cross there is no longer question of the use Our Lord would make of His life, or that He should spend His life only in the spirit of obedience. Ah, no, there is question of something far more and very different from this. Here it is a question of nothing less than that Jesus should completely sacrifice and immolate Himself as God-man, and submit to a painful and shameful death. His life as God-man, more valuable, more precious than the lives of all creatures, including the angels and saints, should be immolated, immolated on the cross. It was in such a thing as this that Jesus was to be obedient at the close of thirty-three years of a life spent in obedience. Surely the Divine Heart of Jesus must have resisted, horror-stricken, such a demand as this. And indeed, beloved, when He had to assent to this demand, the agony of death came upon Our Lord, and He begged and implored His heavenly Father to avert, or at least lessen, this ordeal; and after the third

repetition of this prayer an angel came bearing the chalice
to strengthen Him and to comfort His soul, that was sorrowful even unto death. Now the moment had come, the
last moment, when He must say the yes or no that should
determine our destiny, say it bindingly and irrevocably,
and He loved us enough to say this awful yes. But, O
beloved, it cost His Heart something to say it, for " His
sweat became as drops of blood trickling down upon the
ground."

It is an obedience exceeding our power of comprehension
And again we note that it was difficult for St Paul to find
the right words to express this obedience. For he restricts
himself to the strongest and most comprehensive expression that there is, saying: " He humbled Himself, becoming obedient unto death, even unto the death of the cross."
More he cannot say, words fail him. But you certainly
understand that to be obedient in such a thing, obedient
unto death, is heroic obedience for a God.

Now behold, my brethren, Our Lord continues this
obedience of the cross in the Blessed Sacrament; here,
too, He lays down His life and is obedient even unto
death; the forcible words of the Apostle of the Gentiles
apply literally to the Blessed Sacrament: " He emptied
Himself and became obedient unto death." And now we
must add· Even unto the death of the *form of bread.*
Must I prove this to you ? Then listen   Consider a moment, my brethren, what is your belief of the Blessed Sacrament   Oh, to-day, and all through the Forty Hours,
you confess your belief in the Blessed Sacrament. The
walls of this church and of all parish churches echo
with the confession of your faith. You sing as with one
voice:

> " Lo, the Good, supreme and best,
> On the altar deigns to rest,
> Is with flesh and blood our Guest."

You sing:

> "Here our God Himself we see;
> Bow the head, and bend the knee."

This is the confession of your belief in the Blessed Sacrament, as you declare it with one voice, as you feel it with one heart. I can say it is the strong, unshaken, unanimous faith of you all; in this faith and for this faith you are willing to die. But do you realize that in these words you also publicly and solemnly proclaim that in the Blessed Sacrament Jesus practises the obedience of the cross, ceaselessly sacrificing His life in the Blessed Sacrament? Consider how Jesus is present in the Blessed Sacrament.

O beloved, if it is certain that Jesus is truly present in the Blessed Sacrament, there can be no more doubt that He has humiliated Himself and become obedient even unto death. For here we see absolutely nothing of life, not the slightest sign of it, and yet the Fulness of life, the Source of life, the Author of life, God Himself, is here present. I see more life in the worm crawling in the dust, for it can raise itself, bend, writhe, gather itself up; but here I see the lifeless, powerless, dead form of bread, and now, when Jesus, the Source of life, is in it, it is as motionless, as still, as lifeless as before. How marvellous! His mere breath quickened the lifeless body of Adam; why does He not create life here? Why does not the form of bread become living when Jesus dwells in it with the fulness of His divine life? For we see that our dear Lord is in the Blessed Sacrament under circumstances that are like to death and annihilation This is certainly true. For, instead of the bread feeling the awful nearness of its Lord and God, and the appearance of bread which still remains becoming living in the solemn moment of consecration when it is changed into the true body of the Son of God, precisely the contrary happens. When the Fulness of all life disdains not to come into the form of bread, and takes upon Himself the laws of this lifeless substance, He renounces completely, renounces forever, the use of His life. All the members of His sacred body are there, but He does not employ them: the hand is there, but is not raised; the foot is there, but does not move; the mouth and tongue are silent Our Lord allows Himself to be brought into a condition in which He makes no use whatever of His life, and can give no sign thereof; a condition in which it is incomprehensible to us how He can be present; a condition which renders it necessary for us to silence all our experience, our senses, and our thoughts, and hold only to Him who hath the words of eternal life in order to believe:

> "Lo, the Good, supreme and best,
> On the altar deigns to rest,
> Is with flesh and blood our Guest."

Behold, my brethren, this is the obedience of Our Saviour in the Blessed Sacrament !

His love was great enough for Him to spend His life in obedience in the house of Nazareth; His love on Calvary was great enough to be so obedient as to allow His life to be taken from Him, and in the Blessed Sacrament His love is so great that He, from whom life can no more be taken, brings Himself into a condition resembling death. Does this obedience of the Son of God seem great to you ? O beloved ! To possess the fulness of all life, to be Life itself, the Author and Source of life, and then to assume a condition like to death, a condition wherein He can perform no action, give no sign of life, —truly this is great obedience, so great there is no name for it. And if St. Paul, in enumerating the obediences of the incarnation and of the cross, finds it good to use the strong expression, " He humbled Himself," " He emptied Himself," then, my brethren, it will content you if, in contemplating the obedience of Jesus in the Blessed Sacrament, I say to you, "Jesus has emptied Himself, and become obedient unto death, even unto the death of the form of bread." Our Lord's obedience is heroic because He is obedient in such a matter. And the obedience of Jesus in the Blessed Sacrament is heroic for still another reason, and that is because of the circumstances in which we find He is thus obedient.

Second Point.—It is not only the thing in which one is obedient that makes his obedience great, wonderful, heroic, but it may be so because of the circumstances under which he is obedient   The more lowly and humiliating the circumstances, the greater, the more heroic the obedience becomes, even though the matter in which one had to obey were insignificant, and therefore easy. But when both are united, when the matter in which one must obey is the most difficult, and the circumstances most humiliating, then the obedience is not only heroic, but it is heroic obedience in its greatest perfection, its highest consummation; and this applies to the obedience of Jesus in the Blessed Sacrament, for here the circumstances under which He is obedient are the most humiliating.

Consider three obvious conditions of this obedience in the Blessed Sacrament. Consider when Jesus must be obedient, whom He has to obey, and how He must practise this obedience.

If you consider when it is that Jesus must give up His life, His divine life, and offer it unreservedly in obedience as a sacrifice, then you must see that this circumstance makes the sacrifice already so bitter inexpressibly harder. For the sorrowful time when He fulfilled the work of salvation is over, the bitter time of penance is past, and the glorious time of triumph, of victory, has begun, and must continue for Him. And if it is mysterious, and must ever be so, that Jesus, the consubstantial Son of God, could be so obedient as to be always guided by Mary and Joseph, living only according to the will of His heavenly Father, and never using His prerogative of commanding; if it is a profound mystery how Jesus could be obedient unto death, even unto the death of the cross, surrendering His life in the most awful agony and ignominy, yet in a degree we are reconciled to all this by knowing that at the time He bore it Jesus was solving the problem of the work of salvation, paying to God in our stead the honor due Him, and wiping out the insult to God of a creature disobeying his Creator, and suffering for our sins, performing a penance in our stead which should annul the punishment of eternal death which our crime deserved. For, beloved, though I cannot understand how that which actually happened could be possible, and an incarnate God could be obedient even unto the death of the cross, yet in this great mystery I perceive two glorious, wonderful truths. On the one hand I see the marvellous proportion between man's sin and its punishment, and the saving practice of virtue and penance. Man fell by disobedience, and the God-man saved Him by obedience, man was to suffer eternal death, and the God-man obediently endured the death of the cross. On the other hand I see the perfect satisfaction given for man's sin, and its punishment; for the divine majesty is more honored and glorified by the obedience of a God-man than it was dishonored and insulted by the disobedience of a creature, and it is more horrible that a God-man should die as a malefactor on the cross than that all creatures should suffer in the eternal pain of hell.

But now, my brethren, Jesus has fulfilled this work of salvation; now is the glorious time of His triumph; now are all the fruits of grace growing out of His work ripe, and over-ripe, on the tree of the cross in the glow of Jesus' love. Now is the glorious time when these innumerable, un-

limited graces are to be spent; now is the time when for a
twofold reason Jesus is in the possession of His prerogative
of ruling and governing all earthly creatures, for He has also
merited by His death on the cross the right to govern and
to rule which was His by nature. And now, in the time
of His triumph, He has descended still lower in the scale
of obedience; now when He is glorified, and reigning over
all the universe, He becomes obedient even unto death, even
unto the death of the form of bread. What shall I say of
this ? Be satisfied if I say it is heroic obedience in its
highest perfection. Nor is this yet all; we must consider
to whom He must be obedient in this time of His triumph.
For this may make the obedience very humiliating and
therefore very heroic.

If we were to see that a lawgiver, a lord and ruler, was
obedient to one of his subjects, allowing him to give him
orders to which he submitted, we should be greatly edified,
and call such obedience heroic. Hence we recognize it as
an edifying, pathetic, profoundly touching mystery that
Jesus, the divine and infinite Majesty, the great Creator,
Lord and Lawgiver of the whole universe, was obedient to
the work of His hands, to poor creatures brought forth
from nothing, His feeble images of clay But in this mystery it consoles and gratifies us that Our Lord selected a
virgin full of grace, and a just man; that it was Mary and
Joseph to whom He was submissive. For if a lawgiver
were to be obedient to an inferior we should expect him
to whom he thus demeaned himself to have eminent qualities. And when we see in the crucifixion that the men to
whom Jesus had to show obedience were rude, unjust,
criminal, it is still a certain consolation to know that on
this obedience the work of salvation depended; that this
obedience then gave the decision and struck the first blow
for the redemption of fallen humanity Here indeed a truth
dawns upon my mind, namely, that it is just as monstrous

and terrible for a creature to be disobedient to his Creator as for a God-man—provided He can and will be obedient —to submit Himself to criminals. I see, too, that by *this* humiliation *that* crime becomes entirely blotted out and expiated.

But now, beloved hearers, the work of redemption is accomplished; now is Jesus' time of triumph; and if it is amazing that in the Blessed Sacrament Jesus is obedient even unto death, at least we should expect Him to choose as priests, to whose word He was to be obedient, only such souls as would be, if not equal to His Mother, full of grace, and to the just St. Joseph, at least not unworthy to stand beside them.

But, my brethren, though it is true that Our Lord makes it the duty of the priests to whom He gives power over His sacred body, and at whose word He conceals Himself in the form of bread, to struggle after holiness of life, and though it is true that He chooses the priests Himself, yet again and again He chooses souls which have not only not attained to such sanctity as Mary's and Joseph's, but are exactly like all other sons of Adam, lamentably imperfect, fallible and weak. Yes, it is actually true that He not only changed a Saul into a Paul, but that He has repeatedly gone into the ranks of His enemies, and converted souls who were His persecutors, and given them the vocation to the priesthood, becoming obedient to their word in the holy sacrifice of the Mass. And though it is true that most priests, before they speak the Godlike, creative words, prove themselves, whether they be pure enough to utter them, and though it is true that the average believer before he eats this Bread proves himself, lest he eat to his condemnation, yet it is also true that Our Saviour must endure to see guilt-stained souls, with enmity in their hearts toward Him, committing the new sacrilege of profaning their God in the Most Holy Sacrament.

O beloved, the voice of an unworthy priest who speaks the solemn, creative words of consecration, the villainous heart of a hardened sinner who comes to receive holy communion—how these things put the obedience of Our Lord to the test! But, surely, only that He may prove it more plainly and more heroically. For you know that even if it is a second Judas who speaks the words of consecration, Our Lord is obedient enough to let this traitor's voice call Him into the sacred Host, and to be abused by the tiger-claws of his criminal, sin-stained hand. And you know when a wolf in sheep's clothing comes to holy communion, no fire and brimstone fall upon his tongue when he opens his mouth; no, Jesus is obedient enough to remain in the sacred Host and enter a soul that is a robber's den, the shelter of Satan. What do you say to this? Truly, beloved, such submission on the part of His divine majesty is not merely heroic obedience; it is heroic obedience carried to the highest perfection. Moreover, my brethren, I can present to you a third consideration which shows us how Jesus practises heroic obedience in the highest perfection in the Blessed Sacrament: it is the manner in which He practises and must practise this obedience.

What I mean is that Jesus must practise and really does practise this obedience in profound silence, making no outward demonstration of His grandeur. Bear in mind that obedience under such conditions was not required of Jesus in fulfilling the work of our redemption, wherein He became obedient even unto the death of the cross. When Our Lord was visibly on earth, great signs and wonders solemnly and publicly proclaimed that the God of armies, the King of all kings, had taken upon Himself the form of a servant.

Consider only the three great chapters in the history of the work of Christ's redemption. The Son of God came upon earth, was born, assumed the garb of penance, bore the form of a servant, and would perfect the great work by renouncing His right to command, taking upon Himself the deep humiliation of obedience. He began to write in the great living Book, whose title-page reads: "That I may Do the Will of My Heavenly Father." No one could see that He was the everlasting King, the Creator of all things; but behold, Heaven sends its messenger; the angel appeared in the sky, singing, "Glory to God in the highest." The celestial spirits loudly and solemnly proclaimed to earth, "The God of Israel, the God of heaven and earth, hath come."

Now Our Lord so employs His life that in all that He has to do He is guided by the commands of Joseph and Mary, and is so dependent on their will that the sole prerogative, the distinguishing characteristic of His entire life in Nazareth, is, "He was subject to them." And again, beloved, the world did not recognize this great work of condescension and self-renunciation of its God, did not grasp it; it saw only the son of the carpenter in the obedient Jesus of Nazareth, and not its Creator, Lord and Master. But behold again, it is Heaven that interferes to show the world that this obedient Jesus of Nazareth is almighty God in the form of a servant, and it proves it magnificently. One day the chosen people were gathered in a countless multitude at the river Jordan, assembled from all parts of the country, and Jesus came among them. All eyes were turned in astonishment upon Him, when John the Baptist spoke the words, "I ought to be baptized by Thee, and comest Thou to me?" But the people were dumb with wonder at what they saw and heard when Jesus was baptized. Then they saw the heavens open, and the Holy Ghost descend upon Him in the form of a dove, and from the open heavens they heard a voice, the voice of the God whom they feared and adored, saying, "This is My beloved Son, in whom I am well pleased." Behold how

magnificent is the proof by which Heaven appealed to the
world; behold, wonder and adore ! Thy Lord and thy God
has emptied Himself, is in the form of a servant, is like
to thee, is obedient.

And finally, beloved, when Jesus fulfilled the obedience
by which, according to the decrees of the eternal Father,
the work of redemption was accomplished, when He gave
up His life, allowed Himself to suffer the deepest humiliation and agony, when He was obedient unto death, even
unto the death of the cross, what happened as a proof ap-
pealing loudly to the world and showing it that it was its
God who was obedient even unto the death of the cross ?
From all inanimate, lifeless nature a cry arose. At bright
midday the sun was overcast, the earth shook to her pro-
foundest depths, the ancient rocks were burst asunder,
the sealed graves yawned, the mouldering bones were enlivened, and the skeletons of the dead wandered through
the terror-stricken streets. O beloved, what a marvellous
proof ! How loudly, how convincingly, how irresistibly it
proclaims to the world: God, Life itself, the Author and
Source of life, has become obedient even unto death, even
to the death of the cross ! Behold, my brethren, thus
by magnificent proofs has Heaven loudly and solemnly proclaimed and glorified Jesus in the midst of the deepest
humiliation, even in the obedience by which He consummated the work of redemption, proclaimed Him as the
King of kings, the Sovereign and Ruler of the whole universe, as the living God, the Lord of heaven and earth.
But now, my brethren, when Jesus has accomplished the
work of redemption, now when for Him the time of His
eternal triumph and glory at the right hand of His eternal
Father has begun, now He practises on earth an obedience
which, though not greater than His obedience of the cross,
yet surely is equal to it. He sacrifices His life anew; He
possesses all life, yet allows all employment of it to be

taken from Him, even the slightest exercise of it, and becomes obedient even to the unbloody death in the form of bread. Oh, we should certainly fancy Heaven would interfere, and that, as on the plains of Bethlehem, in the waters of the Jordan, on the heights of Golgotha, it would give some wonderful sign that here we must recognize Jesus, the King of glory, the Son of the living God, who has emptied Himself and become obedient unto death, even to the death of the form of bread.

But what happens in the most awful moment when the Lord of heaven and earth humbles Himself to His creatures in and by obedience, when He appears more insignificant than the worm of the earth crawling in the dust, when He descends even into this lifeless substance ? Beloved, what happens ? No angel voices proclaim Him; the heavens do not open, nor is the voice of the heavenly Father heard; there is no sign in the sun; the earth is not shaken; the rocks are not burst, nor do the graves open. No, never does the altar change upon which this awful Omnipotence descends; never does the hand of the priest shine in which the divine majesty rests. Unnoticed, in perfect silence, with no perceptible change in anything around Him, Jesus comes at the word of a priest under the form of bread.

Now, since Jesus is triumphant in heaven, we should have expected to see in the moment when He becomes obedient even unto death, even unto the death of the form of bread, the greatest proof of His divinity; yet no sign appears, no sound is audible making known to us that it is the King of kings who is obedient even unto the death of the appearance of bread. Thus, beloved, the obedience practised by Jesus in the Blessed Sacrament is not merely heroic obedience, but it is heroic obedience in its greatest perfection. Hence it is true that Jesus has not ceased doing out of love for us that which is and ever must be a mystery—being obedient.

Now I may say, for now it will not seem exaggerated to you, that never has a prince renounced his throne more completely and under more humiliating circumstances than has Jesus in the Blessed Sacrament. There is no depth of obedience to which He will not descend, if it is required of Him, in this Sacrament. In this lowly state He wills to be with us in this Blessed Sacrament, He on whom heaven and earth depend! And it would seem that all treasures are His except that treasure towards which His longing desire is directed—the treasure of man's free heart. For He submits to all this to win our hearts, and, moreover, in order to obtain it He will be our bondman, as Jacob served for Rachel, but not for merely twice seven years, but even to the end of the world.

Therefore it is fitting that we should assemble before Our Lord in the Blessed Sacrament to place upon His head the humble crown of our love, in return for the crown of splendor that He has relinquished for love of us.

Therefore it is fitting that we should consider whether on our part we cannot do something that is more than the *Gloria in excelsis* of the angels on Christmas morn, more than the "This is My beloved Son," uttered by the heavenly Father at the Jordan, more than the terror of inanimate nature on Good Friday, proclaiming still louder and more convincingly: He who is obedient even unto the unbloody death of the form of bread is Jesus, the King of glory; Jesus, the King of our hearts, praised through all eternity.

Perhaps you think that this is a bold conception, and that such a thing cannot be done. And yet, beloved, it not only can be done, it is done, and done by the Forty Hours. Yes, my brethren, this magnificent homage, this sublime celebration at which we Christians fall on our knees before

the Most Holy Sacrament, and publicly and solemnly adore
it, is even greater than the glorification of Jesus on the
plains of Bethlehem, in the waters of the Jordan, and on
the heights of Golgotha; it is a tribute rendered to His
obedience even to the form of bread. You must say that
I am right in this. For greater glory cannot be given Jesus
than the adoration of those who bend the knee before Him,
where through obedience He has made Himself unrecognizable, devoutly exclaiming, "Blessed be the Most Holy
Sacrament!" and singing, "Here our God Himself we
see," and chanting, "Ave Jesu!" although they behold
nothing more than the form of bread. Oh, that is a spectacle for angels and men! And this week, when it is our
turn to place on our dear Lord's head the crown of glory
which for love of us He renounced, this must be to us a
more powerful, a more irresistible inducement to solemnly
confess by our unwearying, devout adoration of the Blessed
Sacrament that Jesus, the King of glory, has humbled
Himself and has become obedient even unto death, even
unto the death of the form of bread.

And now I will not say a word more, and I cannot say
a word more, to urge you to glorify your Lord in this Holy
Sacrament for His voluntary, heroic obedience. No, now
I will turn to Jesus Our Lord in the Blessed Sacrament,
in your name, and say to Him: "O Thou King of kings,
and Lord of heaven and earth, Thou Lord of glory, Thou
who art obedient in the Blessed Sacrament even to the
form of bread, and who for this didst renounce the angels'
hymns of praise, the voice of Thy heavenly Father, the
wonderful cries of inanimate nature, Thou who awaitest
and desirest our praise, oh, accept the praise which we pour
forth to Thee; accept it when we unwearyingly pray:

"O Sacrament most holy! O Sacrament divine!
All praise and all thanksgiving be every moment Thine.

Accept also our prayer that Thou Thyself may be in this life our consolation, in death our Viaticum, and in eternity our reward; that with Mary, Thy glorious Mother, and all Thy blessed angels and saints, we may behold Thee face to face, love, praise and adore Thee for evermore." Amen.

SERMON XVII.

JESUS IN THE BLESSED SACRAMENT A HIDDEN GOD.

"Verily Thou art a hidden God, the God of Israel, the Saviour."
—*Is.* xlv. 15.

THE Church teaches and encourages us, her children, to show our respect to Our Lord in the Blessed Sacrament in manifold and significant ways. Among the demonstrations of respect established by her are two especially magnificent and solemn—the beautiful Corpus Christi procession and the solemn Forty Hours. The Church celebrates Corpus Christi to express her gratitude to Our Lord for this gracious Sacrament, and, as it is a memorial of the day of the coming among us of the King of heaven and earth in the Blessed Sacrament, she strives to pay Him corresponding honor; she bears Him in solemn, triumphal procession through the streets of the city and the meadows and fields. But Jesus has, moreover, come to us in such manner as never more to forsake His own, remaining with us for all time in this Mystery of love, and the Church requites this trait of the love of Jesus by a corresponding feast, the Forty Hours, during which, from early morning even till night, from one parish to another, ceaselessly, from hour to hour, Our Lord is publicly and solemnly adored in the Blessed Sacrament. Oh, it is a magnificent homage paid to Our Lord when the faithful flock hither, fall on their knees before the Most Holy, and never weary of saying in adoration and thanksgiving: "Blessed be the Most Holy Sacrament!"

Now this is what we shall do this week, and surely you will again respond to this invitation of the Church, for you well know that it is but a feeble proof of reciprocal love which we can give Our Lord in return for His immeasurably great love proved to us by His abiding with us in the form of bread. To-day I shall make clear to you how immeasurable is the love of Jesus in the Blessed Sacrament by dwelling on the fact that He has chosen to be with us in concealment,—as a hidden God.

I.   The greatest of all concealment is that in which Our Lord dwells with us in the Blessed Sacrament.

II.   He has assumed this great concealment for love of us.

First Point.—In the Blessed Sacrament Our Lord has brought Himself into the deepest concealment possible; nay, more, He has sunken and buried Himself in it. In saying this I have said much, but surely, my brethren, you do not think that I have exaggerated; you feel as strongly as I feel, you are as truly convinced as I am that I have spoken nothing but the truth. For you are Christians who hold fast and unshaken the faith that your Lord and God is truly present under the form of bread, you confess publicly and solemnly:

> " In the monstrance is adored
> Christ, our undivided Lord."

Hour after hour you cry to your Lord:

> " From the sacred Host is fled
> All the substance of the bread:
> Jesus Christ is here instead."

But verily, my brethren, if this that you sing be true, then certainly there is no more silent solitude, no greater seclusion, no deeper concealment than this in which Our Lord has placed Himself among us. For here everything, most truly everything of Himself is hidden, vanished, buried; here Jesus is hidden in His entire being, hidden in all His actions.

We wonder, and wonder justly, at the hidden life of Our Lord in the crib and in the house of Nazareth. Who would not wonder when he reflects that the Creator of the world lies a little feeble baby in the crib, while the brute beasts—the patient ox, the despised ass—stand there where the kings of the earth are not worthy to stand ? Oh, how veiled is the majesty of the divine Son that these beasts fearlessly stare at Him with their mild, meditative eyes! How veiled the splendor of His glory when the beasts stand there breathing out their warm breath over Him ! How hidden His divine power that His inanimate creatures, the heat and cold, the rain and wind, day and night make no distinction for Him, but exercise their agreeable and disagreeable influence on Him as on men,—exercise them in the same degree and with the same regardlessness ! How completely hidden His heavenly power that like a helpless, suffering human being He was subject with unresisting patience to all the sensations and feelings, all the deficiencies and weaknesses, all the pains and difficulties which are the ordinary portion of childhood ! And how wonderful had the fulness of divine wisdom that was in Him as He lay in the crib, as He grew in Nazareth, as He spake the words of eternal life, and spake as one having authority, so that all the people wondered and exclaimed: "A prophet has arisen, and the Lord has visited His people;" how had this fulness of divine wisdom put on in Bethlehem the garment of littleness and insignificance ! Since He had assumed the impenetrable, the inconceivable disguise of a child, the infinite Wisdom has shown to us, and shown for the long space of thirty years, that it was docile and yielding of heart to His creatures. Truly this life of Our Lord was a hidden life; if ever there was anything amazing it is this hidden life of Our Lord.

But, beloved, you will agree with me when I say that great and amazing as is the concealment of the crib and the house of Nazareth, it is far, far, further than anything words can express from the concealment in which Our Lord places Himself in the Blessed Sacrament. For, beloved, though you see that in Bethlehem and Nazareth He clothed the radiant splendor of His majesty in the flesh and blood of a feeble child, a poor laborer; and concealed the mighty hand that sustains the great earth and vast celestial bodies in immeasurable voids of space under the tender finger of a child, under the weak hand of a man; though He veiled the fulness of divine wisdom, that established the heavens and by exact laws set the bounds of the deep, that restrained the winds and distributed the watercourses, that gave the waters commandment not to overflow their limits, that apportioned the earth its strong foundations, that penetrates the depths of human hearts and makes the night as light as day; though He veiled this wisdom in the dependence, and the docility and subjection of a dutiful son: it is nevertheless true that He still went about among us in a living, recognizable human form, able to increase and grow, waxing greater in body and soul—a form fitted and able to give in itself signs of life But here in the Blessed Sacrament we see a form which has not the slightest degree of life, which cannot improve, nor increase, nor develop; a form belonging to the class of substances which are perfectly lifeless, insensible, motionless and unchangeable, so that it is actually true that not only the splendor of His divinity is hidden in the *human form,* but the divine Majesty is again concealed in the *form of bread.*

Let me say, however, in the Blessed Sacrament Jesus is not idle : He here performs the most sublime, the greatest works, and they happen and repeat themselves

so ceaselessly that it is impossible to enumerate them all
He sacrifices Himself for His people; He pleads and intercedes for them night and day; He enlightens and ad-
monishes them; He touches, rouses, protects, defends, delivers, supports, strengthens, inspires their hearts,—hearts
in such sore need of help. And yet I cannot say that the
least sign of any action, much less of such great and holy
actions, is to be perceived; I must say that though all these
sublime works are actually performed, they are completely
hidden; the sacred Host, in which and by which they
come to pass, remains motionless, and even the great work,
the great action in which He sacrifices Himself is consummated without any exterior sign; the priest in whose
hand it is accomplished must give the sign of it, or have
it given,—for everything is so completely hidden that only
to the Father who seeth in secret is it visible.

Surely, my brethren, you see, you feel, that the concealment of our dear Lord in the form of bread exceeds
by far His concealment in the crib, His concealment in
the house of Nazareth; exceeds it so far that we have no
words to express it. For as great as is the difference between the human form and the form of bread—and this
difference is great beyond all naming—even so great is
the difference between the concealment of the Son of God
when He enveloped the divine majesty in the form of a
servant, and when in this form of a servant He enveloped
Himself in the form of bread. And you must also see and
feel that much more than we can say was required of Our
Lord in bringing Himself into such utter concealment.
And I imagine you say to yourself: I should very much
like to know what has made Our Lord consent to hide
Himself forever, even to the end of time, in this greatest
of all concealment.

Now, beloved, you can learn this, you shall learn this,
for it is exactly this that I would have you consider in

your hearts. Dear brethren, the motive that has led Jesus into this greatest of all concealment is His love for us.

Second Point.—Jesus Himself has said plainly, and has caused it to be told to all men by His servants, that the true, last and sole motive for all that He has done for us is this: Because He loves us. Therefore it is always our duty to discover and consider what great love for us burns unquenchably in the Heart of Jesus, that we may constantly remind ourselves of this thought: "Behold thus thy Lord loves thee, this has thy Saviour done for love of thee."

It is in speaking of this work, wherein, in order to be with us always, in all places, He has confined Himself in the most profound, unbroken solitude and concealment, that He has especially told us, and told us by the beloved disciple who rested on His breast when the work was wrought, that therein He has revealed all the fulness of the love burning in His Heart: "Having loved His own who were in the world, He loved them to the end."

He says to us: I have loved you always, and in all that I have done; when I lay in the crib; when I fled to Egypt; when I was in Nazareth; when I went about Judea; when I bled on the cross, tortured by a thousand wounds; but when I hide Myself in the form of bread, when I reduce Myself and all that I have and am to almost nothing, and thus dwell with you at all hours and in all places, then have I done the last that a loving heart can do for its own whom it loves.

But perhaps you ask me: How is it His *love* for us that has prompted Him to remain concealed beneath the sacramental veil? O beloved, you know how it is in our own case when we love some one deeply and warmly Then we desire these two things: we like to be with the person we love, and in return we would have that person glad to be with us; we would not have him uneasy in our presence, but wish him to be familiar and confidential toward us. Our Lord has revealed this twofold desire; He says to us: "It is My delight to be with the children of men," and again: "Come to Me, all you that labor and are burdened,"—come as a child to its father. Surely you already feel and understand what His love would bring about, what He would attain in hiding Himself in the form of bread. He has found the means for perfectly satisfying the desire, the yearning and thirst of His Heart for us Surely you know now why He has taken up His abode in the form of bread, and there established His dwelling ? He conceals Himself in the form of bread, He remains in the form of bread, and He does it for love of us, for only thus can He be at the same time in all places, and at the same moment with all of His own.

It is this that He has at heart, and He counts it nothing that so much is required in order that He may lead such a hidden life in all places, even to the end of time. He conceals Himself under the appearance of bread, and remains there, and He does it for love of us, for only thus we venture to approach Him with confidence and desire. Were we to catch but a glimpse of His splendor, were He but to appear in the form of man, we should be confused, timid and anxious before the Blessed Sacrament; our hearts would never know love, longing and peaceful joy. When St. Peter was a witness of the power of the Saviour, he cried out: "Depart from me, for I am a sinful man, O Lord," and as he beheld the shadow of the heavenly glory in the transfiguration he fell helpless to the ground. How then would it be with us if Our Lord showed us His living form, if He gave us even a glimpse of His heavenly splendor when we approached Him ? Oh, I am sure those would be uncomfortable hours which we spent before the Blessed Sacrament; our hearts would throb with fear and anxiety while we were in His presence,

and each time we came to Him the coming would be an
ordeal, and especially would it be hard for us to pray to
Him, or receive Him into our hearts, if He showed us
His heavenly splendor, His divine glory. Then our
Forty Hours, our communion days would be hard days,
days of martyrdom, during which we would suffer
fear, instead of being filled with joy. Do you not
think so ? For you know, my brethren, that if we have
but to speak before a person who is our superior, and of
higher station than ours, or if we have to speak or plead
on an occasion that greatly moves or stirs us, we are confused and anxious, embarrassed in uttering a word; we
are possessed by a feeling of fright and cowardice which
overcomes us, and the greater the superiority of the person, or the more the occasion affects us, the more unable
we feel to speak calmly and collectedly, if we can speak
at all. Think of Mary Magdalen the first time that she came
to Our Lord She had so much to say to Him her heart
was full, and she had betaken herself to Him for the very
purpose of revealing it; yet when she was in His presence
she could not utter a word, she could not support herself,
she could only fall on her knees and sob and weep. What
had made her mute and speechless ? Wherefore was she so
awe-stricken and frightened ? Very many things led to
this, and naturally would have led to it, but the main reason was this: As Magdalen came close to Our Lord and
caught sight of Him, His greatness appeared clear to her,
and she was completely overcome by His majesty and holiness as well as by her own lowliness and sinfulness. It
was this, dear brethren, that so completely disconcerted
Magdalen.

And again when Our Lord passed unexpectedly through
closed doors and stood before His apostles, they were so
confused that they were unable to do what they should
have done, make reparation to Him for their treachery,

pour forth to Him thanks for this great proof of His love toward them, and beg Him to receive them again. All this, and more, would surely be in their hearts. Why, then, having so much to say to Our Lord, were they silent ? Oh, we can readily understand that the occasion affected them too deeply

Now, my brethren, do you not think that our Forty Hours would be difficult and hard days were Our Lord to suddenly lift the veil of His concealment and show us only a little of the splendor of His majesty and holiness, omnipotence and justice ? Then we should fare no better than Magdalen and the apostles. Then during the Forty Hours all hearts would be filled with anxiety and fear, and tears and sobs would burst forth from all sides. But now they are among the most beautiful, most joyful, most desired days of our life; now they are days of tender emotions, sweet consolation and ardent devotion. And whence comes this ? It comes from the fact that Our Lord is present in the Blessed Sacrament in the greatest concealment. It is these two things—that Jesus dwells with us, but dwells here completely hidden—which take from our hearts all fear, anxiety and confusion when we come to give Him a proof of our love in return for that great love by which He dwells here in our midst. Now we can open our hearts to Him; now it is a joy and comfort to do so, and with sincere delight we repeat again and again:

"O Sacrament most holy! O Sacrament divine!
All praise and all thanksgiving be every moment Thine."

Furthermore, my brethren, whence comes it that we can now go to holy communion with such great tranquillity, devotion and recollection, with so much desire, confidence, peace and joy, that the moment of communion brings such comfort and delight ? O beloved, recognize and consider the reason: it is because in the Blessed Sacrament you possess a hidden God and Saviour.

Behold, my friends, because Jesus is so completely hidden in the sacred Host you can draw near Him with tranquillity and recollection; you can sweetly dwell upon the thought how great an honor it is for you that the great and mighty God should condescend to come down to you, to rest within you, to choose your heart as His living tabernacle; and how great a blessing it is for you that your rich and bountiful God should visit you in your poverty with the fulness of His grace. And when you see yourself thus favored and beloved, in spite of your degradation, misery and sinfulness, by the Most High, the Lord, whose name is holy,—then you will be touched and your heart will be filled with tender emotions, love, confidence and desire, and you will pray with all your soul: "Lord, I am not worthy that Thou shouldst enter under my roof;" but you will add at once with faith, hope and love: "O my Jesus, my Saviour, I long for Thee; come to me now, and when Thou dost abide with me, strengthen and preserve me in Thy grace!" And thus our communion days become the happiest and most peaceful days of our life,—because Jesus in the Blessed Sacrament is a hidden God. Truly, my friends, this is love! A God will be with His creatures, a God will have His creatures perfectly fearless in His presence, and therefore He will be, and therefore in all truth He is a hidden God and Saviour— hidden in the form of bread. How right and just it is, how sacred is our duty to praise, exalt and glorify Our Lord in the Blessed Sacrament!

But we must not be content to do this privately Solemn and public adoration is due Our Lord, and we can give it Him: it is the homage paid Him in the Forty Hours. In the Blessed Sacrament Our Lord is a hidden God and Saviour, but He must not be a neglected and forsaken God and Saviour. No, beloved, Jesus, Our Lord and Saviour, hidden for love of us, shall be to us a Lord and Saviour publicly and solemnly glorified. And at least once a year we will demonstrate this with the greatest possible pomp, with all the splendor at our command. At least once a year the altar must be resplendent with the bright colors of the fragrant flowers, and shine with the flames of myriad burning candles. At least once a year Our Lord must be surrounded with every outward evidence of honor and glory, and then His faithful people must gather in great numbers around their hidden God and Saviour, and hour after hour they must kneel in adoration, praying unweariedly and ceaselessly.

"O Sacrament most holy! O Sacrament divine!
All praise and all thanksgiving be every moment Thine."

Since it is our turn this week to render to our hidden God in the Blessed Sacrament this public and solemn service of adoration, thanksgiving, reparation and prayer, let us do so with all the fervor and devotion in our power

We will spend as many hours as possible in the church during these days; we will praise and magnify, and especially thank Our Lord in the Blessed Sacrament that for love of us He has become a hidden God and Saviour, a God so loving, so condescending, so gracious, that no terror comes from His nearness to us, but rather the impulse to love Him with our whole hearts, to be with Him always, and to bless Him evermore

And how precious to Our Lord, to the Blessed Virgin, to all the angels and saints, to the entire court of heaven must be the Forty Hours thus celebrated ! For thus the intention and desire of the Sacred Heart is fulfilled. There are souls who have understood why He is a hidden God and Saviour, and value this properly. And these souls are to be congratulated, for they have reason to hope that because they have loved, adored and praised their hidden God and Saviour He will be their God for all eternity, but their God who will unfold to them His heavenly glory. O dear Lord, grant this to us all. With St. Thomas we cry to Thee:

> " Jesus, whom for the present veil'd I see,
> What I so thirst for, oh, vouchsafe to me:
> That I may see Thy countenance unfolding,
> And may be blest Thy glory in beholding."

Amen.

SERMON XVIII.

JESUS IN THE BLESSED SACRAMENT A HIDDEN GOD.
(Continued)

" Verily Thou art a hidden God."—*Is.* xlv. 15.

THE world loves display. It takes trouble for what is intrinsically worthless, even wicked and pernicious, if it be exteriorly dazzling and speciously beautiful. And as in other matters, so in this, the world has to-day many followers Man's most eager, emulative effort generally is to make an ostentatious parade. Many who have scarcely enough to eat deprive their bodies of even this scant nourishment that they may wear fine clothes Others do not hesitate to load themselves with monstrous debts, which means making themselves poorer, only to be considered rich and prosperous. On the other hand, nearly everything man deals in is false, though he calls it by a finer name— *imitations, copies* Gold, silver, precious stones, velvet, silk, furs, the materials of luxury—how many of them are imitations ! Yes, the greater proportion of human beings even disguise their faces, have false hair, false teeth, false complexions, and all merely to appear beautiful. In a word, all trades more than ever attain deplorable success in making the imitation pass for the real.

Not thus does the Lord our God act, the infinitely wise and almighty, the infinitely perfect Spirit; He is a deadly enemy to all empty display. Mankind is wont to keep the worst for within and turn the finest outside; but God, the eternal Wisdom and Omnipotence, does precisely the reverse of this, and turns the most trifling and valueless toward the outside, hiding within the most beautiful and precious.

Look at the sacred Host! Can one find a simpler, a more insignificant, a more valueless appearance? And yet Heaven is there!

> "Lo, the Good, supreme and best,
> On the altar deigns to rest;
> Is with flesh and blood our Guest."

Oh, blessed he who, with his Church, really grasps this truth! He does not join with the world in allowing himself to be misled by his senses, disdaining so sublime and invaluable a treasure, as if the infinite God were not actually present in His glory and majesty because our eyes cannot perceive Him. He trusts to the omnipotence, the wisdom and truth of his God, who has said, "This is My body." He knows that, "God Himself is here, as faith declares." And he believes this of the Blessed Sacrament, prizing it as he should, feeling grateful to Our Lord for this adorable Sacrament, and rejoicing that in the Forty Hours he has an opportunity to show a little of his love and gratitude to Our Lord in the Holy Eucharist.

Perhaps sometimes the wish has arisen in your heart that Our Lord might appear on the altar in His splendor; perhaps sometimes the question has come into your mind why, since Our Lord will only be in the Blessed Sacrament for our welfare, He has not perfected His kindness by appearing visibly there; and perhaps the thought has occurred to you that we could pray better, and more devoutly; that our devotion would be more profound and earnest, were Our Lord visible to us in the Blessed Sacrament. Now, my brethren, our holy faith does not lack a satisfactory answer to these suggestions.

It is God's delight, the inclination of His innermost

being, to dwell on earth veiled. " Verily Thou art a hidden God; " thus He had Himself announced. This is one answer, and with it each believing heart can and must be content. But our holy faith has another answer, and as we are to celebrate the Forty Hours I will enter into a detailed explanation of it. For what we shall hear will strongly incite us to keep this beautiful and sublime feast with more joyful gratitude. We learn that Jesus overwhelms us with more kindness in thus remaining hidden in the Blessed Sacrament than He would have shown us had He dwelt there openly; we learn that it is our best good which led Him to be a hidden God in the Blessed Sacrament. Yes, this is true; for by concealing Himself in the appearance of bread Our Lord has—

I. Made the use of the Blessed Sacrament easier to us;

II. Has certainly made it much more profitable and meritorious for us.

First Point.—We all understand that beholding the face of Christ as it is now when He is reigning glorious in heaven, and beholding it as it was while He was still on earth, are two very different things. And I ask where are the human eyes which, like the eagle's, can look upon the sun; or could behold Him in such bright, resplendent, burning light, and not be blinded ? Oh, truly, it was to our advantage that Our Lord ordained to veil His divine beauty and glory under that form of bread in which He dwells among us, for now we can come before the majesty of our God as it is not only our duty, but also our honor, and happiness, and blessedness, to do; adore Him on our knees, even receive Him into our hearts, with no fear of being crushed by the splendor of His infinite beauty, but consoled and glad in knowing we are with our God, and He with us.

Oh, now that Our Lord is in the Blessed Sacrament a hidden God, the use of this gracious Sacrament has been made exceedingly easy, I must say even perilously easy, to us, so that now we must guard ourselves from the guilt of irreverence.

Furthermore, I ask, which one of us, had he once beheld the divine beauty, and majesty, and grandeur, would venture to come to Our Lord familiarly ? Could we then pray to Him—I will not say with childlike confidence, freely, and with all our hearts—but could we in any way pour out to Him our cares, our necessities, our wishes, our desires ? And having beheld such great majesty, how could a man, a poor sinner, dare draw near Him and receive Him in holy communion ? Could he venture to take into his heart his Lord, who had shown Himself to him in all His splendor ? I know not whether one individual might be brought to do this in peace, tranquillity and courage; but I do know that, as we men are constituted, courage and readiness to do this would in most cases disappear in the vision of the divine beauty and glory, and we should be filled with fear, confusion and awe.

Reflect a moment on the remarkable thing told us by Holy Writ of Judith. The sacred history tells us that this heroine, a woman of unequalled beauty as she was, went entirely alone among an uncontrolled, arrogant, unbridled host; and it adds that of this multitude of impudent soldiers, addicted to excesses, which she addressed, not one committed a single bad deed; not the slightest injury was done her, and none dared say to her the least unseemly word And we are told that she not only had decked herself in the most splendid habiliments, but that God Himself actually coöperated to make her yet more charming and beautiful, so that she was surrounded by an unearthly splendor. " The Lord increased her beauty so," says the Holy Scriptures, " that she appeared to all men's eyes incomparably lovely "

Whence comes it, then, that alone among so many uncontrolled men, and with such beauty, none dared inflict upon her the most trifling insult ? Certainly this is to be ascribed first of all to God's great care and protection, at whose inspiration she went there. But besides this first and principal reason, do you know whence it came ? It came precisely from the fact that her beauty was so great, so extraordinary, so transcendent. It is the characteristic of ordinary beauty to captivate, to entangle, the hearts of those who look upon it. But what is the effect of the highest beauty ? It makes the beholders wonder, filled with awe, mute and subdued; they draw back in reverential awe, amazement and confusion. And, indeed, my brethren, what was the first feeling that overcame each of these fierce men when he saw Judith ? Was it desire, sensuality, passion at the sight of her beauty ? Oh, no; it was wonder and surprise. We read in the Holy Book: " And when these men had heard her words they beheld her face, and their eyes were amazed, for they wondered exceedingly at her beauty." Have you grasped this ? It does not say, " They were filled with desire; " it says, " They wondered exceedingly." This is exactly the first effect on us of true greatness, real nobility, highest beauty; we wonder at it, falling into amazement and confusion.

Now, my brethren, if the vision of a perishable face like Judith's made all who saw it motionless with surprise, even those who were so unbridled; if the beauty which was imprinted on her face was to them so resplendent, so awe-inspiring, then a glimpse of the eternally, divinely beautiful face of Christ would not merely fill us with wonder, amazement and confusion; but the glimpse of such a face must take from us all feeling, all consciousness, almost deprive us of life, through fear, anxiety and anguish; through the terror that would penetrate our inmost being. And if this be so, who would ever dare remain near Him ?

Where are they who would come to Him familiarly, and tell Him that they loved Him; that they had such a wish, that they needed such a grace, or longed for a certain consolation ? Who would dare receive Him into their hearts ? Oh, we should be blinded and affrighted by such great beauty, forced to close our eyes and shrink from the glory we could not bear ! It would be with us as with the bat, if at noonday it fluttered from its hole and raised its eyes to the sun; and when we were before the Blessed Sacrament the awful words of the Lord would literally be fulfilled in us when He said, " He shall go into the clefts of rocks, and into the holes of stones from the face of the fear of the Lord, and from the glory of His majesty." We should be unable to frame a thought before the Blessed Sacrament, or utter a word; anxiety, fear and awe would overwhelm us.

Great, therefore, great beyond all words, is the kindness which Our Lord shows us in the Blessed Sacrament; for in order that we may fearlessly and confidently approach Him, and remain with Him, He condescends, as He did to Moses when he stood upon the mountain, to veil His face, but with such a veil as lets none of His radiance shine through. " Thereby He spared our weakness," says the wise Hugo of St. Victor, so simply and tenderly, " not revealing Himself openly in the brightness of His majesty, but concealing Himself as under a veil." For our good has He ordained to be a hidden God. Surely this is true, and that you may see it better, and it may become more vivid to you, I will make it clear by two incidents related in the Old Law.

Surely Daniel was endowed with strong celestial vision. Yet, behold, when merely an angel was sent to him as a messenger, and when Daniel saw his countenance, he felt such terror that according to his own words he not only fell powerless, but he became unconscious. " There remained no strength in me," he says, "and I fainted away."

Tobias, Josue and Gideon, and others of their like —men who by prayer and meditation drew near to heaven confidently—in such moments as this, fell to the earth like dead men. And in the last years of his life King David always felt such aching cold in his limbs and bones that he could not be warmed, even when he was wrapped in purple garments. "When he was covered with clothes he was not warm," says Holy Writ. Do you know the cause of this unusual chill ? It came from the terror caused him by the sight of the angel who appeared to him by the threshing floor of Areuna the Jebusite, bearing in his hand a sword, although he was on the point of sheathing it Yet you know what a man of prayer King David was, and that to him heaven and the angels were nothing strange.

Now, my brethren, if this be so, and the glimpse of a mere angel effected such tremendous perturbation in these holy, divinely inspired souls, familiar with the dwellers of heaven, what would it be to us poor miserable beings if we were to behold, not an angel, but the Lord of all the angels, in His infinite beauty ? Could we bear His presence, and abide therein ? Could we surround Him confidently, pray to Him, and tell Him our troubles ? Could we receive Him into our hearts ? And how far beyond all self-control should we be in our terror; in what death-like swoon should we fall upon the earth ! When columns totter and fall, could weak reeds still stand upright ? But Our Lord has concealed all His splendor. His divine beauty, under the form of bread; He has made the Blessed Sacrament easily approachable for us. Now we can draw near to this, our great, our true and hidden God in this great Sacrament, stay with Him, pray peacefully before Him, and confidently receive Him. For here in the Blessed Sacrament do you know what He has actually done ? Let us consider it more fully.

Sometimes a monarch comes among his people *incognito,* which means unrecognized. Then he no longer bears the signs of his high rank either in his clothing or his retinue, but appears to be of the simple rank of a citizen. When this is done two things are certain: First, it shows that the king wishes to remove every trace of fear, and shyness, and embarrassment, from all who come in contact with him, and he also wills that his subjects shall be freed from acting according to the strict requirements of court etiquette. You see in this a figure of what our dear Lord has actually done, and what was His intention in coming to us and dwelling among us with His true form hidden. He wished to show us that He is in the Blessed Sacrament not so much as prince and king, but rather to come to us as our consoler, and thus be with us. He gives us to understand that He does not require from us the honor peculiar to His divine grandeur, but is content if we give Him such homage as is in our feeble power to pay; he wishes to encourage us miserable mortals to come to Him. Oh, verily, it is for our good that Our Lord has ordained to dwell with us hidden under the form of bread; for now a glimpse of the Sacrament cannot blind us, nor make our life unendurable; now we cannot shrink from it in fear and anxiety; now we feel drawn with full confidence to this great, overflowing fountain of grace; and oh, how easy is the use of this great Sacrament made to us; easier than if it were in any other form; yes, so easy that we careless, unreliable men are ever in danger of not being sufficiently reverential toward the Blessed Sacrament. But not only is the use of the Blessed Sacrament made easy for us, it is also made more meritorious and profitable for us.

Second Point.—Be assured, beloved, that the Blessed Sacrament is a treasure of grace, more profitable the more hidden it is. For, allowing that we could bear the splendor of the divine countenance, that we could bring ourselves to approach Our Lord resplendent in the light of His glory, speak to Him, eat with Him, and receive Him into our heart, what were then our merit ?   True belief consists in walking in the way of faith in everything, advancing in it steadily, not turning aside to any other way.   What, then, is faith, according to the Apostle inspired by the Holy Ghost ?   Nothing else, beloved, than "the substance of things to be hoped for, the evidence of things that appear not" (Hebrews xi. 1).   This, according to the clear definition of the Holy Ghost, is faith.   We strongly and surely hold as true everything our religion teaches, not because we can see or understand, but because God, the eternal, infallible Truth, has revealed it to us.   Faith, then, as St Augustine tersely and comprehensively says, is "to hold that true which thou seest not."   We have knowledge of what we see with our eyes, and understand with our reason—we have certain evidence and assurance of it; but we have not faith in it.   Why did St. Peter bestow such high praise upon those newly converted Christians to whom he wrote ?   Because they believed in the Christ whom he had seen, though they themselves had not beheld Him   For he wrote them, saying, "In whom now also you believe though you see Him not"   And wherein does our merit consist when we believe in the Blessed Sacrament ?   Precisely in the same thing; we believe in Jesus, our dear Lord, though we have not seen Him.   And this merit is so great that Our Lord calls those blessed who thus believe. " Because thou hast seen, Thomas," He said to the apostle, " thou hast believed: blessed are they who have not seen and yet believed."

Oh, then it is truly for our good that Our Lord has ordained to be a hidden God in the Blessed Sacrament, for how great is now our merit in believing in the Blessed

Sacrament, and of the Blessed Sacrament what we have not seen. Moreover, the merit of our belief in the Blessed Sacrament grows greater and mounts higher the more closely we examine it For we believe of the Blessed Sacrament not only what we do not see, but precisely the contrary of what we see, and should naturally think was true. We lay more weight on the hearing, on that which we hear from the lips of Jesus, and we know that what appears bread is not bread, but the true body of Our Lord Jesus Christ.

This resembles in many points what befell the aged patriarch Isaac, when instead of blessing Esau he blessed Jacob under Esau's form, and our faith can be beautifully illustrated by this story. Isaac was deceived by sight, touch, smell and taste; only the hearing deceived him not The eyes deceived him because he thought that he saw the true Esau before him; while it was not Esau, but Jacob in Esau's garments. The hand deceived him because it imagined the hairy skin it felt to be that of Esau, and it rested on furry hide, the nose deceived him because it fancied the odor which arose was that of Esau, while it was but the sweet-scented garments of Jacob; and the tongue deceived him because it imagined it tasted the wild game of Esau; but it was not, it was the flesh of a tame animal prepared by Jacob in the place of game. But did the ear join with the other senses in deceiving him ? Ah, that did not err. It was strong in the assertion, "The voice is the voice of Jacob." And had Isaac trusted rather to the ear than the other senses he would not have been deceived.

Now behold, something similar to this happens in the Blessed Sacrament. As often as the priest, like a new Isaac, raises his hand to make the sign of the cross over the sacred Host, one might fancy that which he has before him to be but bread, as it appears to be. But it is Jesus

Christ under the form of bread, just as it was Jacob under the garments of Esau. And the substance that we see, the taste that we perceive, are, as we all know, but the husk, the appearance of bread, but are in no wise the bread itself. Nevertheless, all the senses—the sight, smell, feeling, taste—will draw their conclusions as to the substance from the appearance, as is their custom. And they all cry out as with one voice, " This is bread." But the hearing courageously resists them all, proclaiming decidedly and confidently, " Not so; it is Christ, the Son of the living God." Who is it in this case also who is deceived ? Only he who, like Isaac, trusts to the eye, the hand, the nose, the tongue and the palate. But he who trusts his ear, believing in his divine Teacher, his Lord, when He says, " This is My body," corrects all the other senses, and never falls into error in his faith And he confesses joyfully and gratefully with St. Thomas Aquinas:

> " Sight, touch, and taste in Thee are each deceived;
> The ear alone most safely is believed:
> I believe all the Son of God has spoken,
> Than Truth's own word there is no surer token."

You see, my brethren, wherein the great merit of our faith in the Blessed Sacrament consists Here we not merely believe the hearing, as in the case of all the other mysteries of our faith, for all faith comes, and must come, by hearing, here we believe the ear in defiance of the other senses, however many there be which clamor against us in conspiracy. But were Christ, now enthroned in the Blessed Sacrament, to reveal Himself to us in His glory, it would be very different Then all the senses would unite to bear witness to the truth, and then we should be deprived of the merit of this belief, for then it would no longer be faith; as St Gregory the Great says, " Belief

has no merit when based on human reasoning." Then
how great is our merit in believing in the Blessed Sacrament! We not only believe what we do not see or understand, but believe the contrary of what we see and understand. Surely then it was for our good, our great profit,
that Our Lord ordained to be a hidden God in the Blessed
Sacrament, hidden under the veil of bread. And I can
give a further and greater thought on this point, a sublime
thought from St. Thomas Aquinas. You know where our
ruin began. It began in paradise, in the credence given
the arch-enemy by our first parents, when under the form
of wholesome food he offered them what was certain death.
They believed the serpent rather than God, and ate of the
forbidden fruit containing the death of the human race.
It is truly appropriate, says St. Thomas, that our restoration has its beginning in yielding faith to the words of
Christ, Our Saviour, when He says that He gives us life
under the form of perishable food

Again do you not see that Our Lord had our great
profit in view when He made Himself a God hidden under
the veil of bread in the Blessed Sacrament? Now He
gives us an opportunity as often as we adore Him, hear
Mass, or receive holy communion, to practise great and
heroic virtues; the most lively faith, the deepest humility,
the purest, most sincere attachment, the most perfect submission. And does not this prove that Our Lord has
shown much greater benevolence to us by being present
in the Blessed Sacrament in a hidden manner than if He
had revealed Himself to us in His glory? Now this great
Sacrament is not merely more fitted for our use, but it is
also far more meritorious and.profitable for us.

But if there were nothing gained, O beloved, what an
exquisite happiness it is for us that we can in this way
prove to our dear Lord the tender and great love for Him
that fills our hearts! Yes, my brethren, this is so true

that if the seraphim, the spirits of love, could feel envy, they would envy us that we can thus love our dear Lord and God whom we have present unseen among us. And now listen to one thing more. You know in what attitude these angels were once shown to the prophet Isaias. With two wings they ceaselessly flew before their Lord in sign of greatest joy. But do you know what they did with their four other wings ? They sought to conceal God from themselves. "With two they covered His face, and with two they covered His feet." And why did they do this ? We interpret this action correctly when we say that they did this to show their profound veneration and awe; but if we explain it also by saying that they did this to see if they could love Him equally when He was concealed from them, the suggestion is not to be rejected, but rather merits consideration and approval. Ah, dear friends, what a heavenly lot it must be to adore a hidden God if the citizens of heaven covet it for themselves ! And this has been our portion, not theirs ! Who, therefore, can say how great our merit will be if we know how to profit continually by such a great source of grace ?

So you see that it was for our best good, doubly for our best good, that Our Lord ordained to be present in the Blessed Sacrament as a hidden God. Thereby He has made the use of this great Sacrament truly easy to us, and certainly more meritorious and profitable for us You also see that this must be a new inducement to Christians to adore, praise and love Our Lord in the Blessed Sacrament But alas, this very fact is the cause of so many failing to show Our Lord in the Blessed Sacrament the honor due His great majesty, and even doing presumptuous things, whereby He is disregarded, dishonored, insulted; of their actually ignoring Him, behaving as though He were not present while they look around, chatter and laugh. Would they dare do this if they saw His divine face unveiled, or heard an admonishing word from His almighty lips ? What terror this would cause them !

You know the effect of one single glance of His omniscient eyes, one single word from His almighty lips, on the mob which in the Garden of Olives were rushing forward to seize Him. They were made powerless and deprived of their senses. " They fell backward to the ground," and remained lying there motionless. Yet then Our Lord was still lowly and humiliated; then He was in a condition to be judged. Now He dwells with us as He who will judge us. Who would dare to be irreverent if he had Jesus, his Judge, visibly before him ? Do you think any one would dare insult Him here were He present unveiled ? But He dwells here veiled, and therefore men presume to be irreverent toward Him. " His countenance is covered and despised." But is He not actually and truly present in His own Person in the Blessed Sacrament, although He does not allow Himself to be seen ? Oh, how sad it is to see that He is not more sincerely believed in, not more honored, even by Christians !

When the famous judge of Athens sat in judgment to pass sentence, a great curtain was drawn before him to hide him from the eyes of the accused. Would the criminal have chattered, laughed, amused himself, would he have shown even trifling disrespect to his judge ? Now, here, actually present, is Jesus, our Judge, the Judge of the living and the dead. He has a curtain before Him that conceals Him from us; God is hidden, that I admit. But is it more allowable to insult Him than if He were present here unveiled ? Surely not, my brethren, nor shall it go unpunished. Oh, may it be clear to you at least that precisely the fact that Our Lord abides veiled among us must be an incentive to us to love Him more !—certainly not make us despise Him It would be the easiest thing to Him to unveil Himself, and many times and for many souls has He done so; that He does not do so constantly is, as we now sufficiently know, only for our best good. He will thus make the use of the Blessed Sacrament easier for us, and more meritorious. To attain this end, and to procure for us this great gain, He gave no thought to all the many and great injuries and insults which He would receive if He kept the splendor and sublimity of His divine majesty hidden under the form of bread.

Now, my brethren, show to all the world that precisely because Our Lord is a hidden God in the Blessed Sacrament He has your love, gratitude and veneration; and celebrate the Forty Hours not only so that you all bear your share in it with zeal and perseverance, but also celebrate it so that you adore and praise Him with the greatest exterior and interior devotion and reverence; that you give all your being to your dear Lord and hidden God in the tiny Host. Yes, O Thou, our divine Saviour, the smaller, the more insignificant, the more unrecognizable, the more hidden Thou art in the Blessed Sacrament, the more worthy of praise, exaltation, reverence, adoration and glory Thou art in it; for we know that only for exceeding great love of us Thou art such a hidden God; and behold, what nature and human skill can offer of beauty, adornment, splendor and value we have brought and spread before Thee, and we prostrate ourselves before Thee, rejoicing in this splendor, and praying in deepest emotion, " Blessed be the Most Holy Sacrament ! " and singing in jubilant inspiration, " Ave Jesu ! "

And now, O my Jesus, Thou, our hidden God and Saviour, we have one prayer to offer to Thee; hear it, we beseech Thee. Show us in Thy kingdom the splendor of Thy divine glory, and bless those that dwell in Thy house, that they may praise Thee for all eternity. O divine Saviour, take us also into this kingdom; let us also behold Thy divine glory, make us blessed in Thy brightness, let us sing Thy praise in heaven for all eternity. O Jesus, here where Thou art hidden Thou art our God; oh, be also our God there in heaven where Thou dost reveal Thyself in Thy glory! Amen.

SERMON XIX.

JESUS IN THE BLESSED SACRAMENT FILLED WITH RE-PROACHES.

"He shall be filled with reproaches."—*Lam.* iii. 30.

THIS was the lot ordained for Jesus, for Jesus the Messias, the Expected of nations, the Saviour promised to the world. And hard, painful, heartrending as was that which was ordained for Him, it was in no degree lessened, no part was remitted Him, nor was anything taken from it; no, He had to endure everything appointed Him, and endure it as long as was ordained. This was His portion: "He was filled with reproaches."

This prophecy was fulfilled, as you know, in the cruel hours of His bitter agony and death. Ah, could we but add: But then it ended; now He is never more, nor will be ever more filled with reproaches ! But instead of this we must say: But that was not the end ! Ah, shame upon us that we must say: From that time even to this hour, in countless places and countless times, every day Our Lord is filled with reproaches. And we must add the horrible statement : Even to the end of the world, every day, in countless ways and in countless places, He will be filled with reproaches. And we must add the unnatural statement· Jesus, the Good Shepherd, is filled with reproaches in this Blessed Sacrament, where He has given the greatest proof of His love, going so far that it is not too much for Him to graciously dwell with us in

His own Person day and night in all places, under the insignificant form of bread. Behold, beloved, thus is the excessive love of Our Saviour requited: He is filled with reproaches. This is so true that it is the principal reason why the Church has established the Forty Hours. Surely, then, when we keep the Forty Hours we should give Our Lord a feeble proof of the love we bear Him in return, and it should be done to make fitting reparation for the insults heaped upon Him in the Blessed Sacrament. For this reason, and because of her wicked children, the Church causes her worthy sons to pray to Our Lord in the Blessed Sacrament. " O dearest Jesus ! May Thy blessed Mother, together with all Thy angels and saints, bless Thee for all the insults and offences which Thy ungrateful creatures have committed, or ever will commit to the end of time, against Thee the supreme Good." You see, my brethren, that I act exactly according to the intention of our Church in calling upon you to make proper reparation before the supreme Good exposed here, and seeking to excite your compassion and sympathy by showing you how Jesus is filled with reproaches in the Blessed Sacrament. We see this when we glance—

I. At His dwelling;

II. At His visitors;

III. At His reception.

First Point.—Jesus is filled with reproaches in the Blessed Sacrament because of the dwelling-places prepared for Him. There have been children who have assigned to their poor parents as an abode a little nook, a miserable corner, a hole more like a stable than a room, and have put into it the worst, oldest, most dilapidated and scantiest furniture, while they could not be content with any number of rooms, nor satisfied with the finest and most expensive furnishings for themselves. Such conduct was inhuman, cruel and heartless; the more so if in their excessive love for these children the parents had stripped themselves for their sake and given them everything. The very thought of such cruel conduct makes us shudder; how should we feel were we obliged to endure it ? Now, this shows us in a measure the greatness and bitterness of the pain that Jesus bears in the Blessed Sacrament. For what children have done in rare cases in giving their parents a wretched hovel as a dwelling, and any miserable contrivance for their use, is done by men often and in many places to our dear Lord in the Blessed Sacrament.

Our Lord has deigned to dwell with us here in His own Person; is it more than just that we should not merely give Him a clean dwelling, but should ornament this dwelling with all the beauties of art and nature ? No; it is but right and just that the most beautiful, the most precious things that man's skill can procure should be given for this dwelling of Our Saviour And since Our Lord dwells with us in such a manner that an altar, a tabernacle, linens, lights and other accessories are necessary, besides sacred vessels and vestments, it is not more than just that all these appointments be not merely complete and clean, but that they be also fitting, beautiful and precious.

Now, beloved, throughout our diocese the churches are in good condition; it cannot be generally said that they are too plain, old, or not kept in repair, or that they are untidy; and, where they are so, everything is being done according to circumstances to remedy this bad condition. We certainly have churches remarkable for their art, beauty, and even wealth of ornament ; and in each -church the greatest effort is made that all the appointments should be clean, complete, beautiful and precious. Even in the smallest churches there is a sufficient store of everything, so that variety may be had, and on feast days our altars are decked with the most splendid of these things. But, beloved, it is not so everywhere. There are Christians, nor is their number small, whose church is like anything else rather than God's house. When one enters it he starts in horror at the thought that this should be the shelter of Our Lord, and fancies he sees before him the stable in Bethlehem—so poor, so old, so dirty, so damp, so gloomy, so tumble-down is everything. And in what miserable, wretched, utterly unfit condition are the appointments of the church! how many congregations are poor in this respect! There is nothing in them but what is indispensable, and since this little is in constant use, how worn, untidy and in need of repair it is! Now, my brethren, if a congregation is so poor that it can give no better dwelling to Our Lord and make no better arrangements for Him, then it is certainly very hard and pitiful; but Our Lord is not offended, and if care is taken that everything, though it be old and poor, is still kept as clean and whole as possible, He is content; yes, He even dwells there with pleasure, as in a second Nazareth, where, too, everything was very simple and poor, but yet was really beautiful, because Mary and Joseph took care that all about it should be clean and whole.

But there are Christian congregations in good circumstances, even rich, which could, if they united, build a worthy house of God and provide suitable appointments for it with no inconvenience to themselves; yet they have a miserable church, and all its furnishings are extremely meagre, and it does not trouble them in the least; they never seem to think that it is high time for them to restore their house of God and its appointments. If its condition should be remarked, or they were called upon to repair it, they would not consent; they would refuse point blank, and have the effrontery to say that this was good for a long time yet, and delay the work of restoration, perhaps even try to prevent it. Oh, then occurs again the cruelty St. John records: "He came to His own, and His own received Him not;" there is repeated the treatment of Bethlehem, for such people tell Him: "There is no room for Thee."

My brethren, what do you say to this? Surely it pains you, and it makes you cold to think of what the Divine Heart of Jesus must feel, which has to bear such treatment. For it is a great offence to Him, and He is filled with reproaches each time and as long as any one gives Him, or allows Him, such an unworthy dwelling and such unseemly appointments. Therefore, beloved, I call upon you to make heartfelt reparation for this most unworthy treatment which Our Lord has to endure. Yes, beloved, pray with all your heart: "O dearest Jesus! May Thy blessed Mother, together with all Thy angels and saints, bless Thee for all the insults and offences which Thy ungrateful creatures have committed, or ever will commit to the end of time, against Thee the supreme Good."

But this is not the only dishonor inflicted on our dear Lord; still another reproach is His in the Blessed Sacrament: consider the visits paid Him there.

Second Point.—There are different ways of treating a friend or relative, by which sharp pain can be given him, and not the least among them is treating him as a stranger, whom one scarcely takes notice of, and to whom one is not bound by gratitude. What pain it causes one to be forsaken by his kindred, and how it hurts to have relations who never come to visit one and are utterly unconcerned about one! Ask a father who is thus treated by one of his children what he feels, and hearken to his reply. When a child treats his father as a complete stranger, coming to see him as seldom as possible, perhaps never, and taking no interest in his affairs, how the parent suffers, how the pain gnaws at his heart, what sighs burst from his oppressed bosom, what burning tears flow from his sorrowful eyes, how disconsolate is his speech ! Truly such parents are to be commiserated, and it pains us to think of such treatment, or hear of it being inflicted on any one. What should we do if we had to bear it ?

Now, beloved, this faintly shadows forth the greatness and bitterness of the pain which Jesus has to bear in the Blessed Sacrament. For in the Blessed Sacrament Our Lord is not spared this heartrending treatment; this great sorrow also is His. The forgetfulness toward a parent in not visiting him, in treating him as a stranger, shown now and then by some unnatural child, is repeatedly inflicted on our dear Lord in the Blessed Sacrament by an exceeding number of men, and for very long, and in many—nay, I must say in all places. Since Our Lord dwells most graciously and continually in the tabernacle; since He does this precisely in order that we may come to Him with all our necessities; since our needs of body and soul for time and eternity are so many and great; since it is from the Blessed Sacrament that He gives us His touching invitation: " Come to Me all ye that labor and are burdened, and I will refresh you," it behooves us to show our respect and veneration to Our Lord in quite a different manner from that which we pay to the great and mighty ones of this earth. We are not to keep ourselves at a distance, as we are accustomed to do with regard to the princes of this world; but rather to come to Jesus in the tabernacle frequently and to abide long in His presence, according to His wish. If, therefore, there be a place in the whole world that ought to be frequently visited, certainly this place is the church. But, my brethren, is the contrary not the case ? The streets are alive; men flock to the theatres in crowds; there are numerous assemblies in the public places; the pleasure halls are overfilled; only the churches, only God's house, only the

sanctuary of the Lord, only the holiest and happiest place
in which Our Lord dwells in His own Person, day after
day for hours, is quite empty, quite forsaken; seldom is
any one seen kneeling before the tabernacle.   How incalculably great is the number of Christians who let day
after day, week after week, month after month, and even
a whole year, go by without once coming to their Lord in
the Blessed Sacrament ! Yes, there are those who let their
whole life go by and never make a single visit to the
Blessed Sacrament; they live as though it were nothing
for them to treat their Saviour in the Sacrament of His
love like the most unknown and insignificant stranger.
And the number of such persons is not small; they form
a vast multitude. Nor do all these of whom I am speaking keep away from their loving Saviour and leave Him
thus alone for lack of time or opportunity to come to Him;
for we see, on the one hand, that these Christians have
plenty of time for unnecessary things, and waste a great
deal of time, and on the other hand every opportunity
is surely given them to come. for the churches are open
and it is possible to visit Our Lord all day long.   No;
there is another cause.   They remain away because they
care nothing for Our Lord in the Blessed Sacrament, and
because it seems to them quite unnecessary, quite superfluous to visit Him; because they set little value on Jesus
abiding with them.   Verily, my brethren, this treatment
of Our Lord must be pronounced unjust, improper, wrong
in the highest degree; it expresses disregard and contempt
too plainly; thus Our Lord becomes in truth filled with
reproaches.

And if you but glance around you at the conduct and
demeanor of many when they are in church at divine service, you will be witness to any number of insults and
offences inflicted on our dear Lord   Since for a twofold
reason our churches are so holy, first, because they are

sct aside as the houses of God, in which we offer to the Almighty the homage of our adoration, and second, because they are the dwelling-places of Jesus Christ, wherein He abides in His own Person, it is proper, just and necessary that Christians behave therein with interior respect and exterior decorum. The most profound quiet and silence must reign in the church; we must kneel on both knees, the hands folded, the eyes drooping, or fixed on the altar, and we must kneel there quietly and peacefully, saying recollected and heartfelt prayers, praising and blessing Our Lord, glorifying and adoring Him, thanking Him and making reparation to Him, imploring His mercy, begging for prosperity, blessing, help and grace for body and soul, for time and eternity This should be our behavior in church in the presence of Our Lord. And is this our conduct ? O beloved, how disgraceful, how shameful for us is the answer that must be given ! Who prays from the beginning of divine service to the end ? Who prays devoutly ? Who tries to pray one prayer, even one " Our Father " devoutly ? A prayer is repeated expressing the glorious praise of God, the warmest thanks, the most heartbroken contrition, the most earnest supplication; but we do not think of what it expresses, and instead of Our Lord hearing from our lips a heartfelt prayer, He hears but empty words from thoughtless lips that are like a tinkling bell shaken by the wind. And what kind of thoughts must Our Lord see in the hearts of His people below the utterance of their lips ? Bold thoughts, unfitted to His presence on His throne, which must be banished from one's mind before the altar; worldly, earthly thoughts, thoughts of business, of work, of friends, of amusement, pleasure, even thoughts which under no circumstances should be entertained; forbidden, sinful, wicked, improper, unjust, angry, envious thoughts Our Lord must see.

And would that the exterior behavior were such as it should be before Our Lord ! But if there be a place where people fearlessly permit themselves all sorts of liberties, where they act without propriety and consideration, it is the church. How unmannerly and irreverent are the positions and demeanor one sees; people stand and sit instead of kneeling and bowing. They lean on their elbows or lounge; they bow a little at the consecration and the blessing, but the hands are not folded, the arms hang loosely, or are crossed, and the head and eyes are not at rest a moment, but are continually turning from side to side. If these people make the sign of the cross or beat their breast, how meaningless and absurd these actions appear, and these irreverent Christians are sometimes seen laughing and chatting with one another, as if the church were a theatre

Beloved, no one would dare behave thus before an earthly dignitary, yet we behave thus toward the Lord, our God, and this behavior is not the conduct of a few, but of very many Oh, thus is renewed what Our Lord had to suffer on the cross ! In His bitter agony He was forsaken by so many; those who were present grieved Him, some more, others less, and only a few came to Him out of love and true devotion. And here in the Blessed Sacrament how many leave Our Lord quite alone, and of those who come nearly all sin against Our Lord by their behavior —one more, another less—and only very few are they who from true love, veneration and respect toward Him take the pains to kneel before Him properly and quietly, praying to Him with recollection and from their hearts. What do you say to this ? Surely it grieves your heart to hear it, and you shudder at the thought of what the Divine Heart of Jesus suffers in consequence of such treatment. Therefore, beloved, I call upon you to make heartfelt reparation for this unworthy treatment to which Our

Lord is subjected. Yes, my brethren, let us say with all our heart: " O dearest Jesus ! " etc.

Another great dishonor is inflicted on Our Lord in the Blessed Sacrament. Consider how Christians behave in receiving the Holy Eucharist.

Third Point.—The dishonor inflicted on Our Lord in holy communion is twofold. The first consists in the fact that most Christians receive Him far too seldom, and the second in that most people receive Him so badly. When a proffered kindness is rebuffed, a great, a keenly felt injury is inflicted on the one offering it. And the injustice is greater when the benefit to be conferred is something valuable and costing a great deal, and if he who was to be thus honored and made happy had deserved no kindness or distinction, but really merited punishment and correction. O beloved, how unjustly treated would he feel who for love of another had offered him the most costly and dearest thing that he could give, and it had been contemptuously thrust back upon him; how slighted and despised would he be if the one who treated him thus were his inferior, an inferior deserving punishment, one who were subject to him as his lord, his ruler, his king. Perhaps you think that such a thing could never be; that it is too monstrous, too inhuman. Now, my brethren, if you think so, you will better understand how Our Lord is filled with reproaches in the Blessed Sacrament. For, behold, this treatment is inflicted on Him in this very Sacrament of love.

In His exceeding love the Lord has done what no one could have anticipated or deemed possible. He has bestowed Himself completely on us; we receive Him as the nourishment of our souls, and take Him into our hearts by receiving holy communion He did not shrink from reposing in the virginal womb of Mary, and neither does He shrink from entering our heart and resting there, though it is so dry, so sin-stained, so poor in grace. Oh, what happiness, what honor, what grace for us ! In doing this Our Lord truly gives us the greatest, the most precious, the holiest thing that He could offer us, or that there is in heaven above, or in earth below. There He offers us not many, not great graces, not rare, not special graces, but Himself, the Fulness, the Source, the Author of all graces, with all His virtues and merits. Yes, even to those who might be glad to have this exceeding grace, but fear to receive into their hearts Jesus, the Holy of holies, because they know their sinfulness and unworthiness, even to them Our Lord says: I offer it to you too; I command you to receive it, and I will punish, severely punish those who will not let Me show them this love; I will consider it the greatest offence, a frightful sin, a sin that robs you of the life of grace and consequently of the life of heaven. "Except you eat the flesh of the Son of man, and drink His blood, you shall not have life in you." Behold, my brethren, so earnest is Our Lord in this offer to come to us in holy communion ! He says to you: Your insignificance and poverty, your misery and lowliness, your black ingratitude and treachery, are not reasons for your remaining away; they are rather reasons that you should come to Me, the Fountain, the Fulness and Author of all grace and sanctity. " Come to Me all you that labor and are burdened, and I will refresh you."

Now, my brethren, since the honor that Our Lord bestows upon us in coming to us in holy communion is so great; since He so earnestly desires to enter our hearts by this food of angels, and since the needs of our soul are so manifold, and so perfectly relieved at the holy table, one would imagine that all Christians ought to hail most joyously this love of the divine and compassionate Saviour, and that what happened in the lifetime of Our Lord; that as He then was surrounded by those who suffered and

sought physical relief, so our altars would be besieged by
all Christians who labor and are burdened, that their
soul might be refreshed; one would imagine that Christians would receive holy communion very often, and with
true delight. Is it so ? O beloved, how full of reproach,
how shameful to us is the answer we must give ! We are
actually forced to say that the contrary is the case ! Is
it possible, is it conceivable ? Yes, it is true; alas, it is
actually true. If there be anything in our religion which
some Catholics do unwillingly, which instead of doing
gladly they would like to escape doing, and which is a
martyrdom, a torture, a burden to them, it is the receiving of holy communion. If there be anything in our religion that is seldom performed, that is deferred—not from
day to day, nor from week to week, but from month to
month, from quarter to quarter, from half year to half year
—it is receiving holy communion Yes; Christians are even
capable of the enormity of letting years elapse without
receiving holy communion, and the Church 'has found it
necessary to command us to receive holy communion at
least once a year, under penalty of being excluded from her
fold, and forbidding Christian burial to him who does not
fulfil this law. Thus, my brethren, is Our Lord treated
in the Sacrament of His love. The greatest of all favors
that He could possibly do us, purchased so dearly at the
price of His blood, and offered us so urgently, is thrust
back upon Him contemptuously, rejected, by not merely
a few, but by many, very many—perhaps by the majority
of Christians.

Oh, such treatment is too cruel, too indecent, too out-
rageous; such treatment too plainly expresses contempt
and disregard for Our Lord; but how it increases the base-
ness of such treatment to an incalculable extent; how unprecedented it is when one considers that those who inflict this sorrow, this ingratitude on Our Lord are poor,

miserable sinners, sinners deserving eternal punishment, sinners for whom He came, to whom He has taught the way to avoid this punishment, to whom He has given the power to become children of God, for whom He has purchased the right to become fellow-citizens of the saints in heaven, and of the household of God. O beloved, when it is such as these who dislike to receive into their hearts Jesus, their Deliverer, surely the words of the prophet are fulfilled: "I have brought up children and exalted them: but they have despised me" And again: "He came unto His own, and His own received Him not." And: "There was no place for Him." Here the prophetic words are verified: "He was filled with reproaches." And, beloved, He is not only filled with reproaches because so incredibly many omit communion; still another reproach is given Him. It is that there are so many bad communions.

Do not think, my brethren, that in speaking of the reproach inflicted on Our Lord by bad communions I have in mind that horrible profanation of the Holy of holies— an unworthy or a sacrilegious communion. For such a horror and sacrilege, for such a crime the term "bad communion" is much too feeble; we really have no words strong enough to designate the vileness and meanness of such guilt. "Judas communion," "The communion of the devil"—these terms describe it in a measure, and yet we would express ourselves more strongly if we could. No, beloved, when I say that so many afflict Our Lord with reproach in the solemn and blessed moment of their communion by making it so badly, I have something very different from this in my mind; I am thinking of how most Christians behave in receiving holy communion

If it is certain that in holy communion we receive our great God, then it goes without saying that it is our sacred duty to behave exteriorly with the greatest reverence, and that as to our interior disposition we should bring Our

Lord into a well-prepared heart. Beloved, how penetrated and overwhelmed with holy awe one should be when
the solemn moment has come to go up to the King of
kings, and how it should be shown in exterior signs; it
must be seen in the gait, the carriage, the whole demeanor.
As a king has a master of ceremonies, who charges the
guests at the king's banquet as to court etiquette, so has
the Church, the representative of Our Lord, inspired and
enlightened by the Holy Ghost, specifically instructed all
Christians how to approach the banquet of the King of
heaven and earth, how to go up to the communion-rail.
We were shown this, and rehearsed in it, before the most
beautiful, holiest and happiest day of our life, before the
day of our first communion. We learned then that with
hands folded on the breast, with downcast eyes and slow
steps we must go to the communion-rail, and it was impressed upon us that we should always go to the communion-rail thus, for Our Lord never loses His divine
dignity; He remains forever the King of heaven and earth,
and as often as we communicate we go to the banquet of
the King of kings. At their first communion practically
every one goes up to the table of the Lord in this manner;
have they kept to it ? Do they come thus to-day; do all,
do even the majority thus approach the communion-rail ?
How different it has all become ! People are ashamed to
approach the celestial banquet as they should, and as
they were taught to come, and venture to go up to it in
an unseemly manner, such as one would not dare assume
before an earthly lord and ruler. And they who do this
are not few, but are many—the majority of Christians.
How many still go to the communion-rail as on the day
of their first communion ? They are so few that one can
count them But how many are they who rush up hur-
riedly, making a great noise; whose hands are not folded,
but whose arms hang down, swinging hither and thither,

or whose hands, if folded, are badly folded, and not on the breast, but much below it; whose eyes are not downcast, but are wandering to all sides ? Oh, these cannot be numbered; they are the majority. What a sight for Our Lord ! What disrespect, what disregard, what insult lies in such behavior !   And Our Lord must see this, and suffer it patiently

And only consider the condition of the heart which most Christians offer Our Lord, and whether it can be agreeable to Him, or whether new dishonor is not thereby inflicted on Him.   The chamber in which a king or prince is to dwell must be perfectly clean and fair, at least in the moment in which the mighty lord enters it; it must not be the abode of any other, least of all of his enemy.   And a great wrong would be done the sovereign were these conditions not observed.   Now, my beloved, at holy communion you can see how Our Lord is filled with reproaches, because at His coming these conditions are not fulfilled.

He who goes to holy communion must have a heart that is pure and fair.   There should not be the least stain of venial stain there through his own fault or negligence. Our Lord must find no other occupant in the heart of him who goes to holy communion, least of all an inmate disagreeable and inimical to Him.   Your inclinations, your passions must no longer dwell in your heart when your Lord comes to you; must no longer control and command you; the dear Lord must see that you have given warning to this evil inmate; that you have driven this tyrant from his throne.   He must see a strong purpose to no longer heed and hear the suggestions of your passions; to give way no longer to their continually repeated instigations and solicitations; to hear only your Lord's teaching, and to live exactly by it.   It is certainly His due, and it is our most sacred duty to bring to Our Lord a heart thus disposed.   Is this done ?   O beloved, once more how shame-

ful, how reproachful is the answer! The heart of the
Christian kneeling at the rail is not as pure and lovely as
it should be; he brings here to his Lord a heart in which
venial sin is still to be found through his own fault, besides many imperfections and evil inclinations. Thus is
Jesus brought into hearts in which are occupants that are
displeasing to Him, absolutely insupportable to Him, and
He must be united to that which He abominates. For
hearts are offered Him to dwell in of which God has but
the smallest portion; divided hearts, in which wicked inclinations have undisturbed place and control beside Our
Lord; hearts which will not sacrifice for Him their anger,
their impatience, their pride, their unkindliness; hearts
in which the glimmering fires of concupiscence are never
quite extinguished; hearts in which a ruling passion ever
increases, getting stronger foothold, and striking deeper
root; hearts in which God and Belial shall ever contend,
and which, if they do not, like the reprobate, resign themselves entirely to the world and its pleasures, yet never,
like the righteous, give themselves wholly to God and His
commandments. Hearts such as these are offered to Our
Lord; hearts wherein remain, even as He descends into
them, other and base tenants. Nor are these cases few,
nor even many, nor merely very many; the majority of
Christians bring such hearts as these to Our Lord in holy
communion Verily, this is great indifference to Our Lord,
great disregard of the Holy of holies! Thus He is sorely
dishonored; thus He is in truth filled with reproaches.

And our dear Lord is also filled with reproaches by
what Christians do after holy communion. God poured
very many and great benefits on the worthy, pious, God-
fearing family of Tobias through the archangel Raphael.
The angel made himself known to them, announced his
tidings to them, and at once disappeared. Now what did
this highly favored and happy family do? They fell on

their knees, full of gratitude, praising and adoring their God, and could not weary, nor ever cease pouring out their grateful hearts in wonder before the Lord, and for full three hours they thus employed themselves.

Now, my brethren, in holy communion we are more honored, made richer and happier than was the family of Tobias. For something more than an angel or archangel, more than the cherubim or seraphim, yes, more than all the angels and saints together, has descended and visited us. Oh, what has happened to us in the solemn moment of holy communion; what great thing has the Lord done for our soul ? The majesty of God itself, Jesus Christ, the Fulness, the Source, the Author of grace and blessedness, has descended into our heart; but not, like the angel, at once to disappear: He rests there. Oh, how right and just, what a sacred duty it is for us to be profoundly moved and carried away with wonder and emotion ! We should fall on our knees, praise and adore God, and ceaselessly thank Him for His great, incomprehensible love, goodness and mercy in deigning to come to us sinners, and enter our poor souls. How right and just, what a sacred duty it is for us to beg many graces for ourselves and for those dear to us, and for all men while still the Fountain and Author of all grace rests in us ! How right and just, and what a sacred duty it is for us to remain long sunken in profound prayer, and never weary of pouring forth this prayer and praise before Our Lord !

But when, after holy communion, instead of doing this, one immediately hastens away as if nothing marvellous, nothing worth considering, had taken place, and goes back to worldly affairs, completely forgetting the memorable event that has happened; in short, when one has Jesus with him, and never thinks of Him, what kind of conduct is this ? When one stays in the church awhile but does not know how to fill up the time, and the few minutes he

is there seem long to him; when in these few moments
that his Lord is in his heart, and he should have so much
praise and gratitude and supplication to pour forth to Him,
he scarcely knows what to say, but is quickly through, and
then kneels there, full of distractions What must we say
to such conduct ? However moderate we may be we can but
say that it is shameful conduct; that it is unspeakably ungrateful and indifferent to Our Lord, who there is indeed
filled with reproaches. For we know well, and feel
strongly, that to receive kindness and favors, and in receiving them prove one's self ungrateful, as if one had received nothing of any value, is conduct that can but
wound; for it proves indifference and disregard, and thus
reproach is inflicted on the giver. And we know well, and
feel strongly, that the greater on the one hand is the kindness received, and the greater on the other hand is the
indifference shown toward it, the more reproach the giver
endures.

Now, beloved, that is precisely what Our Lord must
suffer when in holy communion He descends into the
hearts of Christians. I need not dwell long on this; it is
sufficiently understood. I will only say this one thing:
In holy communion divine love exhausts itself; there Our
Lord gives us the greatest and best gift that He has to
bestow; yes, that there is in heaven or on earth. There
under the veil of bread He gives that which unveiled is
the satisfaction, the blessedness of the saints; He gives
Himself in His own divine Person and majesty, with the
entire fulness of His grace and merits. And yet there
are Christians who behave as if that which they receive
were worth nothing, as if it were ordinary food ! And
there are others who act as though that which they receive were not worth much; they do not rejoice in it; they
can scarcely praise and pray to God properly, and they
absent themselves from holy communion for long periods.

Nor are they few, nor even very many; they are the majority of Christians who behave thus after holy communion ! Now what do you say to all this ? Surely it pains you to hear it, it makes you shudder when you think: What must the Heart of Jesus feel under such treatment ? For it shows great indifference toward our dear Saviour, and He is filled with reproaches each time that any one goes away so quickly after holy communion, and each time that after receiving Him any one kneels there so cold and distracted.

Therefore, my brethren, I call upon you to make earnest reparation for such unworthy treatment endured by Our Lord. Yes, beloved, say with all your heart: " O dearest Jesus ! " etc.

You see, my brethren, that in the death of Jesus His sufferings did not end, but are continued in the Blessed Sacrament; there day after day, ceaselessly, in numberless places, by numberless Christians, Our Lord is filled with reproaches. In many places how unworthy is His *dwelling,* how unseemly its appointments ! And as to the *visits,* how Our Lord is neglected in the Blessed Sacrament, and how disrespectfully people behave in His presence ! And as far as the *reception of this most precious gift* goes, how coldly, how badly the majority of Christians receive holy communion ! In all three regards we see conduct full, overflowing with disrespect, disregard, indifference to Our Lord. He is filled with reproaches.

It is incomprehensible that Christians can act thus toward our dear Lord in a Sacrament wherein He bestows so much honor, such great happiness on them. But still more incomprehensible is it that to give us this Most Holy Sacrament Jesus placed Himself where He knew that even to the end of time the majority of Christians would fill Him with reproaches. For here it is not a question of such gift as many parents and friends have mourned, saying: Had I known that I should have been so treated I would not have opened my hand. No, my brethren, Our Lord foresaw that He would be so treated; He knew it perfectly, foresaw it in each individual case. Oh, then how marvellous, how incomprehensible, how wonderful it is that He has established this Sacrament, and that His words, His blessed words, " Do this for a commemoration of Me," were ever uttered ! The overwhelming flood of indifference and neglect which Jesus foresaw could not quench the ardor of His love !

Now, beloved, it is fitting that we who know this love of our divine Saviour, and this ingratitude of His people, should unite to do what devoted children do when they learn that a cruel child has pained their father's heart. How they hasten to him; how they try to comfort him by making amends for the ungrateful treatment of such a misguided child, by renewing and increasing their own love and devotion !

Then, beloved, come to Our Lord during the Forty Hours. Give His bleeding Heart the consolation of your renewal and protestation of love, gratitude and devotion, and with overflowing hearts make reparation to Him for all dishonor and insults inflicted on Him in this Most Holy Sacrament Let the words come from your heart as you pray, " O dearest Jesus ! " etc. And be assured you will not do this in vain; Our Lord will reward you richly for it; for if there is any one on whom He lavishes excessive love, it is he whose heart is compassionate for the suffering and injuries inflicted on Him. A malefactor on the cross ceased to grieve the dying Lord, and began to pity Him, and he heard the blessed words announcing his salvation: " This day shalt thou be with Me in paradise."

You will not weary in making reparation for all the insults and offences inflicted on our dear Lord. You will merit the same words of promise. From the sacred Host

Our Lord responds to your cry, " Blessed be the Most Holy Sacrament ! " and He says: " You have been constant to Me in My trials, and I will prepare for you the kingdom that My Father has prepared for Me, that you may eat and drink at My table in My kingdom." Let us glorify Jesus on earth, and we shall be glorified with Him in heaven.

> " O Sacrament most holy! O Sacrament divine!
>   All praise and all thanksgiving be every moment Thine."

Amen.

SERMON XX.

" And the Word was made flesh."—*St. John* i. 14.

THE intention of Jesus in establishing the Blessed Sacrament was to reveal His great love for us. His love for us was not content until it had brought Him into a condition in which He could dwell with us always and everywhere, and by which He could come into our hearts. This is quite certain, for He has revealed it to us by the Holy Ghost. "Having loved His own who were in the world, He loved them to the end;" loved them, then, in giving them this Blessed Sacrament. But Jesus had still another intention in establishing this Sacrament. He therein had Himself in view, and especially His sacred humanity, His holy body and precious blood. He wanted to exalt, honor, glorify His sacred body and precious blood.

Perhaps this seems to you a strange statement. For you have often heard what a great humiliation it was for Jesus to take up His abode in this little, miserable form of bread; and yet I say that it is for the glorification of His sacred body that He has a sacramental existence. If it be true that it is humiliating for Jesus to be present in the Blessed Sacrament, it seems impossible for it to be also an exaltation; one contradicts the other. At least it seems so, but it is only apparently so. For in truth it is both exaltation and humiliation.

317

When we consider what the true faith teaches of the Blessed Sacrament, that there Our Lord completely conceals His sacred humanity and gives it a hidden existence under the form of bread, it is surely a humiliation, and even a humiliation that goes so far that it is self-renunciation, and like to annihilation. But when on the other hand we further consider the teaching of the true faith on the Holy Sacrament of the Altar, what efficacy and what attributes the sacred body of Jesus has in the Blessed Sacrament, we must say that He has glorified His sacred body in giving it a sacramental existence, we must say that He could give His sacred body no greater glory than by making it a holy sacrament, and especially the Most Holy Sacrament of the Altar. And I think, my brethren, that it is appropriate for us to make this clear in the beginning of the Forty Hours. For if we fully realize how much Jesus has in view the highest honor of His sacred body in the Blessed Sacrament, it will be a stronger, more irresistible inducement to us to do what we have to do in adoration of Our Lord in the Blessed Sacrament, and especially of His holy body, with greater perseverance, love and self-denial. With this intention, therefore, and to attain this end, I will show you—

I. That the sacred body of Jesus is worthy of all honor;

II. That in the Blessed Sacrament and by the Blessed Sacrament Jesus shows His body the greatest honor.

First Point.—It was right and just that the flesh of Jesus should be glorified; yes, it was fitting that Jesus should take upon Himself to procure His sacred flesh the divine honor that is its due. And there are two reasons why this should be. The first reason is that He allows His flesh to share the inexpressibly, inconceivably great honor of being united to Him, and by His incarnation being associated with His divine Person. And the other reason is the extreme humiliation which His sacred body

underwent. It is very remarkable that St John, inspired
by the Holy Ghost, used the expression that he did in
telling us of the great, insurmountable mystery of the
incarnation He did not say: The Word was made man;
he did not say· The Word united Himself to a reasonable, intelligent nature, like the nature of an angel;
he did not say: He took a soul like to ours; no, he said
quite simply: " And the Word was made flesh." " Is not
that striking, is not that strange," exclaims St Augustine.
" The flesh of man is that which is the most worthless, the
lowliest part of him. It is precisely that in which the
dumb brute resembles him. Why, then, has the Holy
Ghost inspired His apostle to announce the great, the wonderful mystery of a God becoming man by saying, ' The
Word was made flesh ' ? Oh, that," replies this teacher, " is
to make us understand what God has done for us; what
God has become, and how deeply He has humiliated Himself for love of us; humiliated Himself so profoundly that
God as He was and is, He has not disdained to become
flesh." This is true, but precisely because this is true so
is another thing equally true, and it is this: The Holy
Ghost would thereby give us to understand how important
it is to know and realize the value, the majesty, the nobility
of the flesh of Jesus. For by virtue of the divine expression, " The Word was made flesh," I must now by all the
rules of faith say and believe: The flesh of Jesus is the
flesh of a God, the flesh of Jesus has no existence in itself
and outside of God; it is borne by God, by the Person of a
God, and the flesh of Jesus is, so to speak, a part of that
whole which is God. As in the incarnation the Word of
God was made flesh, so also by the incarnation the flesh
of man became the flesh of a God Therefore is that truth
self-evident of which I will remind you, that there is no
honor, no glory, no homage, no reverence, that is not due
the flesh of Jesus, and Our Lord having once consented to

such a noble, honorable union, cannot do too much to
honor His sacred flesh,.though He do all in His power.
And Our Lord would do this the more that in His sufferings He subjected His flesh to the most extreme, keenly
felt humiliations. For it was precisely this venerable
flesh that was overwhelmed and filled with reproaches; it
was defiled by the hands of executioners, it was torn by
scourges; and, to sum it all up, bore, if I may use the expression, all the costs of our salvation. It was really not
so much the soul of Jesus Christ, which by sacrifice
merited our salvation; it was His sacred, His divine flesh.
It was His sacred flesh that He immolated on the altar of
the cross; this flesh was perfectly holy and spotless, and
He made it bear the curse and rejection of God; this
flesh was worthy to receive all veneration and homage
from men, and He suffered it to be given over to their
insults.

Thus, in a sense it is obligatory, and it is certainly just
and right, that He indemnify it, remunerate and glorify
it in proportion to its humiliation; or rather as He humiliated it. Our Lord has done this in the Blessed Sacrament, and through the Blessed Sacrament; it was among
the intentions which He had in establishing the Blessed
Sacrament. In the Blessed Sacrament, and by the Blessed
Sacrament, He shows the greatest honor to His body.

Second Point.—The adorable body of Our Lord receives more honor, and greater honor, by the Most Holy
Mystery of the Altar than by all the other glorious mysteries which we celebrate, and at which we marvel. And
great as was the majesty, and splendor, and glory shared
by Jesus with His body as it rose triumphant from the
grave, it does not equal that glory which He has given,
and daily gives, His sacred body in the Holy Eucharist.
Perhaps this idea is new to many, and possibly some will be
troubled by it, considering it exaggerated, and that I have

fallen into that error which frequently occurs, when in order to praise one thing a person belittles another. No, my brethren, that is not the case. You see I have thought that some one might make this objection, and I assure you that nothing is further from my intention than to depreciate the glory given by Jesus to His body in the resurrection; on the contrary, I declare, wondering at them as I speak, that the attributes which the risen body of Jesus possesses are absolutely marvellous and peculiar to itself. But, beloved, I will consider the qualities which the sacred body of Jesus received in His resurrection, and those which it received in the Blessed Sacrament, and compare them. And though I must certainly marvel at the former, I must say that the latter far, far surpass them. I must wonder, my brethren, that the sacred body of Jesus, when it rose from the grave, was never more subject to death, to corruption, nor to pain, but possessed the glorious gift of incorruptibility, for that a body could be like this is truly wonderful. And it must also make me wonder that the sacred body of Jesus after His resurrection shone radiant and brilliant, that it had the glorious gift of brightness, for I know that ordinarily the human body never gives out light, radiance, or brilliancy. And we must surely be overwhelmed with wonder when we learn that the glorious risen body of Jesus sped fast as light—fast as thought—through universal space, soaring even to the throne of the Most High, having now the gift of agility. And when we learn that the body of Jesus, after the resurrection, retained its form and dimension, and yet was able not merely to pass through empty space, but through strong and naturally impassable substances; that it went forth from the grave before the stone that still securely closed the tomb had been rolled away by the angel; when we learn that He entered through closed doors the room where the apostles were assembled; when we learn that after the resurrection the body of Jesus had the gift of subtility, we are dumb with wonder. For these gifts. incorruptibility, brightness, agility, subtility, are certainly qualities belonging only to spirits It is a marvellous and a stupendous thing to see these qualities in a body, and the body possessing them is glorified and distinguished from all others. But you must note that they are qualities belonging to creatures, although they belong naturally to spiritual beings.

But if qualities and attributes and powers which are peculiar to God, which belong to the uncreated Spirit, are given, not to a spirit, but to a body, then surely of all the glories that can be conferred on a body this is the greatest; nothing can be conceived of to exceed it. Precisely such are the qualities, the powers possessed by the body of Jesus in the Blessed Sacrament. We shall see this if we do but consider what holy faith teaches us on this point. Listen: Boundlessness—that is to say, existing, or being present not in one appointed place at a time, but being present at the same time in all places, everywhere—is an attribute of God alone; none of the angels possess it. Is it not a kind of immensurability that is received by the body of Jesus in the Blessed Sacrament, since He is not in this Sacrament in one appointed place, but is present, not merely with His divinity, but also with His humanity, and especially in His humanity at the same time in so many places, in numberless places in the world, and could be present in still more places ? Build more churches, erect more altars, fill the world with them, and the body of Jesus is present in them all. How wonderful, how glorious this is ! Yet it is not all.

That quality which we admire in the boundlessness of God, namely, that He is present in each object, and each constituent part of each object, Our Lord has given His sacramental body In this Holy Sacrament He is present with His entire humanity in the whole Host, and in each portion of it. If the sacred Host, the form, is divided, Jesus is at the same time present as many times as there are divisions of the form of bread, be they ever so tiny. How wonderful, how glorious this is! And there is still more in the Blessed Sacrament for us to wonder at. The body of Jesus in the Blessed Sacrament, and by the Blessed Sacrament, is in a certain sense eternal and indestructible.

God alone, as you know, possesses the whole of life at one time, and exists always; while creatures, even spiritual beings, live their life little by little, as drops fall, and therefore in them there is continual increase and decrease. But here in the Blessed Sacrament the consecrated humanity of Our Lord possesses at once its entire life; and it is, and remains, strong in this Sacrament, even to the end of time. Yes, and more than that! Jesus dies daily in the Blessed Sacrament, but dies a death more glorious than the immortality glorifying His humanity in heaven. For He is constantly born with His whole life, through the words of a priest, in a most wonderful manner; born truly, with His entire life, but into a life that by this birth is reversed to a condition which appears like death.

Behold, my brethren, these are all magnificent actions of divine omnipotence, and they are wrought that the body of Jesus may be glorified. And how much the sacred body of Jesus is glorified by them! There it shares the attributes belonging properly only to the divine majesty of God!

But the great miracle which includes all the others, and on which Our Lord lays so much stress in the Gospel —that miracle which unfortunately Christians value so little, but which cannot be sufficiently considered, and which indisputably is the most glorious for Our Lord—is that the flesh, the body of Jesus in the Blessed Sacrament, is the nourishment of our souls. How marvellous, my brethren ! The flesh of Jesus is exactly like our flesh, an earthly, a corporeal substance, and it possesses the strength to enliven our spirit, our soul ! Does not this seem to you unprecedented, marvellous ? Yes, beloved, Our Lord has said this plainly to the Jews when He spoke to them of this Most Holy Sacrament. He did not say to them, " I am really a food," but " My flesh is food indeed " You see how clearly and comprehensively Our Lord expressed Himself.

. In this Holy Sacrament, as our faith teaches us, are truly found with the flesh of Jesus His soul and His divinity also; but that is because they are inseparably, livingly united to His body; but what is primarily and especially given us as the nourishment of our soul in this Holy Sacrament is not, according to the unmistakable words of Jesus, His soul, nor His divinity; no, it is His most holy body, His sacred flesh. To nourish our soul, to strengthen it, to preserve it in the life of faith, to bring it to full development, this is the work of the flesh, the body of Our Lord.

Surely then, my brethren, you feel that flesh which is enabled to do this, flesh that makes us spiritual, that bestows on us grace, that makes us live a supernatural life, is indisputably raised to the highest summit of honor and glory. Yes, beloved, I may say that this miracle alone raises the flesh of Jesus to a supernatural order and height. For only the flesh of a God could work such miracles, and though God has become flesh, has assumed flesh, He could not honor it more than by endowing it with the ability and strength to perform these miracles.

All this belongs to the body, the flesh of our dear Lord in the Blessed Sacrament, and the Church always whispers it in our ear in the solemn moment when in holy communion she lays on our tongue the body of Our Lord; for at the command of the Church the priest speaks the memorable, mysterious words: "The body of Our Lord Jesus Christ preserve thy soul to life everlasting." Oh, truly marvellous words, expressing an unfathomable miracle! Receive, Christian soul, says the Church, the body of thy Lord and thy God,—and wherefore? To preserve thy soul to everlasting life! Behold there, my brethren, the inestimable prerogative of the sacramental body of Jesus In the order of nature it is the soul which preserves the body; in the order of grace it is the body of Jesus which preserves our soul; and this order, which is for us an order of grace, is for the body of our dear Lord an order of glory, an order of honor,—but the highest glory, the most sublime honor.

If, then, Our Lord has so exalted His divine flesh, His sacred body, and has so glorified it, what wonder that He also presented it to us in this Holy Sacrament to receive the homage of our adoration? For what should we adore with more justice than this holy flesh, this divine body, the fountain and source of our life and immortality? In this Blessed Sacrament Our Lord has truly bestowed on His sacred body the almighty power of quickening our soul to the life of grace, and animating our spirit for heaven. "Yes," says St. Ambrose, "we pray daily to the divine body of Our Saviour, and pray to it in the Holy Mystery which He has established, and which we daily celebrate on our altars" And he adds: "This flesh of our divine Saviour is made precisely as ours is, out of clay, and in the Holy Scriptures the earth is called the footstool of God, as the heavens are called the throne of God But this footstool," he proceeds, "contemplated in the Person of the Son of God, and in the Sacrament of

His body, is more worthy of honor than the heavens, the throne of God itself, for it is God's flesh, God's body, and therefore we adore this flesh, this body, this footstool of God." "Oh, yes," St. Augustine exclaims gratefully, "my Lord and my God, no longer am I ignorant of what Thou wouldst say to us by Thy prophet when at Thy bidding he cries out: 'Adore His footstool,' which is the earth. I could not understand how one could do this without impiety, but I have found this hidden mystery: in this Holy Sacrament have I discovered it. For in this Sacrament we adore Thy divine flesh, adore it before we receive it, adore it not only without superstition, but with all the merit of faith. Yes," he exclaims to the Christians, "we must adore this flesh if it is of earth, of God's footstool, for it is the Food of salvation, and far from being sinful for us to worship the flesh of Our Saviour in the Blessed Sacrament, we are criminal if we refuse to adore in it the hidden body of Our Lord and Saviour Jesus Christ."

Now, beloved, since worship is due Our Lord in the Blessed Sacrament, and especially due His sacred body, the Church has instituted the feast of the Forty Hours. It is not enough that we adore Him all the year in silence, and by short visits make Him reparation; we Christians, each in his own parish, must also set apart a whole day, during which, from morning till night, Our Lord is continually adored by us, publicly and solemnly, and reparation made Him. Surely you will respond to the call of the Church, and bear your share piously and perseveringly in the Forty Hours.

As you have heard how much the body of Our Lord merits being glorified, and as you have heard how greatly Our Lord glorifies it in and by the Blessed Sacrament, how He allows it to be preserved in the tabernacle, and exposed in the monstrance for our adoration, surely you rejoice to have an opportunity in the celebration of the Forty Hours to bring this well-merited homage of adoration and reparation to your Lord in so solemn and sublime a manner. For you yearn to follow Our Lord's example and intention, and it is your consolation, your joy, your delight to know that you are one with Him. And since you see that in the Blessed Sacrament Jesus has in view the honor and glory of His sacred body, it inspires you with a joy that shall not be taken from you to hasten hither and honor and adore this Most Holy Sacrament, and glorify this hidden body of your Lord

Therefore, I will refrain from further exhorting you to take a proper part in this solemn adoration and reparation of the Most Holy Sacrament No, my brethren, I will no longer detain you; I will only say this: Do now what your heart urges you to do. Fall down and adore your hidden God and Saviour. Your "Blessed be the Most Holy Sacrament!" will be the more heartfelt the oftener you say it; your "O dearest Jesus!" will be more reparative the oftener you pray; your "Ave Jesu!" will be warmer the oftener you sing it, and the Te Deum, with which you conclude the sublime festival, will be the expression of the joy with which your heart is overcharged.

But Thou, O Lord Jesus, our hidden God and Saviour, let our praise and adoration and reparation be pleasing to Thee, and graciously hear us as we pray:

> "When the hour of death is near,
> And my soul is numb with fear,
> Jesus, Lord and Saviour, hear.
> Give this food to be my stay;
> Lead me on my journey's way
> Into realms of endless day."

Oh, yes, most loving, compassionate, divine Lord, hear us as we each of us cry to Thee: "In the hour of my death call me, and bid me come to Thee, that with Thy saints I may praise Thee for all eternity." Amen.

SERMON XXI.[1]

THE LIFE OF JESUS IN THE BLESSED SACRAMENT.

"He hath made a remembrance of His wonderful works."—
Ps. cx. 4.

DEARLY beloved, a pious French author writes: "How often do we say to ourselves: I should indeed have been happy if I had lived at the time when Jesus was visibly on earth, going about teaching and preaching from hamlet to hamlet in Judea and Galilee, working miracles and 'doing good to all.' Oh, to have sat at His feet on the mountain, or by the seaside, or away in the loneliness of the desert, where He went to pray! What a joy! What a help! What a consolation! How His adorable presence would have solaced and sanctified my soul! And surely He, who fed the hungry, and gave sight to the blind, and forgave the worst sinners, and even rescued the dead from the grave and gave them once more to their mothers that mourned them, surely He would have given me all I stood in need of—and how holy and how happy I should have been! My friends, what you would then have done you can do this very hour. Jesus is near you

---

[1] This sermon is taken, for the greater part, from Dr. Lierheimer's German work, "*Jesus mit uns.*" We intended it as a substitute for the four last sermons in Dr. Scheurer's "*Das grosse Gebet.*" It will be found useful and practical not only for the Forty Hours but also for all occasions on which Eucharistic Sermons are in order.—F. X. L.

still. In the church, on our altars, is the same Jesus who
was on the mountain, and by the seaside, and in the lone
desert; and He has the self-same loving Heart and the
self-same divine power to aid. He is veiled, indeed, under
the appearances of bread; you do not see Him, it is true,
with your bodily eyes, but neither did the blind people
whom He cured, they believed that He was there, and
their faith led them to follow Him. What matters it that
Jesus is hidden beneath the eucharistic veils? We know
that He is there; we see Him with the eyes of faith. Reflect, moreover, that when Jesus was preaching in Judea
it would not have been easy for you to have gained access
to Him, and to have spoken to Him alone   Many of the
crowds that followed Jesus beheld Him only from a distance, and it was but a small number of privileged souls
who had the happiness of private conversation with Him.
Far happier are we, for we can approach Him at any time.
In the Blessed Eucharist Jesus waits to speak with each
one of us in particular, that we may tell Him the wants of
our inmost heart and obtain from Him all graces particularly necessary for us."

The sentiments of this pious author suggested to us
the thought of elucidating on this occasion, preparatory
to the opening of the Forty Hours, how true it is and how
consoling that in the mysteries of the Blessed Sacrament
are reproduced the *active* life, the *suffering* life, and the
glorious life of Jesus. In other words, we shall see how
the Blessed Sacrament is the faithful picture or reproduction of the earthly life of Jesus, of the thirty-three
years that He sojourned in the world, and also of His life
of glory in heaven.

The life of Jesus on earth began with the moment of
His incarnation. When Mary, after she had received the
message of the archangel, gave her consent and spoke her
fiat, "Be it done to me according to thy word," in that

moment " the Word was made flesh," the Son of God became man by taking upon himself human nature in Mary's
womb and dwelling therein for nine months, like as a
prisoner in close confinement. The Lord was then already
in the world, yet hidden from the eyes of man; nevertheless He disclosed even in this hidden life His wonderful
power. For when the Blessed Virgin visited her cousin
Elizabeth, and the latter, divinely inspired, greeted her
with these words, " Whence is this to me that the Mother
of my Lord should come to me ? " then it was that a
stream of sanctifying grace poured forth from the blessed
Fruit of Mary's womb, and penetrating to the soul of the
unborn infant—John the Baptist,—who leaped with joy,
cleansed it from original sin.

Now, my dear friends, transfer your thoughts to the
life of Jesus in the Blessed Sacrament. Five words from
the mouth of Mary, " *Fiat mihi secundum verbum tuum,*"
sufficed to cause the Son of God to take flesh in her womb.
Similarly five words from the mouth of the priest, " *Hoc
est enim Corpus meum,*" spoken at the consecration of the
Mass, suffice to bring our blessed Lord Jesus Christ down
upon the altar to dwell in the little Host. And, to use
the words of a pious writer: " The very life of Our Lord
in the sacramental species closely resembles His life in the
bosom of His Mother. In the bosom of Mary His divinity
is hidden in a twofold manner—hidden by the living tabernacle of flesh and blood, which encompasses Him; hidden
by the humanity with which He has clothed Himself. In
the Blessed Sacrament divinity and humanity are alike
hidden—the sacred species concealing the human body
and soul of Jesus in like manner as that human body and
that human soul concealed the Godhead."

And yet, how wonderful are the operations of this
hidden God ! What virtue, what power goes forth from
the silent Prisoner of the tabernacle ! What a blessing

it is to have Our Lord near to us at all times! How
mighty is His influence upon the devout soul that kneels
before Him in the tabernacle! How great and how manifold are the streams of grace that flow from the Blessed
Sacrament into hearts that thirst for the love of God!
How the rays of divine light penetrate into hearts that
seek counsel and help! How the balm of consolation, of
hope and encouragement, is poured out upon troubled
and suffering hearts! How filled with heavenly sweetness
and rapturous joy do pious souls become at the foot of the
altar, by the mere presence of their Lord and Saviour, so
that, like Mary when she had received Elizabeth's inspired
salutation, they chant interiorly the *Magnificat:* "My soul
doth magnify the Lord and my spirit hath rejoiced in
God, my Saviour; for He that is mighty hath done great
things unto me, and holy is His name: He hath exalted
the humble; He hath filled the hungry with good things."

Let me call your attention here to another circumstance. It was Mary who carried Jesus to Elizabeth and
to John. And it is certainly a fact that those who enter-
tain a special love and veneration for Mary, as a rule, also
foster a particular devotion to the Blessed Sacrament;
Mary is for them also a mediatrix who leads them to her
divine Son. The zealous Father Faber writes: "O my
Mother! My Mother! I never have a communion but
to thee I owe it. The tabernacle, the pyx, the monstrance
—the very beauty of the Mystery—is that it is thy Jesus
and not another; the body that was formed from thee,
and not a new one, which consecration brings. And when
I come to thee on thy feasts to look at thyself, to admire
thy beauty, to praise thy grace, to glorify God for all thy
gifts, to kneel before thee and tell thee all my heart in
prayer; for thou art omnipotent in thy intercession, thou
hast Jesus with thee, and makest me feel Him even when
haply I was not thinking of Him in my mind, though

surely I am always loving Him in my heart. All our best life, all our spiritual life, is nothing but a succession of visitations—visitations from Mary, bringing Jesus with her."

This is also the thought of St. Alphonsus Liguori, in consequence of which he has affixed to his " Visits to the Blessed Sacrament " " Visits to Mary."

But let us proceed a step further. The nine months since the incarnation are drawing to a close; we journey with Mary and Joseph from Nazareth to Bethlehem. As the Evangelist tells us: " And it came to pass that when they were there, her days were accomplished, that she should be delivered. And she brought forth her first-born Son, and wrapped Him up in swaddling-clothes, and laid Him in a manger " (Luke ii. 6, 7).

On reading this, how naturally the moment of consecration at the Mass comes to our reflecting mind, when the priest, by genuflecting, first adores the new-born Saviour; then, by elevating the sacred Host, shows Him to the faithful—even as Mary showed the divine Infant to the shepherds and the kings—and finally lays Him down on the linen corporal, which represents the swaddling-clothes; or places Him in the ciborium, or monstrance, which forms, as it were, the manger; while the tabernacle reminds us of the cave, and the church itself Bethlehem.

Bethlehem means *house of bread,* and most truly is the church the *house of bread;* for here the Bread that cometh down from heaven is broken and dispensed—the Bread which gives life to the world.

But all the other mysteries also that have a relation to the birth of Our Lord stand in close affinity to the Sacred Mystery of the Altar. As kings and shepherds once adored the Babe of Bethlehem, so now high and low pay their homage to the Blessed Sacrament. As at the circumcision of the divine Child the blood flowed from His body and

He received that sacred name " at which every knee should bow," so, likewise, all knees are bent before the Blessed Sacrament; and at the separate consecration of the bread and wine the blood is, as it were, separated from the sacred body. As Our Lord was subsequently carried into the Temple, where He was recognized by Simeon and Anna, and proclaimed as the salvation of the nations; as He thus offered Himself to His heavenly Father like a morning sacrifice, which was to be consummated on the cross in the evening of His life, so now also He abides in our temples, offers Himself to His heavenly Father in the unbloody sacrifice every morning, and is acknowledged and adored by the priests and the faithful as their God and their Saviour.

He must leave Bethlehem and flee into Egypt, because a godless prince seeks to take His life. Does not something similar happen to Him in the Blessed Sacrament ? Oh, how many countries in which the Catholic faith once flourished, where grand cathedrals and stately churches once were sanctified by the real presence of Jesus upon their altars, are now robbed of this grace and blessing ! Our Lord was forced to depart from these places and to take up His abode in other lands, because those who belonged to Him would no longer recognize Him nor give Him shelter, but denied and persecuted Him

Now let us for a moment enter the Temple at Jerusalem to contemplate the boy Jesus when He was twelve years old. If we wish to find Jesus we must not look for Him in the streets, nor in play-houses, nor in the palaces of worldly minded people; no, we must seek Him in the Temple; this is His favorite dwelling-place; here He astonishes by His wisdom all who listen to His words; here, as soon as He is found, sorrow departs from troubled hearts, and gives way to peace and joy.

The speech of Our Lord, " Did you not know that

I must be about My Father's business ? " which Mary and
Joseph did not then understand, is now no longer myste-
rious, but perfectly clear to us in its deep significance:
Jesus in the Blessed Sacrament abides evermore in our
temples, because He wishes therein to be at all times our
Teacher, our *Friend,* our *Comfort,* and our *Joy.*

Upon this manifestation of the boy Jesus in the Temple follows Our Lord's hidden life of eighteen years at
Nazareth, which long period of time the Evangelist refers
to and describes by the simple statement, " He was subject to them."

To Mary alone the dignity of her divine Son was fully
revealed. The other inhabitants of Nazareth either knew
Him not at all, or else looked upon Him simply as the
son of the carpenter. Outside the walls of the town
little or nothing was known at that time of His presence.
Is not this mystery of the hidden life of Jesus reproduced
in the Blessed Sacrament ?

His Nazareth is now the tabernacle As at that time
but few people entered the house of the holy family, while
others thoughtlessly passed it by, and others again looked
with disdain upon it, so it goes on at the present day with
regard to the real presence of Our Lord in the tabernacle.
Pious Christians enter the house of God because they believe that Jesus dwells therein; they visit Him, adore Him,
pray to Him, lay before Him their sorrows and necessities,
yet never will they fully fathom the depth of this Sacred
Mystery. Heretics, however, pass by the house of God
and the tabernacle in a heedless manner; they resemble
the inhabitants of Nazareth, to whom Jesus was no more
than a man; they do not believe in the real presence;
the Host is to them merely bread—not the body of Our
Lord. Finally, also, utter strangers to the Christian faith,
infidels, pass along, and they do not take notice of Him at
all; to them the Host is not even a representation or a

remembrance of Christ, the God-man; they absolutely deny
His divinity. And yet, just as Jesus was continually subject to His creatures during those eighteen years that He
lived at Nazareth, so also in the Blessed Sacrament He
has for more than eighteen centuries hidden Himself and
lived a life of obedience without interruption. He obeys
His priests when they celebrate the holy sacrifice; He
obeys, in a manner, each one of His faithful, by coming
to him when he approaches the holy table.

After this long period of His hidden life Our Lord at
length entered upon His public career. It lasted three
years. If we cast a glance over Our Saviour's public life
we encounter again the same three classes of people.
First He was surrounded by His apostles, the pious
women and other beloved disciples and faithful adherents.
Again there were others who, having followed Him for a
time, forsook and abandoned Him in the end; and this,
indeed, they did on the very occasion when He promised
the institution of the Blessed Sacrament. Finally still
others arose against Him and persecuted Him, such as the
obstinate and hypocritical Jews and pagans. But what was
the work that Our Lord accomplished during these three
years of His public life ? He preached to the people
everywhere; He taught them the way of salvation and
scattered His benefactions in all directions; in a word, as
St. Paul tells us, " He went about doing good." Does He
not perform similar good deeds in the Blessed Sacrament ? Does He not scatter His graces broadcast from
the tabernacle ? Oh, how many wise and salutary lessons
does He not inculcate upon those who visit Him there
or receive Him at the holy table ! How many graces, how
many temporal and spiritual benefits He bestows upon
them from His altar-throne ! Jesus in the tabernacle is
now and always will be our God, our Saviour, our
Teacher, our Shepherd, our Physician, our Friend.

And what an example of mercy and charity and all
other virtues Our Lord gave to mankind in His public life ! Did He not even then love solitude and recollection without being on that account unsympathetic,
harsh or repellent ? How often He watched through the
night in prayer, seeking the solitude of the desert, the
mountain or the cave ! How often, when He had wrought
a miracle, He commanded the favored witnesses thereof
to observe silence ! How often He concealed Himself,
when men wished to lavish distinction upon Him ! And
when any one approached Him with faith and confidence,
how good and merciful, how kind and condescending, was
the divine Master ! Above all, how readily did the
Saviour receive and pardon repentant sinners ! And when
persecuted, insulted and calumniated, how patiently He
endured it all ! In a word, did He not truly seek to become all to all, because He wished to win and save all ?

Now, my friends, is Our Lord's conduct not the same
in the Blessed Sacrament ? Here His manner and mode
of operation are even more quiet, hidden and reserved.
He Himself and the entire doctrine of the Holy Eucharist
are a mystery—a deep, a most unfathomable mystery
Here He abides in silence and solitude; here He watches
through the day and through the night—often in greatest
solitude and loneliness, as in Judea—and covers His benefactions even with a more impenetrable veil; for no man
can conceive how grand, how varied, how powerful, how
beneficent, how far-reaching in their effects are the silent
and hidden operations of the Eucharistic Heart of Jesus in
the hearts of those millions who seek refuge at the altar or
present themselves at the holy table. Here He endures
with even greater meekness and humility than in Judea
the countless insults that are inflicted upon Him by those
who look with disdain and malice upon this sacred mystery. Let me call your particular attention to another

great advantage which the real presence of our dear Lord
in the Blessed Sacrament offers us in comparison with
His public life on earth. When in those days He dwelt,
for instance, in a city by the Sea of Genesareth, He could
not be found at the same time in Jerusalem; or, while He
was in Bethany, He could not be seen simultaneously by
people in Nazareth. But now, in the Blessed Sacrament,
He dwells at the same moment, simultaneously, in many
places. We cannot enter a Catholic city nor scarcely a
Catholic village in this or any other country of the world
but that He is really present there in the Blessed Sacrament. He not only now goes about doing good, but He is
at the same time in all places doing good.

Following the three years of Our Lord's public life
comes His bitter Passion and death. Without special reference to the fact that the Holy Eucharist, as a sacrifice,
is the unbloody yet real renewal of the bloody sacrifice
of the cross, consider only the similarity of the life of Jesus
in His Passion and in the Blessed Sacrament of the Altar.
You know what Our Lord had to suffer at the hands of
His wicked and perverse people; how He was falsely accused, struck in the face, mocked and spat upon, scourged
and crowned with thorns, and finally crucified. Oh, would
that our blessed Lord had not to endure similar sufferings
in the Most Holy Sacrament on account of so many who,
like Judas, receive Him in a sacrilegious manner; on account of so many unfaithful disciples, who either betray
Him or deny Him; on account of so many irreverent and
blasphemous people, who abuse the Blessed Sacrament by
cursing and swearing in its holy name; on account of those
low, vile and wretched creatures, who dare with rude and
unholy hands to break open the tabernacle, to cast the
consecrated Hosts upon the ground and even to trample
them under foot; on account of all those who crucify Him
anew by their vices and sinful deeds!

But let us turn away from this sad picture and view the reverse of the same. "And I, if I be lifted up from the eaith, will draw all things to Myself" (John xii. 32). Oh, how perfectly has this word of the crucified Saviour been fulfilled ! For what, indeed, happens on the part of the faithful when Jesus is lifted up, elevated before their eyes in the sacred Host; or when the Blessed Sacrament is exposed for public adoration, especially at the devotion of the Forty Hours ? Does not then the Lord draw all hearts to Himself; do not then the faithful draw near in crowds to the altar-throne of Jesus to make at least partial reparation for all that has been done against Him by Jews, infidels, heretics and bad Catholics; to join in spirit the holy and faithful souls who stood at the foot of the cross —the centurion, the Magdalen, John, and, above all, Mary, the sorrowful Mother—and with them offer Him their compassion, their love and adoration ?

Behold, my friends, thus is the Blessed Sacrament truly a representation, a reproduction, or rather, in a manner, the continuation of the earth-life of Jesus—of the three and thirty years that He dwelt in the holy land. It remains for us yet to point out the similarity of Our Lord's *risen* and *glorious* life and His life in the Mystery of the Altar. After Our Lord had risen from the grave, His body could suffer no more; it was a glorified, a *spiritual* body. For forty days after His resurrection He remained on earth, teaching His apostles and investing them with new powers. He instituted the Saciament of Penance; He constituted Peter the head of the Church by these words: "Feed My lambs; feed My sheep" (John xxi 15); He spoke to His disciples about the kingdom of God, i.e., not only about the kingdom of glory in heaven, where He would soon go to prepare an eternal dwelling-place for them, but also of the kingdom of God to be established on earth—of His holy Church.

Now contemplate Jesus in the Blessed Sacrament. Is not here His glorified body, which can be present everywhere and is subject to no natural power ? Is not here His glorified *risen* body ?

And the actions of Christ after the resurrection and before the ascension, do they not bear a close affinity to the Sacred Mystery of the Altar ?

Is not the Sacrament of Penance a necessary condition to the worthy reception of the Holy Eucharist ? Is not Jesus Himself in the Blessed Sacrament the supreme Shepherd of souls, who feeds and nourishes His sheep and His lambs with His own flesh and blood ? Is not the Blessed Sacrament the very heart and life of the whole Church, just as the adoration of the Holy Eucharist is the spirit of the Church ? And finally, is not this great Mystery the seed of our own future resurrection, the pledge of our eternal glory, and, as it were, the bond of union between our own and Christ's resurrection ? Not in every case did those persons to whom the Lord appeared after His resurrection recognize Him immediately, because He manifested Himself to them under a strange appearance. The two disciples on the way to Emmaus, for instance, mistook Him for a traveller, and Magdalen supposed He was the gardener. But a word, a sign, sufficed to make Him known The two disciples knew Him by the breaking of bread, and Magdalen recognized the divine Master when He called her by name Something similar happens to us with regard to the Blessed Sacrament. The eyes see but the form of bread; but when the bread is broken and offered us at the holy table, or when the Lord speaks to our soul, then our heart, too, " begins to burn within us;" then do we also taste *that the Lord is sweet;* then we recognize and acknowledge Him not only by the testimony of faith, but also by our own interior experience.

And now the time has come at last that the Lord should

leave this world and return to His Father, to enter upon His life of perfect glory, and to celebrate eternal triumphs in heaven. But He has not forgotten His own who are in the world "I will not leave you orphans," He had said. He chose to remain among us, to continue, as in His sojourn of thirty-three years upon earth, His life of abjection and humiliations; and yet, at the same time, to live a life of glory by means of the service of praise and adoration that is offered Him by the Church in the Blessed Sacrament. What the angels do in heaven who stand before the throne of His divine majesty singing, "Holy, holy, holy!"—what the Twenty-four Ancients do, who prostrate themselves before Him and cry with a loud voice: "The Lamb that was slain is worthy to receive power, and divinity, and wisdom, and strength, and honor, and glory, and benediction" (Apoc v. 12). And what the Elect do, who "follow the Lamb whithersoever It goeth in the New Jerusalem,"—that is done by the faithful on earth, by means of solemn processions and hymns of praise at the Forty Hours' Devotion and by the perpetual adoration of the Blessed Sacrament.

In quite another manner, also, Our Lord lives a life of glory here on earth; namely, in all those pious souls to whom He unites Himself in holy communion. For, just as in heaven, He is not only the object of adoration but also the fountain of happiness and joy for the Elect; so likewise in holy communion the heart of the pious communicant becomes a heaven wherein Jesus erects His throne; a heaven wherein He fills the soul with inexpressible delight, a heaven that becomes evermore agreeable to Him in proportion to the love for Him with which He finds the heart inflamed. Behold, my friends, how the Blessed Sacrament is most truly a representation, a reproduction of the mysteries of the whole life of Our Lord and Saviour Jesus Christ—of His infancy, His boyhood, His

manhood; of His incarnation, His nativity, His circumcision, His manifestation to the holy three kings, His pres-
entation in the Temple; of His hidden and His public life;
of His Passion, resurrection and ascension.

In the Blessed Sacrament we find Bethlehem, Nazareth and Jerusalem, Genesareth and Bethany, Gethsemane
and Golgotha—the holy land on earth and the true
fatherland in heaven. Yes, most truly do we find all this,
as we have seen, in the Blessed Sacrament. As it contains
Christ, whole and entire, with soul and body, with humanity and divinity; so likewise it embraces the Child Jesus
and the Man, the suffering and the dying, the risen and the
glorified Jesus,—His life of abasement and humiliation
on earth, as also His life of glory in heaven. In the Blessed
Sacrament we possess Him who has known and loved us
from eternity—our Lord, our Saviour, our God and our
All. The Blessed Sacrament is our life, our joy, our
strength and our hope. Let us therefore be grateful and
fervent adorers of the Blessed Sacrament, especially at the
Forty Hours, and let us frequently say, with hearts glowing
with love,

"O Sacrament most holy! O Sacrament divine!
All praise and all thanksgiving be every moment Thine"

THE LIFE OF THE CHURCH.

By Father Faber.

If the Blessed Sacrament is the greatest work of God, the most perfect picture of Him, and the most complete representation of Jesus, it must needs follow that it is the very life of the Church, being not only the gift of Jesus, but the very living Jesus Himself. . . . Devotion to the Blessed Sacrament is the queen of all devotions. It is the central devotion of the Church. All others gather round it, and group themselves there as satellites; for others celebrate His mysteries; this is Himself. It is the universal devotion No one can be without it in order to be a Christian. How can a man be a Christian who does not worship the living presence of Christ ? It is the devotion of all lands, of all ages, of all classes. National character makes no impression on it. It is not concerned with geography, or blood, or the influence of government. It suits no one rank, or trade, or profession, or sex, or individual temperament, more than another. How can it ? for it is the worship of God turned into a devotion by the addition of the sacramental veils It is, moreover, our daily devotion. All times are its own. As a Sacrifice it is the daily expiation, and as a Sacrament the daily bread, of the faithful.

But the Blessed Sacrament is not only the devotional life of the Church; it is also in itself a life-giving power. Indeed, it seems to embrace the whole Church and make itself coextensive with all the wants of redeemed but

exiled humanity; and it does this in a sevenfold manner
—by Mass, by communion, by benediction, by the tabernacle, by exposition, by viaticum and by procession.
. . . First and foremost is the adorable sacrifice of the
Mass, where God Himself is both Victim and Priest, and
the Majesty to whom it is offered. It is a true expiatory
sacrifice for the living and the dead, not a shadow of the
sacrifice of the cross, but the very self-same, renewed
and continued in unbloody mysteries. . . . From it is
continually rising up to the majesty of the Most Holy
Trinity a perpetual incense of adoration, intercession,
thanksgiving, satisfaction and supplication, itself in man's
imperfect words equal in worth to the worth of the uncreated God. . . . The sacrifice, as it proceeds, exhibits
the history of Our Saviour's Passion, sets forth the resurrection of the redeemed soul, and pictures the fate and
fortunes of the mystical body of Christ. In a word, the
earth lives and moves and has its being in the sacrifice
of the Mass. There is no good on earth of which it is not
the sufficient cause. There is no stay put to the ravages
of hell but through the Mass. There is no alleviation in
purgatory which is not distilled like balm from its abundant chalice. There is no increment of heavenly glory but
through the sacrifice, and no new inmate of heaven whom
the Mass has not landed in his secure immortal rest.

Communion is the second sacramental mystery. Theologians truly say that the greatest action of worship
which a creature on earth can pay to his Creator is to receive Him as his food in this tremendous mystery. When,
therefore, we reflect that communion is to the whole
spiritual world among men what food is to the natural
world, we shall perceive the way in which it is at all hours
acting with divine force and in innumerable holy mani-
festations upon the entire race of man. . . . Were we to
collect into one all the human actions that have ever been

done in the world, with all that was noble, generous, heroic, gentle, affectionate about them, and place them by the side of the act which a man performs in receiving communion, they would seem less than nothing—a shadow of a shadow. It is brighter than all glories, deeper than all sciences, and more royal than all magnificences. But what are all these ways of measuring the dignity of communion but like the leaves of the forests and the sands of the sea which we play with when we try to make a little child understand eternity, and which in truth we ourselves understand as little as he.

Benediction is as it were the evening sacrifice, as it is when noon is past that it is most usually given. It is as if the sense and instinct of Catholic devotion would fain fill the afternoon with the Blessed Sacrament as Mass fills the morning, as if it could not wait from morning to morning without some manifestation or use of the sacramental Jesus, or at least without Him could not keep His own feasts or those of His Mother, the angels, or the saints. Moreover, as if to correspond to this affectionate craving in the multitude of believers, the Church seems with the more facility and abundance to allow the various worships of the Blessed Sacrament in proportion as the wickedness, heresy and ignorance of the world outrage and blaspheme the mystery of love. St. Philip Neri once beheld Our Lord in the Host at Exposition giving benediction to the kneeling crowd, as if it were the natural attitude and customary occupation of His goodness in the Blessed Sacrament. It would be difficult to find words to express the greatness or the reality of the graces which our dear Lord imparts to us at benediction. They fall not only on the cares and sorrows, the troubles and temptations, the faults and unworthinesses, which we venture to spread before Him at the moment; but they light also on all the weak points of our soul, of which we ourselves are ignorant, and on our present circumstances, the danger of which we are unable to perceive, and on the evil spirits around us, making them stupid and nerveless, and on our dear guardian angel, rewarding him for his charitable toils, enlightening and invigorating him in his blessed office. We must remember also that the grace of benediction is not only in the faith and love which it excites in our souls, great as is that boon, but that it comes from Him solid, powerful, substantial, purifying and creative, because it participates in the reality of the Blessed Sacrament itself. Everything that has to do with this mystery enters behind the veils of this awful reality, and thus has a characteristic life which is like nothing else in our devotions. In this reality lies the attraction of the Blessed Sacrament.

The Gospels mention three especial benedictions of Our Lord, and to some one or other of these we may spiritually unite all the benedictions of the Blessed Sacrament which we receive: one, while He blesses little children, as in the tenth chapter of St. Mark, and we may in spirit prostrate ourselves beneath the shadow of His outstretched sacramental arms as if we were little ones, and desired nothing so much from Him as an increase of that childlike simplicity with which He Himself is so intensely pleased. Again, we read that at the ascension, when He was parted from the apostles, He lifted up His hands and blessed them, and at once their sorrow was turned into exceeding joy, and their timidity into bravest zeal for souls. There are times and duties when we are fain to have these graces of joy and zeal multiplied in our sad and weary souls. Again, there is the Doomsday benediction which He describes Himself as giving: " Come, ye blessed of My Father, enter into the kingdom prepared for you before the formation of the world." We may unite ourselves to His benediction to obtain the grace of final perseverance, the dearest of His gifts, because it is one so altogether His. There are some, if I may dare to recommend a practice myself, who are so overwhelmed with the extent and variety of their own wants and of Our Lord's gifts, that at the moment of benediction they bow their heads, and at each sound of the bell repeat that prayer of one of the saints of the desert, *Sicut scis et vis, Domine*—" As Thou knowest and willest, Lord !" and then add, remembering that we are blessed that moment by the very substance which was taken from Mary, those words of the office, *Et innumerabilis honestas cum illa,* " and all kinds of purity with her;" as if these two ejaculations concentrated all they had to say, and all that they would fain in that brief moment lay before the Sacred Heart of their dear Redeemer.

The tabernacle is the fourth sacramental mystery. How beautiful is the silent, patient life of that prison-house of love ! Everything about Our Lord has such endurance. It does not come and go like a transient flash of grand lightning, deepening the darkness of the night. It is not a visitation which is over before we have realized it. But just as He stood quietly among His apostles in the amazing beauty of His resurrection, and said, " Handle Me and see," so does He abide with us in the Blessed Sacrament, that we may get to know Him, to outlive our tremulous agitation and the novelty of our surprise, and to grow familiar with Him, if we can, as our lifelong Guest. There we can bring our sorrows and cares and necessities at all hours, when there is no ceremonial of the Church. We can choose our own time, and our visit can be as short or as long as duties permit or as love desires. There is an unction and a power in the mere silent companionship of the Blessed Sacrament which is beyond all words. The ways of visiting the Blessed Sacrament must be as various as the souls of men. Some love to go there to listen, some to speak, some to confess to Him, as if He were their Priest, some to examine their consciences, as before their Judge, some to do homage as to their King; some to study Him as their Doctor and Prophet, some to find shelter, as with their Creator. Some rejoice in His divinity, others in His sacred humanity, others in the mysteries of the season. Some visit Him on different days by His different titles, as God, Father, Brother, Shepherd, Head of the Church, and the like. Some visit to adore, some to intercede, some to petition, some to return thanks, some to get consolation, but all visit Him to love, and to all who visit Him in love He is a power of heavenly grace and a fountain of many goods, no single one of which the whole created universe could either merit or confer.

The fifth sacramental mystery is Exposition, than which the Church bestows upon her children no more thoroughly maternal boon. Da Ponte says that the sight of the Blessed Sacrament is the " richest vein of prayer," and he would have us look up humbly at the elevation at Mass, to catch a glimpse, like Zacheus of old, amid the branches of sycamore, of the Saviour momentarily passing by. What riches then for the spirit of prayer, when for long quiet hours the Church exposes Him for our adoration and delighted love ! . . . We may approach Him, at it were, in the company of all His creatures, and present ourselves to Him for His blessing, and give free expression in our hearts to the loyal joy we feel in being His creatures, for to be a creature, rightly considered, is our highest honor and our most precious right. Or again, which I have already spoken of, we may look upon Him as our Judge, comparing the silent, gentle majesty of the Host with His blaze of glory at the great assize, and we will be beforehand with the terrors of His judicial royalty by making peace now with His sacramental meekness.

Viaticum is the sixth mystery of the life of the adorable Host, and who can tell its power ? for it comes on the verge of life, and stretches out beyond it, and clasps and buckles together life and death, time and eternity, mortal suffering and immortal bliss. We die in the strength of the Viaticum, our judgment is tempered by its weakness, and our purgatorial pains are cooled beneath its shadow, and its energy waxes not feeble till it has landed us, with more than angelic hand, at the feet of God in heaven. Foregoing life, the coming journey, the untold spiritual and invisible combat, the many-sided act of dying—all find their mysterious completion in the plenitude of the Viaticum, and the very flesh falls to dust and is resolved into its original elements, bearing away with it the unseen force, the indiscernible, and immeasurable, and indivisible Seed which will one day call it back, make it cognizably and numerically the same, and bathe it in a flood of immortal beauty in a glorious resurrection.

The seventh mystery of the Blessed Sacrament is its procession, the highest culminating point of ecclesiastical worship and Catholic ceremony. In it is expressed the notion of triumph Our sacramental God proceeds around the Church, with all the pomp the poverty of human love can shed around Him, as the Conqueror of the human race. It is then that we feel so keenly He is our own, and that the angels can claim less in Him than we. Procession is the function of faith, which burns in our hearts and beams in our faces and makes our voices tremulous with emotion as our *Lauda Sion* bids defiance to an unbelieving world. It is the function of hope, for we bear with us our Heaven which is on earth already, our Reward who has put Himself into our hands, as it were, in pledge, and so we make the powers of hell to tremble while we tell them by shout and song how sure we are of heaven, and the adorable Sacrament meanwhile flashing radiance unbearable into the terrified intelligences of our unseen foes.

Such is the sevenfold manner in which the Blessed Sac-

rament is the life of the Church and its grand life-giving
power. But nothing can show its power more wonderfully
than that the very shadow of it should itself be one of the
greatest powers on earth. I speak of spiritual communion,
which is in truth the communion of the angels. . . . The
Council of Trent recommends it to the faithful, and St.
Thomas says, " They are considered to be communicated
spiritually, and not sacramentally, who desire to receive
this Sacrament; and they eat Christ spiritually under the
species of this Sacrament."

" This food," says St. Catherine of Sienna, speaking of
Our Lord's flesh and blood, " strengthens us little or much
according to the desire of him who receives it, in whatever
way he may receive it, sacramentally or virtually; " and
she then proceeds to describe virtual or spiritual communion St Teresa is speaking of the very great importance
of the soul's remaining alone in Our Lord's presence, and
thinking only of Him during the time of thanksgiving after
communion; and she speaks of spiritual communion by
the way when the immediate subject before her is the disposition we ought to bring in order to receive Our Lord
worthily; and from this she is led to remark that these
dispositions alone, even without the sacramental reception
of Our Lord, are productive of many graces to us. Her
words are as follows: " Whenever, my daughters, you hear
Mass and do not communicate, you can make a spiritual
communion, which is a practice of exceeding profit, and
you can immediately afterwards recollect yourselves within
yourselves, just as I advised you when you communicate
sacramentally; for great is the love of Our Lord which is
in this way infused into the soul. For when we prepare
ourselves to receive Him, He never fails to give Himself
to us in many modes which we comprehend not."

We read in the life of St. Mary Magdalen of Pazzi that
it was the custom in her monastery that when daily com-

munion was hindered by the illness of the priest or any other cause, the nuns should communicate spiritually. The usual signal for communion was given in the morning, and, all being assembled, they prayed for half an hour, and then made a spiritual communion.

What must the reality be of which the shadow is such a power ? If we had been with Jesus in Galilee, He would have been all in all to us when we knew His divinity. He would have been our first thought in the morning, our last at night. So He was with His Mother. So He is with His Church. So should He be with us on earth, as He is at all hours with those in heaven. Sometimes we seem to get a glimpse of the deep abyss of love which the Blessed Sacrament truly is, and we begin to sink beyond our depth in joy and love and wonder. We can pray no prayer, but our silence itself is prayer. We can utter no praise, but then our whole soul itself is praise. Tears begin to burn our eyes with fire, when, alas ! the world has made some noise in our soul, or self has drawn attention to itself, and the light is gone. But in heaven it will not be so. Oh, that we were come, therefore, to that happy shore, to that first unveiled sight of Jesus, which is our beatific welcome to our only true and eternal home !

PRINTED BY BENZIGER BROTHERS, NEW YORK.

STANDARD CATHOLIC BOOKS

PUBLISHED BY

BENZIGER BROTHERS,

CINCINNATI·   **NEW YORK:**   CHICAGO:
343 Main St.   36 AND 38 BARCLAY ST. 211-213 Madison St.

ABANDONMENT ; or, Absolute Surrender of Self to Divine Providence By Rev. J P. CAUSSADE, S. J. 32mo,   *net*, 0 40

ALTAR BOY'S MANUAL, LITTLE Illustrated. 32mo,   ‡0 25

AMERICAN AUTHOR SERIES OF CATHOLIC JUVENILES. 16mo, cloth
  The Blissylvania Post-Office. By MARION AMES TAGGART 16mo, 0 50
  Three Girls and Especially One. By MARION AMES TAGGART 16mo, 0 50
  By Branscome River By MARION AMES TAGGART 16mo, 0 50
  The Madcap Set at St. Anne's By MARION J BRUNOWE 16mo, 0 50
  Tom's Luck-Pot By MARY T. WAGGAMAN. 16mo, 0 50
  An Heir of Dreams By SALLIE MARGARET O'MALLEY. 16mo, 0 50
  A Summer at Woodville By ANNA T SADLIER. 16mo, 0 50

ANALYSIS OF THE GOSPELS. LAMBERT. 12mo,   *net*, 1 25

ART OF PROFITING BY OUR FAULTS, according to St. Francis de Sales By Rev. J TISSOT 32mo,   *net*, 0 40

ASER THE SHEPHERD By MARION AMES TAGGART. 16mo,   *net*, 0 35

BEZALEEL. By MARION AMES TAGGART. 16mo,   *net*, 0 35

BIBLE, THE HOLY 12mo, cloth,   0 80

BIRTHDAY SOUVENIR, OR DIARY. With a Subject of Meditation for Every Day By Mrs A E BUCHANAN. 32mo,   0 50

BLESSED ONES OF 1888. Illustrated. 16mo,   0 50

BLOSSOMS OF THE CROSS Dedicated to My Companions in Suffering for their Pious Entertainment. By EMMY GIEHRL 12mo, cloth,   1 25

BONE RULES ; or, Skeleton of English Grammar. By Rev. J B. TABB. 16mo,   0 50

BOYS' AND GIRLS' MISSION BOOK. By the Redemptorist Fathers 48mo,   ‡0 35

BREVE COMPENDIUM THEOLOGIÆ DOGMATICÆ ET MORALIS una cum aliquibus Notionibus Theologiæ Canonicæ Liturgiæ, Pastoralis et Mysticæ, ac Philosophiæ Christianæ Auctore P. J BERTHIER, M S Quarta editio, aucta et emendata 8vo, cloth, | *net*, 2 50

BUGG, LELIA HARDIN. Correct Thing for Catholics 16mo,   0 75
—— A Lady Manners and Social Usages. 16mo,   0 75
—— Prodigal's Daughter, The, and Other Stories. 12mo,   1 00

CATECHISM EXPLAINED, THE An Exhaustive Exposition of the Christian Religion, with Special Reference to the Present State of Society and the Spirit of the Age A Practical Manual for the use of the Preacher, the Catechist, the Teacher, and the Family From the original of Rev. FRANCIS SPIRAGO Edited by Rev. RICHARD F CLARKE, S J. 8vo, cloth, 720 pages,   *net*, 2 50

> This Catechism is suited to the needs of the day, and may be placed either in the hands of the people or employed as a manual for the use of Priests and Catechists It is divided into three parts : the first treats of faith, the second, of morals, the third, of the means of grace. It aims at cultivating all the powers of the soul : the understanding, the affection, and the will It does not, therefore, content itself with mere definitions. The principal object proposed in it is not to philosophize about religion, but to make men good Christians who will delight in their faith

I

CANONICAL PROCEDURE IN DISCIPLINARY AND CRIMINAL CASES OF CLERICS. By Rev F DROSIE Edited by the Right Rev S G. MESSMER, D D New edition 12mo, *net*, 1 50

CANTATA CATHOLICA Containing a large collection of Masses, &c. HELLEBUSCH Oblong 4to, *net*, 2 00

CATECHISM OF FAMILIAR THINGS. Their History and the Events which led to their Discovery. Illustrated. 12mo, *1 00

CATHOLIC BELIEF. 16mo.
Paper, *0 25, 25 copies, 4.25; 50 copies, 7 50; 100 copies, 12 50
Cloth, *0 50, 25 copies, 8 50; 50 copies, 15 00, 100 copies, 25 00

CATHOLIC CEREMONIES and Explanation of the Ecclesiastical Year. By the Abbé DURAND. With 96 illustrations. 24mo
Paper, *0.25, 25 copies, 4 25, 50 copies, 7.50; 100 copies, 12 50
Cloth, *0.50; 25 copies, 8 50, 50 copies, 15.00; 100 copies, 25 00

CATHOLIC FATHER, THE A Manual of Instructions and Devotions By Bishop EGGER 640 pages, thin paper, 32mo, †0 75

CATHOLIC MOTHER, THE. A Manual of Instructions and Devotions 32mo, cloth, †0 75

CATHOLIC HOME ANNUAL *0 25

CATHOLIC HOME LIBRARY. 10 volumes. 12mo, each, 0 45

CATHOLIC WORSHIP. BRENNAN Paper, *0 15; per 100, 9 00
Cloth, *0 25, per 100, 15 00

CATHOLIC TEACHING FOR CHILDREN. By WINIFRIDE WRAY. 16mo, cloth, 0 40

CHARITY THE ORIGIN OF EVERY BLESSING. 16mo, 0 75

CHILD OF MARY. A Complete Prayer-Book for Children of Mary. 32mo, †0 60

CHILD'S PICTURE PRAYER-BOOK Illustrated in colors. Small 32mo, †0 25

CHILD'S PRAYER-BOOK OF THE SACRED HEART. 32mo, †0 25

CHRISTIAN ANTHROPOLOGY. By Rev J. THEIN. 8vo, *net*, 2 50

CHRISTIAN FATHER, THE. Paper, *0.25; per 100, 12 50
Cloth, *0.35, per 100, 21 00

CHRISTIAN MOTHER, THE. Paper, *0.25, per 100, 12 50
Cloth, *0.35, per 100, - 21 00

CHRISTIAN PHILOSOPHY A Treatise on the Christian Soul. By the Rev. JOHN T. DRISCOLL, S.T.L 12mo, |*net*, 1 25
An attempt to set forth the main lines of Christian philosophy as enunciated in the Catechism and as systematized by the Schoolmen, especially St. Thomas

CHRIST IN TYPE AND PROPHECY. By Rev. A. J MAAS, S J 2 vols, 12mo, *net*, 4 00

CIRCUS-RIDER'S DAUGHTER, THE. A novel. By F. V. BRACKEL 12mo, 1 25

COLLEGE BOY, A A Story. By ANTHONY YORKE. 12mo, cloth, 0 85

COMEDY OF ENGLISH PROTESTANTISM, THE. Edited by A. F. MARSHALL, B.A Oxon. 12mo, *net*, 0 50

COMPENDIUM SACRÆ LITURGIÆ Juxta Ritum Romanum. WAPELHORST, O S F 8vo, *net*, 2 50

CONFESSIONAL, THE By Rt. Rev. A. ROEGEL |*net*, 1 00

CONNOR D'ARCY'S STRUGGLES. A novel. By Mrs. W. M. BERTHOLDS. 12mo, 1 25

COUNSELS OF A CATHOLIC MOTHER to Her Daughter 16mo, 0 50

CROWN OF MARY, THE A Complete Manual of Devotion for Clients of the Blessed Virgin. 32mo, †0 60

CROWN OF THORNS, THE; or, The Little Breviary of the Holy Face. 32mo, 0 40

DATA OF MODERN ETHICS EXAMINED, THE. By Rev. JOHN J MING, S.J. 12mo, *net*, 2 00

2

DE GOESBRIAND, RIGHT REV. L. Jesus the Good Shepherd. 16mo,
net, o 75
—— The Labors of the Apostles 12mo, net, 1 00

DEVOTIONS AND PRAYERS BY ST. ALPHONSUS. A Complete Prayer-
Book 16mo, †1 00

DEVOTIONS AND PRAYERS FOR THE SICK-ROOM. By Rev. Jos. A.
KREBS, C SS R. 12mo, cloth, net, 1 00

DION AND THE SIBYLS. A classic novel. By MILES GERALD KEON
12mo, 1 25

DORSEY, ELLA LORAINE. Pickle and Pepper. 12mo, o 85
—— The Taming of Polly. 12mo, o 85

EASY LANGUAGE LESSONS. 12mo, o 50

EGAN, MAURICE F. The Vocation of Edward Conway. A novel. 12mo, 1 25
—— Flower of the Flock, and Badgers of Belmont. 12mo, o 85
—— How They Worked Their Way, and Other Stories. o 75
—— The Boys in the Block 24mo, leatherette. o 25
—— A Gentleman 16mo, o 75

ENGLISH READER. By Rev. EDWARD CONNOLLY, S J. 12mo, *1 25
EPISTLES AND GOSPELS 32mo, ‡o 25
EUCHARISTIC CHRIST, THE Reflections and Considerations on the
Blessed Sacrament. By Rev. A. TESNIERE. 12mo, net, 1 00

EUCHARISTIC GEMS A Thought About the Most Blessed Sacrament for
Every Day By Rev. L C. COELENBIER 16mo, o 75

EXAMINATION OF CONSCIENCE for the use of Priests who are Making a
Retreat By GADUEL. 32mo, net, o 30

EXPLANATION OF THE BALTIMORE CATECHISM of Christian Doctrine. By Rev. THOMAS L. KINKEAD. 12mo, net, 1 00

EXPLANATION OF THE COMMANDMENTS, ILLUSTRATED By Rev.
H. ROLFUS, D D. With a Practice and Reflection on each Commandment,
by Very Rev F. GIRARDEY, C.SS R 16mo, o 75
The most popular exposition of the Commandments published It is full
of interesting stories, and contains also a reflection, practice, and prayer on
each Commandment. Beautiful full-page illustrations adorn the book The
low price of 75 cents is possible only in the anticipation of large sales, which
the publishers confidently expect for this excellent book.
Most Rev Sebastian Martinelli, D.D , Apostolic Delegate. ". . I congratulate you for this publication, which, both for the subject and the
popular style in which it is written, will be of great advantage for every
one ."

EXPLANATION OF THE GOSPELS Illustrated. 24mo.
Paper, *0.25 ; 25 copies, 4 25; 50 copies, 7.50; 100 copies, 12 50
Cloth, *0 50 ; 25 copies, 8.50; 50 copies, 15.00; 100 copies, 25 00
EXPLANATION OF THE HOLY SACRAMENTS, ILLUSTRATED. By
Rev H. ROLFUS, D D With a Reflection, Practice, and Prayer on each
Sacrament, by Very Rev. F. GIRARDEY, C SS.R 16mo, o 75
The most popular and the best explanation of the Sacraments and the
Sacramentals.
This book has been approved by His Excellency Sebastian Martinelli, D D..
Apostolic Delegate, Right Rev. Thomas Grace, D.D , Bishop of Sacramento,
Right Rev J. S Michaud, D D , Coadjutor Bishop of Burlington; Right Rev,
A. J Glorieux, D.D. Bishop of Boise City; Right Rev James Aug Healy,
D D , Bishop of Portland ; Right Rev. H Gabriels, D.D., Bishop of Ogdens-
burg , Right Rev. M. J. Hoban, D D., Coadjutor Bishop of Scranton ; Right
Rev Ign. F Horstmann, D D., Bishop of Cleveland ; Right Rev. N C. Matz,
D D , Bishop of Denver, Right Rev. Wm. Geo. McCloskey, D.D., Bishop of
Louisville, Right Rev Thomas M Lenihan, D.D., Bishop of Cheyenne
Right Rev H P Northrop, D D , Bishop of Charleston; Right Rev. E. J.
O'Dea, D D , Bishop of Nesqually, Right Rev. James Schwebach, D D ,
Bishop of La Crosse

EXPLANATION OF THE MASS. By Father VON COCHEM. 12mo, 1 25
This work is compiled from the teachings of the Church, of the early
Fathers, of theologians and spiritual writers It is written in an agreeable
and impressive manner, and cannot fail to give the reader a better acquaintance with the Mass, and to inflame him with devotion to it.

3

EXPLANATION OF THE OUR FATHER AND THE HAIL MARY
Adapted by Rev. RICHARD BRENNAN, LL D   16mo,   0 75

EXPLANATION OF THE SALVE REGINA. By St. ALPHONSUS LIGUORI.
16mo,   0 75

EXPLANATION OF THE PRAYERS AND CEREMONIES OF THE MASS,
ILLUSTRATED   By Rev. D. I. LANSLOTS, O.S.B   With 22 full-page
illustrations.   12mo,   1 25

EXTREME UNCTION.   Paper, *0.10; per 100,   5 00

FABIOLA   Illustrated Edition.   By Cardinal WISEMAN.   12mo,   0 90
Edition de luxe,   *6 00

FABIOLA'S SISTERS.   (Companion volume to "Fabiola")   By A. C.
CLARKE.   Three editions printed in three weeks.   12mo,   0 90
The most successful novel of the year.

FINN, REV FRANCIS J., S J.   Percy Wynn.   12mo,   0 85
—— Tom Playfair.   12mo,   0 85
—— Harry Dee   12mo,   0 85
—— Claude Lightfoot   12mo,   0 85
—— Ethelred Preston.   12mo,   0 85
—— That Football Game   12mo,   0 85
—— Mostly Boys   12mo,   0 85
—— My Strange Friend   24mo, leatherette.   0 25

FIRST COMMUNICANT'S MANUAL   Small 32mo,   ‡0 50

FIVE O'CLOCK STORIES.   16mo,   0 75

FLOWERS OF THE PASSION,   Thoughts of St Paul of the Cross   By Rev.
LOUIS TH. DE JÉSUS-AGONISANT.   32mo, *0.50; per 100,   25 00

FOLLOWING OF CHRIST, THE   By THOMAS À KEMPIS.
With Reflections.   Small 32mo, cloth,   ‡0 50
Without Reflections   Small 32mo, cloth,   ‡0 45
Edition de luxe   Illustrated   French sheep, gilt edges,   †1 50

FOUR GOSPELS, THE   32mo,   net, 0 10

FRANCES DE SALES, ST   Introduction to a Devout Life   32mo,   ‡0 50
—— Guide for Confession and Communion   Translated by Mrs. BENNETT-
GLADSTONE   32mo,   †0 60
—— Maxims and Counsels for Every Day.   32mo,   net, 0 35

GAME OF QUOTATIONS FROM CATHOLIC AMERICAN AUTHORS.
Series I,   net, 0 25
Series II,   net, 0 25
Series III,   net, 0 25

GENERAL PRINCIPLES OF THE RELIGIOUS LIFE.   By Very Rev.
BONIFACE F VERHEYEN, O.S.B.   32mo,   net, 0 30

GLORIES OF DIVINE GRACE   From the German of Dr. M JOS SCHEEBEN,
by a BENEDICTINE MONK.   12mo,   net, 1 50

GLORIES OF MARY.   By St. ALPHONSUS.   2 vols.   12mo,   net, 2 50

GOD KNOWABLE AND KNOWN.   RONAYNE.   12mo,   net, 1 25

GROU, REV J, S J.   The Characteristics of True Devotion   A new edition,
by Rev SAMUEL H. FRISBEE, S J   16mo,   net, 0 75

—— The Interior of Jesus and Mary.   Edited by Rev. SAMUEL H. FRISBEE,
S J   16mo, 2 vols,   net, 2 00

GOFFINE'S DEVOUT INSTRUCTIONS   Illustrated Edition.   Preface by
His Eminence Cardinal GIBBONS.   8vo, cloth,   1 00
10 copies, 7 50; 25 copies, 17.50; 50 copies,   33 50
" . . . You have conferred a great benefit on the Catholic community
. . . The work is elegantly published "—His Eminence Cardinal GIBBONS
" . .   The type and illustrations are excellent."—His Eminence
Cardinal VAUGHAN.
"It is a very extensive and invaluable collection of instructions and
devotions."—His Eminence Cardinal LOGUE
" . .   You deserve many thanks and congratulations for the attractive
and finely illustrated and economical edition. . . ."—Most Rev. M. A.
CORRIGAN, D. D., Archbishop of New York.

4

"GOLDEN SANDS." Books by the Author of:
Golden Sands Little Counsels for the Sanctification and Happiness of
    Daily Life   32mo, 3 volumes, each,   0 50
Book of the Professed. 32mo,
    Vol. I   {net, 0 75
    Vol II   } Each with a steel-plate Frontispiece.   {net, 0 60
    Vol III.   {net, 0 60
Prayer. 32mo,   net, 0 40
The Little Book of Superiors. 32mo,   net, 0 60
Spiritual Direction   32mo,   net, 0 60
Little Month of May. 32mo, flexible cloth, *0.25; per 100,   15 00
Little Month of the Poor Souls   32mo, flexible cloth, *0.25 ; per 100,   15 00
Hints on Letter-Writing   16mo,   *0 60

HANDBOOK OF THE CHRISTIAN RELIGION. By Rev. W. WILMERS, S J
    Edited by Rev. JAMES CONWAY, S J. 12mo,   net, 1 50

HAPPY YEAR, A   Short Meditations for Every Day   By ABBÉ LASAUSSE.
    12mo,   net, 1 00

HEART OF ST. JANE FRANCES DE CHANTAL, THE.   Thoughts and
    Prayers 32mo,   net, 0 40

HELP FOR THE POOR SOULS IN PURGATORY   Small 32mo,   †0 50

HESCHENBACH, W   Armorer of Solingen, The. 16mo,   0 45
—— Wrongfully Accused 16mo,   0 45
—— Inundation, The. 16mo,   0 45

HIDDEN TREASURE ; or, The Value and Excellence of the Holy Mass   By
    ST LEONARD OF PORT-MAURICE 32mo,   0 50

HISTORY OF THE CATHOLIC CHURCH. By Dr. H. BRUECK. 2 vols ,
    8vo,   net, 3 00
    The characterizing merits of this work are *clearness, precision*, and *con-
    ciseness.* What is aimed at is a compendium which will be *reliable, accurate,
    succinct,* and yet, by means of the abundant and very valuable references it
    contains, also copious. This the learned author has attained It is conceded
    to be the best work of its kind in English.

HISTORY OF THE CATHOLIC CHURCH   Adapted by Rev. RICHARD
    BRENNAN, LL D   With 90 illustrations. 8vo,   1 50

HISTORY OF THE MASS and Its Ceremonies in the Eastern and Western
    Church. By Rev JOHN O'BRIEN, A M   12mo,   net, 1 25

HISTORY OF THE PROTESTANT REFORMATION IN ENGLAND AND
    IRELAND   Written in 1824-1827   By WILLIAM COBBETT   Revised, with
    Notes and Preface, by FRANCIS AIDAN GASQUET, D D , O S B. 12mo,
    cloth, *net*, 0.50 ; paper,   net, 0 25

HOLY FACE OF JESUS, THE. A Series of Meditations on the Litany of the
    Holy Face 32mo,   0 40

HOLY GOSPELS, THE FOUR 32mo,   net, 0 10

HOURS BEFORE THE ALTAR , or, Meditations on the Holy Eucharist. By
    Mgr. DE LA BOUILLERIE. 32mo,   0 50

HOW TO COMFORT THE SICK. Especially adapted for the Instruction,
    Consolation, and Devotion of Religious Persons devoted to the Service of the
    Sick. By Rev. JOS. ALOYSIUS KREBS, C SS.R   12mo, cloth.   net, 1 00

HOW TO GET ON   By Rev BERNARD FEENEY. 12mo,   1 00

HOW TO MAKE THE MISSION   By a Dominican Father. 16mo, paper,
    *0.10 ; per 100,   5 00

HUNOLT'S SERMONS   *Complete Unabridged Edition.* Translated from the
    original German edition of Cologne, 1740, by the Rev J. ALLEN, D D
    12 vols , 8vo,   net, 30 00
    His Eminence Cardinal GIBBONS, Archbishop of Baltimore · "
    Contain a fund of solid doctrine, presented in a clear and forcible style
    These sermons should find a place in the library of every priest. .   "

HUNOLT'S SHORT SERMONS   *Abridged Edition.* Arranged for all the
    Sundays of the Year   5 vols , 8vo, |net, 10 00

IDOLS , or, The Secret of the Rue Chaussée d'Antin. A novel. By RAOUL DE
    NAVERY. 12mo,   1 25

ILLUSTRATED PRAYER-BOOK FOR CHILDREN. 32mo, †o 25

IMITATION OF THE BLESSED VIRGIN MARY. After the Model of the Imitation of Christ. Translated by Mrs. A. R. BENNETT-GLADSTONE. Small 32mo, ‡o 50
Edition de luxe, with fine illustrations. Persian calf, gilt edges 32mo,†1 50

IMITATION OF THE SACRED HEART. ARNOUDT. 16mo, †1 25

INDULGENCES, PRACTICAL GUIDE TO. By Rev. P. M BERNAD, O.M.I., o 75

IN HEAVEN WE KNOW OUR OWN. Rev. BLOT. S.J. 16mo, o 50

INSTRUCTIONS FOR FIRST COMMUNICANTS. Rev. Dr J. SCHMIDT. Small 12mo, o 50

INSTRUCTIONS ON THE COMMANDMENTS and the Sacraments. By St LIGUORI. 32mo. Paper, o.25, per 100, 12 50
Cloth, o 35 ; per 100, 21 00

INTRODUCTION TO A DEVOUT LIFE. By ST. FRANCIS DE SALES. Small 32mo, cloth, ‡o 50
Combines a course of Christian doctrine and of Scripture history, especially that of the New Testament, putting the whole into language that children will easily understand.

JACK HILDRETH AMONG THE INDIANS. Edited by MARION AMES TAGGART. A series of adventure stories, full of interest, perfectly pure, catholic in tone, teaching courage, honesty, and fidelity
1. Winnetou, the Apache Knight. 12mo, o 85
2 The Treasure of Nugget Mountain 12mo, o 85

KELLER, REV DR JOSEPH The Blessed Virgin Anecdotes and Examples to Illustrate the Honor due to the Blessed Mother of God 16mo, cloth, o 75
—— The Sacred Heart. Anecdotes and Examples to Illustrate the Honor and Glory due to the Most Sacred Heart of Our Lord. 16mo, cloth, o 75
—— The Most Holy Sacrament. Anecdotes and Examples to Illustrate the Honor and Glory due to the Most Holy Sacrament of the Altar 16mo, cloth, o 75
—— St. Anthony. Anecdotes Proving the Miraculous Power of St. Anthony of Padua 16mo, cloth, o 75
The object of these four books is to confirm, perfect, and to spread devotion to the Blessed Virgin, the Sacred Heart, the Blessed Sacrament, and St. Anthony.

KEY OF HEAVEN. Large Type. With Epistles and Gospels Small 32mo, o 40

KLONDIKE PICNIC, A By ELEANOR C DONNELLY 12mo, o 85

KONINGS, THEOLOGIA MORALIS. Novissimi Ecclesiæ Doctoris S Alphonsi. Editio septima, auctior, et novis curis expolitior, curante HENRICO KUPER, C.SS.R Two vols. in one, half morocco, net, 4 00
—— Commentarium in Facultates Apostolicas New, greatly enlarged edition. 12mo, net, 2 25
—— General Confession Made Easy. 32mo, flexible, *o 15

LEGENDS AND STORIES OF THE HOLY CHILD JESUS from Many Lands Collected by A. FOWLER LUTZ. 16mo, o 75

LET NO MAN PUT ASUNDER. A novel. By JOSEPHINE MARIÉ 12mo, 1 00

LIFE AND ACTS OF LEO XIII Illustrated. 8vo, 1 50

LIFE OF ST. ALOYSIUS GONZAGA. Richly illustrated 8vo, net, 2 50

LIFE OF ST ALOYSIUS GONZAGA. Edited by Rev. J F X. O'CONOR, S.J 12mo, net, o 75

LIFE OF ST ANTHONY See ST ANTHONY

LIFE OF THE BLESSED VIRGIN, ILLUSTRATED Adapted by Rev RICHARD BRENNAN, LL D With fine half-tone illustrations. 12mo, 1 25
The most popular, most interesting, and most beautiful Life of the Blessed Virgin published in English.
It is a Life of the Blessed Virgin for the people, written in an instructive and edifying manner, in charming English It is not a dry narrative, but its pages are filled with interesting anecdotes and examples from Holy Scripture, the Fathers, and other sources. There are many fine half-tone illustrations in the book, drawn specially for it.

LIFE OF ST. CATHARINE OF SIENNA   By EDWARD L. AYMÉ, M. D.   12mo, cloth,   *1 00
   A popular life of this great Dominican saint, issued in convenient shape.

LIFE OF CHRIST, ILLUSTRATED. By Father M. V. COCHEM. With fine half-tone illustrations. 12mo,   1 25
   The characteristic features of this Life of Christ are its popular text, beautiful illustrations, and low price It is a devotional narrative of the life, sufferings, and death of our divine Saviour. It is based mainly on the Holy Scriptures, though numerous pious legends are also given Beginning with the birth of the Blessed Virgin, it traces the life of Our Lord step by step, from the manger to Calvary.

LIFE OF FATHER CHARLES SIRE. 12mo,   *net*, 1 00

LIFE OF ST. CLARE OF MONTEFALCO. 12mo,   *net*, 0 75

LIFE OF VEN. MARY CRESCENTIA HÖSS. 12mo,   *net*, 1 25

LIFE OF ST FRANCIS SOLANUS. 16mo,   *net*, 0 50

LIFE OF ST. CHANTAL. See under St. CHANTAL,   *net*, 4 00

LIFE OF MOST REV. JOHN HUGHES. 12mo,   *net*, 0 75

LIFE OF FATHER JOGUES. 12mo,   *net*, 0 75

LIFE OF MLLE. LE GRAS 12mo,   *net*, 1 25

LIFE OF RIGHT REV J. N. NEUMANN, D D. 12mo,   *net*, 1 25

LIFE OF FR. FRANCIS POILVACHE 32mo, paper, |*net*, 0 20

LIFE OF OUR LORD AND SAVIOUR JESUS CHRIST and of His Blessed Mother. 600 illustrations. Cloth,   *net*, 5 00

LIFE, POPULAR, OF ST. TERESA OF JESUS. 12mo,   *net*, 0 75

LIFE OF SISTER ANNE KATHARINE EMMERICH of the Order of St. Augustine By Rev. THOMAS WEGENER, O S A From the French by Rev. FRANCIS X McGOWAN, O.S A. 8vo, cloth,   *net*, 1 50
   The first popular life of this celebrated stigmatisée published in English.

LIGUORI, ST. ALPHONSUS DE Complete Ascetical Works of Centenary Edition Edited by Rev. EUGENE GRIMM, C SS R Price, per vol., *net*, 1 25
   Each book is complete in itself, and any volume will be sold separately.
   Preparation for Death   Victories of the Martyrs
   Way of Salvation and of Perfec-   True Spouse of Christ, 2 vols.
      tion.   Dignity and Duties of the Priest
   Great Means of Salvation and Per-   The Holy Mass.
      fection.   The Divine Office.
   Incarnation, Birth, and Infancy of   Preaching.
      Christ   Abridged Sermons for all the Sundays.
   The Passion and Death of Christ.   Miscellany.
   The Holy Eucharist   Letters, 4 vols
   The Glories of Mary, 2 vols.   Letters and General Index.

   "It would be quite superfluous to speak of the excellence of the spiritual writings of St Liguori—books which have converted and sanctified souls everywhere, and which our Holy Father Pope Leo XIII. declares 'should be found in the hands of all' We have only to observe that the editor's task has been creditably performed, and to express the hope that the Centenary Edition of St Liguori's works will be a very great success "—*Ave Maria*

LINKED LIVES A novel. By Lady DOUGLAS. 8vo,   1 50

LITTLE CHILD OF MARY. Large 48mo,   ‡0 35

LITTLE FOLKS' ANNUAL.   0 05

LITTLE MANUAL OF ST. ANTHONY. 32mo, cloth,   ‡0 60

LOURDES. By R. F CLARKE, S.J. 16mo, illustrated,   0 75

LOYAL BLUE AND ROYAL SCARLET. A Story of '76. By MARION AMES TAGGART. 12mo, cloth,   0 85

7

MANIFESTATION OF CONSCIENCE Confessions and Communions in
Religious Communities. 32mo,   *net*, o 50

MANUAL OF INDULGENCED PRAYERS Small 32mo,   ‡o 40

MANUAL OF THE HOLY EUCHARIST Conferences and Pious Practices,
with Devotions for Mass, etc Prepared by Rev F. X Lasance, Director of
the Tabernacle Society of Cincinnati Oblong 24mo,   ‡o 75
  Embraces a series of beautiful conferences which must undoubtedly be
classified among the best and most successful popular works of our times on
the adorable Sacrament of the Altar, and are calculated to impart a better
understanding of this sublime mystery The second part of the book
consists of devotions, prayers, and pious practices that have a relation to the
Holy Eucharist This is the first book of the kind issued, and will be sure to
be heartily welcomed.

MANUAL OF THE HOLY FAMILY. Prayers and Instructions for Catholic
Parents 32mo, cloth,   ‡o 60

MARCELLA GRACE. A novel. By ROSA MULHOLLAND. With illustrations
after original drawings 12mo,   1 25

MARIÆ COROLLA. Poems by Rev. EDMUND HILL, C.P 12mo,   1 25

MARRIAGE. By Very Rev. PÈRE MONSABRÉ, O.P. From the French, by
M. HOPPER. 12mo,   *net*, 1 00

MAY DEVOTIONS, NEW Reflections on the Invocations of the Litany of
Loretto. 12mo, |*net*, 1 00

McCALLEN, REV JAMES A., S.S. Sanctuary Boy's Illustrated Manual
12mo.   *net*, o 50
——— Office of Tenebræ. 12mo, |*net*, o 50

MEANS OF GRACE, THE A Complete Exposition of the Seven Sacraments
of the Sacramentals, and of Prayer, with a Comprehensive Explanation of
the "Lord's Prayer" and the "Hail Mary" By Rev. RICHARD BRENNAN,
LL.D With 180 full-page and other illustrations. 8vo, cloth, 2 50; gilt
edges, 3 00; Library edition, half levant,   3 50

MEDITATIONS (BAXTER) for Every Day in the Year By Rev ROGER
BAXTER, S J. Small 12mo,   *net*, 1 25

MEDITATIONS (CHAIGNON, S J.) FOR THE USE OF THE SECULAR
CLERGY. By Father CHAIGNON, S.J From the French, by Rt. Rev L DE
GOESBRIAND, D D 2 vols, 8vo,   *net*, 4 00

MEDITATIONS (HAMON'S) FOR ALL THE DAYS OF THE YEAR. By
Rev M HAMON, S S. From the French, by Mrs ANNE R BENNETT-
GLADSTONE 5 vols., 16mo, cloth, gilt top, each with a Steel Engraving
                                                           net, 5 00
  These meditations are published in five handy volumes which can be con-
veniently carried in the pocket.
  The subject of each meditation is first given, together with indications of
the resolutions proceeding from it, and a spiritual nosegay
  Then follows the meditation proper, divided into two, three, or four short
points, either on a mystery of our holy religion, one of the Christian virtues,
or a celebrated saint.
  Morning and evening prayers are included in each volume, so that no
other book is necessary for daily devotions

MEDITATIONS ON THE MONTH OF OUR LADY. From the Italian, by
Rev J F MULLANEY, LL.D. Oblong 16mo,   o 75

MEDITATIONS ON THE LAST WORDS FROM THE CROSS. By Father
CHARLES PERRAUD With an introduction by Cardinal PERRAUD. Trans-
lated at St. Joseph's Seminary, Dunwoodie, N. Y. 24mo, cloth, |*net*, o 50

MEDITATIONS ON THE PASSION OF OUR LORD. By a PASSIONIST
FATHER. 32mo, *0.40; per 100,   20 00

8

MEDITATIONS (PERINALDO) on the Sufferings of Jesus Christ. 12mo,
net, 0 75

MEDITATIONS (VERCRUYSSE), for Every Day in the Year, on the Life of Our Lord Jesus Christ. 2 vols.,
net, 2 75

MISS ERIN. A novel By M. E. FRANCIS 12mo,
1 25

MISSION BOOK, BOYS' AND GIRLS'. 48mo,
‡0 35

MISSION BOOK of the Redemptorist Fathers. 32mo, cloth,
‡0 50

MISSION BOOK FOR THE MARRIED By Very Rev F. GIRARDEY, C.SS R. 32mo,
‡0 50

MISSION BOOK FOR THE SINGLE. By Very Rev. F. GIRARDEY, C.SS R. 32mo,
‡0 50

MISTRESS OF NOVICES, The, Instructed in Her Duties. 12mo, cloth,
net, 0 75

MOMENTS BEFORE THE TABERNACLE By Rev MATTHEW RUSSELL, S J. 24mo,
net, 0 40

MONK'S PARDON. A Historical Romance. By RAOUL DE NAVERY. 12mo,
1 25

MONTH OF THE DEAD. 32mo,
0 50

MONTH OF MAY DEBUSSI, S J. 32mo,
0 50

MONTH, NEW, OF MARY, St. Francis de Sales. 32mo,
0 25

MONTH, NEW, OF ST JOSEPH, St. Francis de Sales 32mo,
0 25

MONTH, NEW, OF THE HOLY ANGELS, St Francis de Sales 32mo, 0 25

MORAL PRINCIPLES AND MEDICAL PRACTICE, the Basis of Medical Jurisprudence. By Rev. CHARLES COPPENS, S J., Professor of Medical Jurisprudence in the John A Creighton Medical College, Omaha, Neb., author of text-books in Metaphysics, Ethics, etc. 8vo, *net*, 1 50 Important, solid, original.

MR. BILLY BUTTONS. A novel. By WALTER LECKY. 12mo,
1 25

MÜLLER, REV. MICHAEL. C SS R. God the Teacher of Mankind A plain, comprehensive Explanation of Christian Doctrine. 9 vols., crown 8vo.
Per set, *net*, 9 50
The Church and Her Enemies. *net*, 1 10
The Apostles' Creed *net*, 1 10
The First and Greatest Commandment. *net*, 1 40
Explanation of the Commandments, continued. Precepts of the Church *net*, 1 10
Dignity, Authority, and Duties of Parents, Ecclesiastical and Civil Powers, Their Enemies *net*, 1 40
Grace and the Sacraments. *net*, 1 25
Holy Mass *net*, 1 25
Eucharist and Penance *net*, 1 10
Sacramentals—Prayer, etc. *net*, 1 00
—— Familiar Explanation of Catholic Doctrine. 12mo, *1 00
—— The Prodigal Son, or, The Sinner's Return to God 8vo, *net*, 1 00
—— The Devotion of the Holy Rosary and the Five Scapulars 8vo, *net*, 0 75
—— The Catholic Priesthood 2 vols, 8vo, *net*, 3 00

MY FIRST COMMUNION · The Happiest Day of My Life BRENNAN 16mo illustrated,
0 75

NAMES THAT LIVE IN CATHOLIC HEARTS. By ANNA T. SADLIER. 12mo,
1 00

NATURAL LAW AND LEGAL PRACTICE Lectures delivered at the Law School of Georgetown University, by Rev. R. I. HOLAIND, S.J. 8vo, cloth,
net, 1 75

NEW TESTAMENT STUDIES. The Chief Events in the Life of Our Lord. By Rt. Rev. Mgr. THOMAS J CONATY, D.D. 12mo, cloth, illustrated, 0 60

NEW TESTAMENT. 12mo. New, large type. The best edition published. Cloth, *net*, 0 75

NEW TESTAMENT, THE. ILLUSTRATED EDITION. With 100 fine full-page illustrations. Printed in two colors 16mo, *net*, 0 60
    This is a correct and faithful reprint of the edition first printed at Kheims, with annotations, references, and an historical and chronological index, and is issued with the Imprimatur of His Grace the Most Reverend Archbishop of New York. The advantages of this edition over others consist in its beautiful illustrations, its convenient size, its clear, open type, and substantial and attractive binding. It is the best adapted for general use on account of its compactness and low price.

NEW TESTAMENT. 32mo, flexible, *net*, 0 15

OFFICE, COMPLETE, OF HOLY WEEK, in Latin and English.
24mo, cloth 0 50 , cloth, gilt edges, ‡1 00
Also in finer bindings

O'GRADY, ELEANOR. Aids to Correct and Effective Elocution. 12mo, *1 25
—— Select Recitations for Schools and Academies 12mo, *1 00
—— Readings and Recitations for Juniors. 16mo, *net*, 0 50
—— Elocution Class. 16mo, *net*, 0 50

ONE ANGEL MORE IN HEAVEN. With Letters of Condolence by St Francis de Sales and others. White morocco, 0 50

ON THE ROAD TO ROME, and How Two Brothers Got There. By WILLIAM RICHARDS. 16mo, 0 50

OUR BIRTHDAY BOUQUET. Culled from the Shrines of Saints and the Gardens of Poets. By E. C. DONNELLY 16mo, 1 00

OUR BOYS' AND GIRLS' LIBRARY. 48mo, fancy boards.
My Strange Friend By FRANCIS J. FINN, S J 0 25
The Dumb Child. By CANON SCHMID 0 25
The Boys in the Block. By MAURICE F. EGAN. 0 25
The Hop Blossoms. By CANON SCHMID. 0 25
The Fatal Diamonds. By E C. DONNELLY. 0 25
Buzzer's Christmas By MARY T WAGGAMAN. 0 25
Godfrey the Hermit By CANON SCHMID. 0 25
The Three Little Kings. By EMMY GIEHRL. 0 25
The Black Lady. By CANON SCHMID. 0 25
Master Fridolin. By EMMY GIEHRL. 0 25
The Cake and the Easter Eggs By CANON SCHMID. 0 25
The Lamp of the Sanctuary. WISEMAN. 0 25
The Rose Bush. By CANON SCHMID 0 25
The Overseer of Mahlbourg. By CANON SCHMID. 0 25

OUR FAVORITE DEVOTIONS By Very Rev Dean A. A. LINGS 24mo, to 60
    While there are many excellent books of devotion, there is none made on the plan of this one, giving ALL the devotions in general use among the faithful It will be found a very serviceable book.

OUR FAVORITE NOVENAS. By the Very Rev. Dean A. A. LINGS. 24mo, to 60
    Gives forms of prayer for all the novenas for the Feasts of Our Lord, the Blessed Virgin, and the Saints which pious custom has established.

OUR LADY OF GOOD COUNSEL IN GENAZZANO By ANNE R. BENNETT, nee GLADSTONE 32mo, 0 75

OUR MONTHLY DEVOTIONS. By Very Rev Dean A A. LINGS. 16mo, cloth, †1 25
    The Church, desirous of filling our minds with pious thoughts from the beginning to the end of the year, has encouraged, and in some cases designated, certain devotions to be practised, and sets aside a whole month in which the prevailing thought ought to be centred on a certain devotion In this volume all these devotions will be found. It is the completest book of the kind published

OUR OWN WILL and How to Detect It in Our Actions. By REV. JOHN ALLEN, D.D 16mo, *net*, 0 75

OUR YOUNG FOLKS' LIBRARY 10 volumes. 12mo Each, 0 45
OUTLAW OF CAMARGUE, THE A novel. By A. DE LAMOTHE. 12mo, 1 25
OUTLINES OF DOGMATIC THEOLOGY. By Rev SYLVESTER J. HUNTER, S.J. 3 vols., 12mo, *net*, 4 50

OUTLINES OF JEWISH HISTORY, from Abraham to Our Lord. By Rev.
F. E. Gigot, S S 8vo, | *net*, 1 50

OUTLINES OF NEW TESTAMENT HISTORY. By Rev F E. GIGOT, SS.
8vo,   *net*, 1 50

PARADISE ON EARTH OPENED TO ALL; or, A Religious Vocation the
Surest Way in Life. 32mo,   *net*, 0 40

PASTIME SERIES OF JUVENILES. 16mo, cloth.
The Armorer of Solingen.   0 45
The Canary Bird   0 45
Wrongfully Accused.   0 45
The Inundation.   0 45

PASSING SHADOWS. A novel. By ANTHONY YORKE. 12mo,   1 25

PASSION FLOWERS. Poems by Father EDMUND HILL, C P. 12mo,
cloth,   1 25

PEARLS FROM FABER. Selected and arranged by MARION J BRUNOWE,
32mo,   0 50

PEOPLE'S MISSION BOOK   32mo, paper, *0.10; per 100,   5 00

PÈRE MONNIER'S WARD. A novel. By WALTER LECKY. 12mo,   1 25

PETRONILLA, and Other Stories. By E C. DONNELLY. 12mo,   1 00

PHILOSOPHY, ENGLISH MANUALS OF CATHOLIC.
Logic By RICHARD F CLARKE, S J. 12mo,   *net*, 1 25
First Principles of Knowledge By JOHN RICKABY, S J 12mo,   *net*, 1 25
Moral Philosophy (Ethics and Natural Law). By JOSEPH RICKABY, S J
12mo,   *net*, 1 25
Natural Theology By BERNARD BOEDDER, S.J. 12mo,   *net*, 1 50
Psychology. By MICHAEL MAHER, S J. 12mo,   *net*, 1 50
General Metaphysics By JOHN RICKABY, S J 12mo,   *net*, 1 25
Manual of Political Economy By C S. DEVAS. 12mo,   *net*, 1 50

PICTORIAL GAME of American Catholic Authors
Series A,   *net*, 0 35
Series B,   *net*, 0 35

PICTORIAL LIVES OF THE SAINTS. With Reflections for Every Day in
the Year 50th Thousand 8vo,   1 00
10 copies, 7 50; 25 copies, 17 50; 50 copies,   33 50
There is nothing "cheap" about this book except the price The paper,
print, and binding are excellent, the type clear, and the illustrations will
please old and young. The price is astonishingly low for such a fine book;
and is possible only by printing a very large edition.
The life of each saint and the history of each great festival are given in
succinct but clear style, and each day closes with a practical reflection. The
book is filled with excellent wood engravings, almost every page being
embellished with an illustration. It can be highly recommended as a text-
book for family reading The children in a home can find no better
instructor, and will turn to its pages with delight

PIOUS PREPARATION FOR FIRST HOLY COMMUNION. Rev. F X
LASANCE Large 32mo,   to 75
A complete manual for a child who is preparing for First Holy Communion All the devotions and practices for a first communicant are contained
therein; with a comprehensive preparation for the First Communion day,
and a triduum of three days; pious reflections on the happy morning,
communion prayers, etc.

POPULAR INSTRUCTIONS ON MARRIAGE By Very Rev. F. GIRARDEY,
C.SS R 32mo Paper, *0 25; per 100,   12 50
Cloth, *0.35, per 100,   21 00

POPULAR INSTRUCTIONS ON PRAYER. By Very Rev F GIRARDEY,
C SS R. 32mo Paper, *0 25, per 100, 12 50. Cloth, *0 35; per 100,   21 00

POPULAR INSTRUCTIONS TO PARENTS on the Bringing Up of Children.
By Very Rev F. GIRARDEY, C SS.R 32mo. Paper, *0 25, per 100,   12 50
Cloth, *0.35; per 100,   21 00

II

PRACTICAL GUIDE TO INDULGENCES, A   Rev P M BERNAD, O.M I.
(Rev DAN'L MURRAY.) 24mo,   o 75

PRAYER. The Great Means of Obtaining Salvation. LIGUORI. 32mo,   o 50

PRAYER-BOOK FOR LENT. Meditations and Prayers for Lent 32mo,
cloth,   to 50

PRAXIS SYNODALIS. Manuale Synodi Diocesanæ ac Provincialis Cele-
brandæ 12mo,   *net*, o 60

PRIEST IN THE PULPIT, THE. A Manual of Homiletics and Catechetics
SCHUECH-LUEBBERMANN. 8vo,   *net*, 1 50

READING AND THE MIND, WITH SOMETHING TO READ. O'CONOR,
S J. 12mo,   ‖ *net*, o 50

REASONABLENESS OF CATHOLIC CEREMONIES AND PRACTICES.
By Rev. J. J BURKE 12mo, flexible cloth, *o 35, per 100,   21 00

REGISTRUM BAPTISMORUM. 3200 registers. 11 x 16 inches.   *net*, 3 50

REGISTRUM MATRIMONIORUM. 3200 registers 11 x 16 inches.   *net*, 3 50

RELIGIOUS STATE, THE   With a Short Treatise on Vocation to the
Priesthood By St. ALPHONSUS LIGUORI. 32mo,   o 50

REMINISCENCES OF RT REV. EDGAR P WADHAMS, D D. By Rev,
C A. WALWORTH. 12mo, illustrated,   ‖ *net*, 1 00

RIGHTS OF OUR LITTLE ONES By Rev JAMES CONWAY, S J. 32mo
Paper, *o 15; per 100, 9 00. Cloth, *o 25; per 100,   15 00

ROMANCE OF A PLAYWRIGHT. A novel. By H. DE BORNIER. 12mo, 1 00

ROSARY, THE MOST HOLY, in Thirty-one Meditations, Prayers, and
Examples By Rev EUGENE GRIMM, C.SS R. 32mo,   o 50

ROUND TABLE, THE, of the Representative *French* Catholic Novelists
containing the best stories by the best writers. With half-tone portraits,
printed in colors, biographies, etc. 12mo, cloth,   1 50

ROUND TABLE, A, of the Representative *American* Catholic Novelists,
containing the best stories by the best writers With half-tone portraits,
printed in colors, biographical sketches, etc. 12mo,   1 50

ROUND TABLE, A, of the Representative *Irish and English* Catholic Novelists, containing the best stories by the best writers With half-tone portraits, printed in colors, biographical sketches, etc. 12mo,   1 50

RUSSO, N, S J De Philosophia Morali Piælectiones in Collegio Georgio-
politano Soc. Jes Anno 1889-1890. Habitæ, a Patre NICOLAO RUSSO Editio
altera. 8vo, half leather,   *net*, 2 00

SACRAMENTALS OF THE HOLY CATHOLIC CHURCH, THE. By
Rev A. A. LAMBING, LL.D. Illustrated edition. 24mo
Paper, o 25; 25 copies, 4 25, 50 copies, 7.50; 100 copies,   12 50
Cloth, o 50; 25 copies, 8.50, 50 copies, 15 00; 100 copies,   25 00

SACRAMENT OF PENANCE, THE. Lenten Sermons Paper   ‖ *net*, o 25

SACRISTAN'S GUIDE A Hand-book for Altar Societies and those having
charge of the Altar. 16mo, cloth,   *net*, o 75

SACRISTY RITUAL Rituale Compendiosum, seu Ordo Administrandi
quædam Sacramenta et alia officia Ecclesiastica Rite peragendi ex Rituale
Romano novissime edito desumptas 16mo, flexible,   *net*, o 75

SACRED RHETORIC. 12mo,   *net*, o 75

SACRIFICE OF THE MASS WORTHILY CELEBRATED, THE By the
Rev Father CHAIGNON, S. J Translated by Rt Rev L DE GOESBRIAND,
D D 8vo,   *net*, 1 50

ST. ANTHONY, the Saint of the Whole World Illustrated by Pen and Pencil.
Compiled from the best sources by Rev THOS F. WARD. Illustrated.
Square 12mo, cloth,   o 75

SACRED HEART, BOOKS ON THE.
Child's Prayer-Book of the Sacred Heart. 32mo,   0 25
Devotions to the Sacred Heart for the First Friday. 32mo,   0 40
Imitation of the Sacred Heart of Jesus. By Rev F. ARNOUDT, S. J   From
  the Latin by Rev. J. M FASTRE, S J. 16mo, cloth,   †1 25
Little Prayer-Book of the Sacred Heart   Small 32mo,   ‡0 40
Month of the Sacred Heart of Jesus. HUGUET. 32mo,   0 50
Month of the Sacred Heart for the Young Christian By BROTHER PHILIPPE.
  32mo,   0 50
New Month of the Sacred Heart. St. FRANCIS DE SALES 32mo,   0 25
One and Thirty Days with Blessed Margaret Mary. 32mo, *0 25, per 100,
  15 00
Pearls from the Casket of the Sacred Heart of Jesus. 32mo,   0 50
Revelations of the Sacred Heart to Blessed Margaret Mary, and the History
  of Her Life   BOUGAUD 8vo,   net, 1 50
Sacred Heart Studied in the Sacred Scriptures. By Rev H. SAINTRAIN,
  C.SS.R. 8vo,   net, 2 00
Six Sermons on Devotion to the Sacred Heart of Jesus. BIERBAUM. 16mo,
  net, 0 60

Year of the Sacred Heart. Drawn from the works of PÈRE DE LA COLOM-
  BIERE, of Margaret Mary, and of others   32mo,   0 50

ST. CHANTAL AND THE FOUNDATION OF THE VISITATION. By
Monseigneur BOUGAUD. 2 vols, 8vo,   net, 4 00

ST JOSEPH OUR ADVOCATE. From the French of Rev. Father HUGUET
24mo,   0 75

SCHMID, CANON, CANARY BIRD, THE. 16mo,   0 45
—— Black Lady, The, and Robin Red Breast. 24mo.   0 25
—— Rose Bush, The. 24mo,   0 25
—— Overseer of Mahlbourg, The. 24mo,   0 25
—— Hop Blossoms, The   24mo,   0 25
—— Godfrey, The Hermit   24mo,   0 25
—— Cake, The, and the Easter Eggs. 24mo,   0 25

SECRET OF SANCTITY, THE. According to ST FRANCIS DE SALES and
Father CRASSET, S J. 12mo,   net, 1 00

SERAPHIC GUIDE. A Manual for the Members of the Third Order of St.
Francis   Cloth,   †0 60
Roan, red edges   †0 75
The same in German at the same prices.

SERMONS See also "Hunolt," "Sacrament of Penance," "Seven Last
Words," and "Two-Edged Sword"

SERMONS FOR THE CHILDREN OF MARY. From the Italian of Rev.
F CALLERIO   Revised by Rev. R. F. CLARKE, S J   8vo, cloth,   net, 1 50
  Concise, devotional, and treat in a practical manner of the duties and
  privileges that appertain to the Children of Mary

SERMONS, FUNERAL   2 vols,   ‖ net, 2 00

SERMONS, LENTEN. Large 8vo,   ‖ net, 2 00

SERMONS, OLD AND NEW   8 vols, 8vo,   ‖ net, 16 00

SERMONS ON OUR LORD, THE BLESSED VIRGIN, AND THE SAINTS
By Rev. F. HUNOLT, S. J   Translated by Rev J. ALLEN, D D   2 vols,
8vo,   net, 5 00

SERMONS ON PENANCE. By Rev F. HUNOLT, S J. Translated by Rev.
J ALLEN, D.D. 2 vols., 8vo,   net, 5 00

SERMONS ON THE BLESSED VIRGIN. By Very Rev. D. I. MCDERMOTT.
16mo,   net, 0 75

SERMONS ON THE CHRISTIAN VIRTUES By Rev F HUNOLT, S J
Translated by Rev. J. ALLEN, D D   2 vols, 8vo,   net, 5 00

SERMONS ON THE DIFFERENT STATES OF LIFE By Rev. F HUNOLT,
S J. Translated by Rev J ALLEN, D D   2 vols, 8vo,   net, 5 00

SERMONS ON THE FOUR LAST THINGS By Rev. F. HUNOLT, S J
Translated by Rev. J. ALLEN, D D. 2 vols, 8vo,   net, 5 00

SERMONS ON THE SEVEN DEADLY SINS. By Rev F. HUNOLT, S J. Translated by Rev J. ALLEN, D D. 2 vols , 8vo, *net*, 5 00

SERMONS, abridged, for all the Sundays and Holydays By ST ALPHONSUS LIGUORI 12mo, *net*, 1 25

SERMONS for the Sundays and Chief Festivals of the Ecclesiastical Year. With Two Courses of Lenten Sermons and a Triduum for the Forty Hours By Rev. JULIUS POTTGEISSER, S J From the German by Rev JAMES CONWAY, S. J. 2 vols , 8vo, *net*, 2 50

SERMONS ON THE MOST HOLY ROSARY. By Rev M J FRINGS 12mo, *net*, 1 00

SERMONS, SHORT, FOR LOW MASSES By Rev. F. X. SCHOUPPE, S. J 12mo, *net*, 1 25

SERMONS, SIX, on the Sacred Heart of Jesus. BIERBAUM. 16mo, *net*, 0 60

SHORT CONFERENCES ON THE LITTLE OFFICE OF THE IMMACU- LATE CONCEPTION By Very Rev. JOSEPH RAINER. With Prayers 32mo, 0 50

SHORT STORIES ON CHRISTIAN DOCTRINE A Collection of Examples Illustrating the Catechism. From the French by MARY MCMAHON 12mo, illustrated, *net*, 0 75

SMITH, Rev S B , D D Elements of Ecclesiastical Law.
   Vol I Ecclesiastical Persons. 8vo, *net*, 2 50
   Vol II Ecclesiastical Trials 8vo, *net*, 2 50
   Vol III Ecclesiastical Punishments 8vo, *net*, 2 50
   —— Compendium Juris Canonici, ad Usum Cleri et Seminariorum hujus regionis accommodatum 8vo, *net*, 2 00
   —— The Marriage Process in the United States 8vo, *net*, 2 50

SODALISTS' VADE MECUM A Manual, Prayer-Book, and Hymnal. 32mo, cloth, ‡0 50

SONGS AND SONNETS, and Other Poems. By MAURICE F. EGAN. 12mo, cloth, 1 00

SOUVENIR OF THE NOVITIATE. From the French by Rev. EDWARD I. TAYLOR 32mo, *net*, 0 60

SPIRITUAL CRUMBS FOR HUNGRY LITTLE SOULS. To which are added Stories from the Bible. RICHARDSON. 16mo, 0 50

SPIRITUAL EXERCISES for a Ten Days' Retreat By Very Rev R. v SME- TANA, C.SS R., *net*, 1 00

STANG, REV. WILLIAM, D D. Pastoral Theology. New enlarged edition. 8vo, *net*, 1 50
   —— Eve of the Reformation. 12mo, paper, ‖ *net*, 0 25
   —— Historiographia Ecclesiastica quam Historiæ seriam Solidamque Operam Navantibus, Accommodavit GUIL. STANG, D.D. 12mo, ‖ *net*, 1 00
   —— Business Guide for Priests. 8vo, cloth, *net*. 0 85
   Contents I. Parish Books 1. Book-keeping. 2. Technical Terms and and Formalities. II. Baptismal Records 1 Baptismal Register 2 Bap- tismal Names III Marriage Record. 1 Marriage Register 2 Marriage Dispensations IV Liber Status Animarum. V. Pew Rent. VI Building. VII Letters. VIII. Last Will.

STORIES FOR FIRST COMMUNICANTS, for the time before and after First Communion By Rev. J. A. KELLER, D.D 32mo, 0 50

STORY OF THE DIVINE CHILD Told for Children in Pictures and in Words By Rev Dean A A LINGS 16mo, 0 75

STRIVING AFTER PERFECTION. By Rev. J. BAYMA, S.J. 16mo, *net*, 1 00

SURE WAY TO A HAPPY MARRIAGE Paper, *0.25 , per 100, 12 50
Cloth, 0 35 , per 100, 21 00

TALES AND LEGENDS OF THE MIDDLE AGES. From the Spanish of F. DE P. CAPELLA. By HENRY WILSON. 16mo, 0 75

TANQUEREY, Rev. Ad. S S.   Synopsis Theologiæ Fundamentalis. 8vo,
net, 1 50
—— Synopsis Theologia Dogmatica Specialis. 2 vols., 8vo, *net*, 3 00

THOUGHT FROM ST. ALPHONSUS, for Every Day. 32mo, *net*, 0 35

THOUGHT FROM BENEDICTINE SAINTS. 32mo, *net*, 0 35

THOUGHT FROM DOMINICAN SAINTS. 32mo, *net*, 0 35

THOUGHT FROM ST. FRANCIS ASSISI 32mo, *net*, 0 35

THOUGHT FROM ST. IGNATIUS 32mo, *net*, 0 35

THOUGHT FROM ST. TERESA 32mo, *net*, 0 35

THOUGHT FROM ST. VINCENT DE PAUL 32mo, *net*, 0 35

THOUGHTS AND COUNSELS FOR THE CONSIDERATION OF CATHO-
LIC YOUNG MEN   By Rev P A. VON DOSS, S J. 12mo, | *net*, 1 25

TRAVELERS' DAILY COMPANION   A 5-cent prayer-book which one can
continually carry about the person. Cloth, †0.05; per 100,   3 50

TREASURE OF NUGGET MOUNTAIN, THE   (Jack Hildreth Among the
Indians) M. A. TAGGART. 12mo,   0 85

TRUE POLITENESS. Addressed to Religious   By Rev FRANCIS DEMORE.
16mo,   *net*, 0 60
" . . . Really fascinating . . . Will be read with avidity and profit."
—*The Republic.*
"This book is entirely practical."—*Sacred Heart Review.*
"Useful for every member of society."—*Messenger of the Sacred Heart*

TRUE SPOUSE OF CHRIST. By ST ALPHONSUS LIGUORI 2 vols., 12mo,
net, 2.50; 1 vol., 12mo,   *net*, 1 00

TRUE STORY OF MASTER GERARD, THE. A novel. By ANNA T. SADLIER.
12mo, cloth,   1 25

TWELVE VIRTUES, THE, of a Good Teacher. For Mothers, Instructors, etc.
By Rev H. POTTIER, S J 32mo,   *net*, 0 30

TWO-EDGED SWORD, THE. Lenten Sermons, Paper. | *net*, 0 25

TWO RETREATS FOR SISTERS. By Rev. E ZOLLNER. 12mo, | *net*, 1 00

VADE MECUM SACERDOTUM. 48mo, cloth, *net*, 0.25; morocco, flexible,
net, 0 50

VENERATION OF THE BLESSED VIRGIN   Her Feasts, Prayers, Religious
Orders, and Sodalities By Rev B KOHNER, O.S B   Adapted by Rev
RICHARD BRENNAN, LL.D. 12mo,   1 25
"We assure the general reader that he will find much interest and edifica-
tion in this volume; to devout clients of the Blessed Virgin it will be
especially welcome. It is an appetizing book; we should think that any
Catholic who sees the table of contents would wish to read the work from
cover to cover."—*Ave Maria.*

VIA CŒLI. A new Book of Prayer. Artistically illustrated, convenient in
form. 32mo, lambskin,   †0 90

VISIT TO EUROPE AND THE HOLY LAND. By Rev. H. F. FAIRBANKS.
12mo, illustrated,   1 50

VISITS TO JESUS IN THE TABERNACLE. Hours and Half-Hours of
Adoration before the Blessed Sacrament By Rev. F. X. LASANCE. 16mo,
cloth,   †1 25
The best work on the subject ever published.

VISITS TO THE MOST HOLY SACRAMENT and to the Blessed Virgin
Mary LIGUORI. 32mo, *0 50, per 100,   25 00

VOCATIONS EXPLAINED: Matrimony, Virginity, the Religious State, and
the Priesthood. By a Vincentian Father 16mo, flexible, *0.10, per 100, 5 00

WARD, REV. THOS F Fifty-two Instructions on the Principal Truths of
Our Holy Religion. 12mo, *net*, o 75
—— Thirty-two Instructions for the Month of May 12mo, *net*, o 75
—— Month of May at Mary's Altar 12mo, *net*, o 75
—— Short Instructions for Sundays and Holydays 12mo, *net*, 1 25

WAY OF INTERIOR PEACE. By Rev. Father DE LEHEN, S. J. From the
German Version of Rev. J. BRUCKER, S. J. 12mo, *net*, 1 25

WAY OF THE CROSS. Illustrated. Paper, *o 05 ; per 100, 2 50

WHAT CATHOLICS HAVE DONE FOR SCIENCE BRENNAN. 12mo, 1 00

WIDOWS AND CHARITY. Work of the Women of Calvary and Its Foundress
By the ABBE CHAFFANJON. 12mo, paper, | *net* o 50

WINNETOU, THE APACHE KNIGHT (Jack Hildreth Among the Indians).
M. A. TAGGART. 12mo, o 85

WOMAN OF FORTUNE, A. A novel. By CHRISTIAN REID. 12mo, 1 25

WOMEN OF CATHOLICITY. SADLIER 12mo, 1 00

WORDS OF JESUS CHRIST DURING HIS PASSION. SCHOUPPE, S J.
32mo, *0.25 ; per 100, 15 00

WORDS OF WISDOM. A Concordance of the Sapiential Books. 12mo,
net, 1 25

WORLD WELL LOST, THE. A novel. By ESTHER ROBERTSON. 16mo, o 75

WUEST, REV. JOSEPH, C.SS.R. DEVOTIO QUADRAGINTA HORARUM. 32mo,
‖ *net*, o 15

YOUNG GIRL'S BOOK OF PIETY. 16mo, ‡1 00

ZEAL IN THE WORK OF THE MINISTRY ; or, The Means by Which Every
Priest May Render His Ministry Honorable and Fruitful. From the French
of L'ABBE DUBOIS. 8vo, *net*, 1 50

BENZIGER'S MAGAZINE.

AN ILLUSTRATED CATHOLIC MONTHLY FOR YOUNG AND OLD.

Subscription, $1.00 a year. Single copies, 10 cents.

STORIES BY THE FOREMOST CATHOLIC WRITERS: Father Finn, Ella
Loraine Dorsey, Katharine Tynan Hinkson, "Theo Gift," Marion Ames Taggart,
Maurice Francis Egan, Mary G. Bonesteel, Marion J Brunowe, Mary C. Crow-
ley, Eleanor C. Donnelly, Mary T. Waggaman, Katherine Jenkins, Sallie Mar-
garet O'Malley, Anna T. Sadlier, Mary E. Mannix, Esther Robertson, David
Selden, etc
SPECIAL ILLUSTRATED ARTICLES on Interesting Subjects.
REGULAR DEPARTMENTS· Current Events, Science and Inventions, Catholic
Teaching, Art, Lessons in Shorthand, Photography, The Household, Amuse-
ments, Games, Tricks, etc, Puzzles and Problems, Letter Box, Prize Question
Box, Story Writing, Penmanship and Drawing Contests
ILLUSTRATIONS : A special feature of "Benziger's Magazine" are the illustra-
tions of the stories and of the articles. Each number is profusely illustrated.

Lightning Source UK Ltd.
Milton Keynes UK
UKHW020740270722
406450UK00005B/653